CREATING
IDENTITY

CREATING IDENTITY

The Popular Romance Heroine's Journey to Selfhood and Self-Presentation

—⫯—

JAYASHREE KAMBLÉ

INDIANA UNIVERSITY PRESS

This book is a publication of

Indiana University Press
Office of Scholarly Publishing
Herman B Wells Library 350
1320 East 10th Street
Bloomington, Indiana 47405 USA

iupress.org

First printing 2023

Cataloging information is available from the Library of Congress.

ISBN 978-0-253-06569-8 (cloth)
ISBN 978-0-253-06570-4 (paperback)
ISBN 978-0-253-06571-1 (ebook)

To
Savitribai Phulé (1831–1897)
and
Jyotiba Phulé (1827–1890)

CONTENTS

ACKNOWLEDGMENTS

MY THANKS TO MY FAMILY—THOSE here and those who live in my memory. My sibling, Sunil, is my rock. Your faith and pride in my work keep me going.

Much gratitude to my patient and generous colleagues in popular romance studies, who have listened and provided feedback at various conferences of the Popular Culture Association and the International Association for the Study of Popular Romance. Among these, special thanks to Eric Murphy Selinger and Hsu-Ming Teo, whose intellectual brilliance pales only in comparison to their kindness. Thanks to Katie Morrissey, who helped me through one of the bleakest times in my life, to Jodi McAlister and Kecia Ali, who talked me through a logistical hiccup, and to Catherine Roach for answering a query about publishing this work.

I am also grateful to my wonderful colleagues at my professional home, LaGuardia Community College, and the City University of New York at large. Particular thanks to Allia Abdullah-Matta, Ece Aykol, Hara Bastas, Linda Chandler, Andy Kai-chun Chuang, Carrie Conners, Linda Dong, Kristen Gallagher, Ximena Gallardo, Natalie Havlin, Bethany Holmstrom, Jacqueline Jones, Demetrios Kapetanakos, Christine Marks, Michelle Pacht, Sylwia Prendable (grant reimbursement champion!), Nichole Shippen, Naomi Stubbs, and Lilla Töke. My thanks to my college Provost and President, past and present, for supporting faculty scholarship, and my library colleagues, who are always willing to answer questions.

My work on this project was assisted by the CUNY Faculty Fellowship Publication Program (mentor and friend Moustafa Bayoumi and the CUNY colleagues in this seminar deserve special mention), a 2017–2018 LaGuardia Community College Academic Affairs Research/Scholarly Work Award overseen by Provost Paul Arcario, LaGuardia EDIT grants, the CUNY Office of Research Book Completion Award (#363), and several PSC CUNY Research Awards. I also attended conferences and visited archives with the aid of grants from the Popular Culture Association and the International Association for the Study of Popular Romance.

My scholarship is informed by conversations with the insightful members of the Brooklyn Word Bookstore's *Bangin' Book Club*, led by Maddie Caldwell. Word also invited me to host a romance course, whose attendees enriched my analysis of romance heroines. Friends and fellow romance enthusiasts Courtney Wetzel and Cassie Montrose provided feedback on different chapters while Alaina Mauro strategized about the publishing process and Sarah Borland went on a citation hunt.

I presented one part of chapter 3, "Work," at the Princeton University Popular Romance Author Symposium, organized by friend and scholar An Goris. Another part of the same chapter stems from a paper I gave at a conference of the American Comparative Literature Association and which I eventually developed into an article for the "Capital Crimes in the Americas" special issue of the *Forum for Inter-American Research*. A special issue of the *Journal of Popular Romance Studies* included parts of chapter 4, "Citizenship," which profited from the comments of the anonymous peer reviewers as well as the feedback of the special issue's editors, Emily Johnson and Julie Cassiday, and the assistance of managing editor Erin Young. Dr. Cassiday convened the symposium Reading for Pleasure: Romance Fiction in the International Marketplace at Williams College, which is where the article originated as a paper. I also shared other sections of that chapter and the conclusion at the International Seminar on Languages and Cultures in Contact in the Romance Novel at the Universidad de Las Palmas (Spain), which was organized by María Isabel González Cruz and which I heard about from María Ramos-García.

My final thanks go to my supportive friends, to the peer reviewers of this book, to my editor, and to my romance community, online and IRL, for its enthusiasm and love of romance.

CREATING
IDENTITY

INTRODUCTION

Who Is the Romance Heroine and What Does She Want?

WHILE LOVE STORIES ABOUND IN all traditions and media, the mass-market romance novel is a specific form of love narrative falling within the category of genre fiction. A twentieth-century creation that gathered steam after the post–World War II paperback revolution, romance fiction inhabits the novel form, descends from the comedy (as opposed to tragedy) mode, and dwells on characters building a romantic bond. For a significant stretch of its history over the last century, the genre has operated with sexual and gender dimorphism as its default, and its protagonists have been cisgender, heterosexual, allosexual, and monogamous. While this study is limited to works with these traits and centers the woman protagonist, romance novels that go beyond these confines are appearing in greater numbers as marginalized identities demand visibility and justice, and as e-readers and apps compete with physical books and offer new stories. The arc of romance novels remains unchanged in some respects, however, bending toward companionate relationships and happiness based on equality and erotic compatibility. All else is fair game for change, for reconsideration, for reexamination. Romance novels may be 180 pages or 500, or a love story may extend across multiple novels. The plot may purely be about courtship and betrothal, as Pamela Regis has defined romance, or it may also involve espionage, making art or money, running a business, solving murders, fighting or assisting vampires/werewolves/ghosts, launching revolutions across the galaxy, raising the dead, or righting the wrongs we have inherited or done. The genre is endlessly pliable, as I argued in my first book, its romance and novel genes allowing it the flexibility to bring in what is romantic and desirable in the present moment and discard themes and structures that no longer serve its goal (Kamblé *Making Meaning*).

In that first book, I studied what a romance hero was made of.[1] When ending that analysis, however, a question became unavoidable—what makes a romance novel heroine? Is the label meant to just indicate the female-presenting/identifying central protagonist in a romance novel or is it someone engaged in acts of heroism? And if the latter, what constitutes said heroism? Scrutinizing this term—used quite unselfconsciously by romance readers and critics alike—can help us understand the mass-market romance genre and its unique appeal to its audience over the last century. I propose that a romance heroine is one who seeks the truth of her own unknown, suppressed, fragmented, or embattled self within a universe that privileges pair bonding and other configurations involving intimacy. My definition is partly inspired by Sandra J. Lindow's work on heroines in folktales. She notes that unlike Joseph Campbell's heroes, these characters embark on journeys not to answer a call to arms or for glory but because home is inhospitable; along the way, they become heroic in the pursuit of truth and proceed to slay their own psychological dragons to become better selves befitting the new homes they make (3–4).

Yet Joanna Russ, writing "What Can a Heroine Do?" in 1972, may not have accepted my label of heroism for the romance protagonist. She argues that female characters are ghettoized into starring only in the love story because women in our patriarchal world don't have access to the options that allow male protagonists their journeys and triumphs in a variety of narratives and thus a claim to being a hero (83–84).[2] The love story, she concedes, contains elements of the bildungsroman and professional as well as personal successes or failures, but the love plot is the chief driver of the action and the female protagonist is limited to it (85). That romance fiction appears to be one of the only literary forms in which the plot centers on a woman but also pivots around her romantic HEA (Happy Ever After) / HFN (Happy For Now) (traditionally with a man) lends credence to Russ's argument. Furthermore, she declares, tongue in cheek, that "successes within the Love Story (which is itself imagined out of genuine female experience) are not important because the Love Story is not important. It is a commonplace of criticism that only the male myths are valid or interesting" (88).

The protagonists of the twentieth- and twenty-first-century romances in this study, however, exemplify how the mass-market romance genre has evolved over the last few decades to offer female protagonists a life of questing for their truth through—and *beyond*—love plots. They serve to complicate Russ's perspective, challenging as they do the primacy of the male myths that she, too, mocks. If the original form that the love story took in mass-market romance was the marriage plot, with the action primarily being a woman finding love and marriage within a social community, the genre has sprouted offshoots around that core idea. It increasingly includes versions of female heroism that neither abandon the love story nor make it the only storyline a heroine can star in or steer; instead, the genre attempts a complex fusion, occasionally even risking anachronistic or historically dubious plots or portrayals—for example, a British Regency noblewoman who falls in love while working as a spy! In other words, romance fiction has a wider imagination for heroic action for women. This imagination opens the door to many kinds of female agency and adventures, which are akin to the roaming point of John Donne's compass, if you will, circling far but always attached to the fixed foot of the love plot, which sits in the center yet leans and hearkens in response to its twin narrative.

This process has taken place over a century, accelerating over the last forty years as the industry has adapted to new developments in publishing technology and market reach, not to mention political change and the growth of the US-based arm of the genre. Mass-market romance publishing, particularly the "category" romance form (numbered, 180–280 page novels), has long been attributed to a single publisher, the British firm Mills & Boon.[3] It was eventually acquired by a Canadian company, Harlequin, which is now the subsidiary of a corporation and continues to have a significant role in the genre. The gradual diversification of Harlequin Mills & Boon into distinct "lines," such as American Romance or Intrigue (romantic suspense), and of the many variations in "single-title" romances (unnumbered longer novels by publishers like Avon) is documented in histories of publishing by jay Dixon, An Goris, Paul Grescoe, Margaret Ann Jensen, John Markert, Joseph McAleer, and Carol Thurston. But the cultural forces that prompted divarication in the genre need more attention. For the most part, as in Jensen's review of romance heroines, scholars acknowledge that romance reflects how women's lives were changing under 1970s' feminist discourse, and they were no longer valuing traditional gender roles alone (86). Jensen sums up these changes in heroines, writing, "They have gone from being [sexually] pure and incompetent to being impure and competent," a pithy claim that is more clever than helpful in understanding the causes of those changes (64). She does quote romance writer Bertrice Small's recollection that the growth of "sub-categories" in the 1970s was an industry effort to find niche markets (59), and she arranges those sub-categories into four groups, each based on traits such as sexual explicitness, practical realism/ verisimilitude, and so forth (63–64).

But practicality (especially in terms of representing the new career options for women) has always had a role in romance fiction, as the original niche subgenre of Doctor-Nurse romances published by Mills & Boon since World War II can attest. So while Jensen's and Small's narrative is accurate, it doesn't account for how the changing lives of women correspond to new subgenres in specific ways, then or now. In other words, what romance criticism has overlooked is that the need for new possibilities and different modes of action for the romance heroine *alongside* the pursuit of a romantic HEA/HFN is linked to women's growing demand for, to paraphrase Russ, access to the options that allow male protagonists their journey.[4]

This reconstitution of women's heroism in terms of having agency in other plots besides the love story has manifested in two primary ways: subgenrification and serialization. Both reflect the expansion of the scope of women's heroism, which results from a long-standing desire in this (women-dominated) genre to see female heroes live complex lives, albeit rooted in the "find partner-marry partner" narrative.

DESIRE FOR FEMALE ACTION I:
SUBGENRES IN ROMANCE

Three main types of plot structures or subgenres in romance speak to the desire for heroic action on the part of the female protagonist and coincide with those in which Russ says one can find "myths that escape from the equation Culture=Male" (90). For her, there are three options in fiction that allow real possibilities of action for heroines because gender roles lose relevance in these narratives: detective stories (ones with "intellectual puzzles" rather than potboilers), late nineteenth- and early twentieth-century supernatural fiction (where strength of character triumphs over gender role restraints), and science fiction (where ingenuity triumphs over physicality and cultural, as well as species, limitations). (These are arguably equivalent to the "integrated and constructive myths" heralded by Carol Pearson and Katherine Pope, as I explain in detail below.) While Russ sees her favored three options as oppositional to the love story, romance novels provide a path to imagining multiple possibilities for female heroism without abandoning traditional narrative (including the love story) as irredeemably tainted by patriarchy. Instead, there is in romance a tendency for dialectical change; once-oppositional forces, such as courtship versus professional success, churn into a new blended narrative, while that which has dated itself is eliminated (a tendency mirrored in changes in the heroine herself).

We can see manifestations of these evolving possibilities in the following romance subgenres, which map onto Russ's conception of stories that make room for heroines:

- The suspense/detective romance, where it is paramount to figure out who disrupted a life or a process and why

- The supernatural/paranormal romance, where intrusions of the unnatural into the familiar require actions that don't conform to traditional gender roles
- Sci-fi/speculative romance, where technological disruption and economic shifts pose challenges to our society and species and need clever solutions

The last includes rethinking gender roles and cultural commonplaces in order to explore a "new world conceptually" (as Russ puts it) on the assumption that true crises and solutions for people require collaboration. In this respect, this romance subgenre again diverges somewhat from Russ, who sees such collective work as incompatible with themes of sex, love, and identity (91–92).

Through the above three subgenres (though not exclusively so), the female protagonist takes up the internal quest to find herself—or *selves*, fragmented by sociopolitical ideology—alongside external action via which she engages with realism and biological determinism, the state and hostile communities, and economic/technological change. The love plot appears in all cases, though its primacy waxes and wanes. The three manifestations of romance heroic action listed above correspond to the subgenre labels used by publishers and readers alike and map well onto Russ's taxonomy, even as there are overlaps between these categories in the broader romance genre. See table I.1 and figure I.1 for two ways to visualize this.

Of the ten novels in this study, Susan Napier's *Love in the Valley* (1985) is closest to the love story that Russ says is the only option given to heroines, while J. D. Robb's sci-fi *In Death* series (1995) and Karen Marie Moning's urban fantasy *Fever* series (2006) range the farthest away. The other texts fall in between those points. Lisa Kleypas's *Dreaming of You* (1994) and Beverly Jenkins's *Indigo* (1996), both historical romances, and the contemporary murder mystery, Linda Howard's *To Die For* (2005), are nearer the center. Kresley Cole's paranormal *Dark Desires after Dusk* (2008), Joanna Bourne's Napoleonic-war thriller *Spymaster's Lady* (2008), Sherry Thomas's *My Beautiful Enemy* (2014)—the second book in her wuxia duology—and Alyssa Cole's contemporary romance *A Princess in Theory* (2018) occupy slightly distant orbits. *Spymaster's Lady* and *My Beautiful Enemy* have espionage plots whereas *Princess in Theory* is a modern fairy tale and *Black Panther* riff. The *In Death* series is both detective romance and futuristic speculative fiction, while the *Fever* series is both murder mystery and urban fantasy. (Steampunk, which I do not include in this survey, could be both detective and sci-fi romance, as in the *Iron Duke* by Meljean Brook, which has human-cyborg hybrid protagonists.) Why do such diverse works qualify as romance novels, one may wonder? The answer is that the love story, with its

Table I.1. Romance novel variants

Love Story	Love Story and . . .
Love in the Valley (1985)—Susan Napier	*In Death* series (1995–)—J. D. Robb
Dreaming of You (1994)—Lisa Kleypas	*To Die For* (2005)—Linda Howard
Indigo (1996)—Beverly Jenkins	*Fever* series (2006–2016)—Karen Marie Moning
	Dark Desires after Dusk (2008)— Kresley Cole
	Spymaster's Lady (2008)—Joanna Bourne
	My Beautiful Enemy (2014)—Sherry Thomas
	A Princess in Theory (2018)—Alyssa Cole

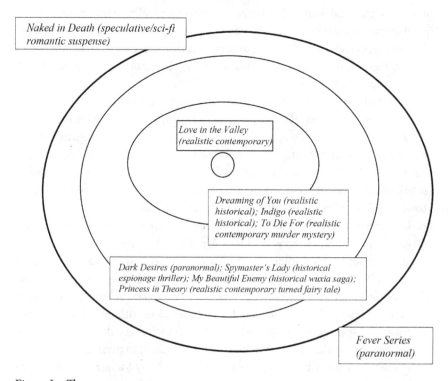

Figure I.1. The romance system.

promise of a happy ending, is the center of gravity; the other plots are tethered to it, even as they allow romance heroines to flex their skills in other realms (and model what kinds of lasting intimate partnerships are desirable in these new worlds). At this moment in time, the genre is a universe of possibilities.

DESIRE FOR FEMALE ACTION II: SERIALIZED ROMANCE

Table I.1 also highlights the development of interconnected romances or serial narrative romances (distinct from the concept of a numbered "category" as in Harlequin Mills & Boon). An Goris has written on this narrative mode in which several novels tell the extended story of one couple's romance ("Happily Ever After . . . and After"). *In Death* is an example of a series about one female protagonist whose love and marriage plot is extended over several books, but the narrative drive comes from other actions on her part in the detective sci-fi mode.

In a departure from this single-couple extended love story, the central protagonists in the first arc or instance of other series may recede to the sidelines in subsequent novels as their friends or family members take center stage in their own love stories in the same narrative universe. *Fever*, for example, is a series in which the resolution of the initial couple's love plot is deferred by the supernatural / urban fantasy plot for several novels, and its heroine gets an HFN rather than an HEA in book five. (The series temporarily moved on to other characters in a supernaturally disrupted world, and then returned to her and her partner as they resumed their paranormal battle against evil.)

In each case, the heroines (Eve Dallas and MacKayla Lane, respectively) are the drivers of one or more whodunit plots (in addition to an ongoing love plot) through which they develop themselves, showing Russ's definition in action. Even *My Beautiful Enemy* and *To Die For*'s heroines have so much agentive potential that it needs two books to be expressed (*My Beautiful Enemy* being a romance with adult protagonists that follows the heroine's Young Adult prequel novel, *The Hidden Blade* (2014), and *To Die For* being book one of a two-book series in which a former cheerleader detects who's trying to kill her). In a variation, *Indigo*, *Dark Desires after Dusk*, *Spymaster's Lady*, and *A Princess in Theory* each belong to a series about a specific narrative world undergoing a geopolitical crisis, and their heroines must do more than love or be loved to survive and play a role in improving that world.[5]

The proliferation of female romance fiction protagonists who act in other spheres besides the traditional one of courtship and marriage is a logical development from having them play lovers alone, and one of many ways in which the genre is always open to change. The impulse expresses itself in two structural ways: one, the rise of subgenres that foreground alternate plots, and two, interconnected stories that make space for the heroines to be on the narrative stage (and happy) in multiple roles—workers, sexual tyros, successful professionals, lovers, wives, mothers, and warriors—and at multiple phases and ages of their narrative lives. The narrative space needed to accommodate the heroine's self-actualization has thus given rise to new subgenres and serialization or what can be termed "episodic novelization."

—ᴍ—

Scholars of folklore and mythology like Russ have examined how women in literature, as in life, have often been given secondary roles that distanced them from the title (and sphere) of hero. But Carol Pearson and Katherine Pope offer a perspective on both women heroines and heroes, defining the latter as female characters who have more independence and free action compared to the former, who are archetypes or stereotypes defined in relation to men (3).[6] They also observe that heroines, a category in which they include the Virgin, the Mistress, and the Helpmate, are limited in their scope and thus unhappy, being variously praised and blamed for not being all three, a bind that all my chapters highlight in varying forms (9).[7]

In contrast, Pearson and Pope see female heroes as freed from sex roles and falling into the categories of the Sage, Artist, and Warrior (9), with the last fully free of playing a supporting part in a man's world (10, 251).[8] Their Sage understands and contests gender-based inequality and patriarchal constraint, a trope that is evident in the detective/espionage romances in this study because the women either know something crucial (particularly in *Spymaster's Lady*) and are looking for a world in which people are willing to accept that, or they're trying to gain knowledge (particularly in *My Beautiful Enemy*, *Fever*, and a *Princess in Theory*) and restructure a community that otherwise clings to traditional notions. If Pearson and Pope's Sage heroes need to either hide their knowledge or pretend that they are ignorant, the Sage figure in romance encounters and overcomes such negative or coping scenarios without deteriorating into death, insanity, or crone status while solving a specific problem. The heroism of this successful romance hero is that she acts in ways she deems necessary and that gains her a community and a romantic partner who celebrate her wisdom, be it a matter of domestic prowess or national security.

The Artist hero includes the subcategory of the Actress who dons a persona in order to persist in an otherwise unlivable world, because "the pressure to play the roles of maiden, mistress, helpmate, and mother makes women into actresses" (196). While literal artist figures of the hero in my study include writer Sara Fielding and chef Julia Fry in *Dreaming of You* and *Love in the Valley*, respectively, the Actress label fits Annique Villiers in *Spymaster's Lady* and Bai Ying Hua in *My Beautiful Enemy* better, though it applies to all of the women protagonists to varying extents. (Pearson and Pope also mention that the "social actress" gives up real emotion and an erotic self for a "controlled and cerebral world," and provide examples of how this can result in schizophrenia and OCD (198)—precisely Holly Ashwin's problem in *Dark Desires after Dusk*.) The Artist/Actress heroes in this study do initiate direct action, however, and while they don different personas, it is because those personas allow them freedom to exercise agency in spaces that are otherwise denied to them; these personas are often identified by the various names the characters give their different selves and serve to facilitate their ownership of disparate parts of themselves.

While Pearson and Pope's Sage and Artist differ slightly from my conception of the heroic woman in romance—one seeking the truth of her sexual needs, gender roles, worth as an economic actor, and relationship to state ideologies—their Warrior hero fits romance well (including my examples, particularly *Indigo*). This hero goes against the establishment in a bid for independence, maintaining a core identity in the face of external pressure, with perhaps some assistance from a male partner (243, 251).[9] While Pearson and Pope insist that a heroic life that effects change and gives satisfaction is seen only in female characters who defy sex-role definitions and act independently (251), romance heroines embrace their preferred versions of sex-role definitions and also act directly; they are not trapped by their accumulated knowledge or permanently forced to choose indirect action—they are all Warriors.

In fact, Pearson and Pope concede that "the traditional woman in her role as lover, mother, worker, or friend may be presented as a warrior" (243), which is certainly true in romance novels: a woman as lover is the standard identity that drives many novels, but many also render her heroic in motherhood, as a laborer, and certainly as a friend, especially to other women. Indeed, romance heroines straddle Pearson and Pope's hero/heroine distinction, in some cases gaining independence through adventure and action (fueled by the knowledge they possess) and in almost every case, role-playing as needed to survive (and thrive) in the process.

A final point of similarity in Pearson and Pope's conception and mine lies in the initial stage of the female hero's journey, with the protagonist being forced from home essentially by patriarchy's chokehold (247–48). Romance novels often narrate (in flashback or the present) this forced movement of the heroine from an inhospitable world to one that she reconfigures—Sara in *Dreaming of*

You experiences it in a subtle fashion while Holly in *Dark Desires* faces it in a more fantastic one, and Hester in *Indigo* escapes chattel slavery—though the initial situation ranges from traditional gender roles to spheres such as political identity and sexual expression. Each romance heroine in this study also reflects the Warrior conception in that she becomes "her own active creator because she must invent the self she wishes to be" (248).

The final stage of romance heroines' journeys may differ, however, from Pearson and Pope's argument that female heroes do not return home because their knowledge or achievements aren't valued in their places of origin. Romance heroines have traditionally returned. (This is one way to read the "society restored" stage in the structure of the romance novel in Pamela Regis's *A Natural History of the Romance Novel* [38].) But the proliferation of serialization in romance and the move from HEA to HFN suggests that a return to the status quo is sometimes undesirable and untenable and that the female hero must go on—and continue to make her home as she goes. In other words, the development of a romance series (such as *In Death*, where one heroine has multiple books that continue to tell her stories) can be read as a way to reconcile the idea of return with the one of journeying onward—a new manifestation of the desire for female heroes and agency in the genre.

Moreover, while Pearson and Pope saw a positive change in the mid-1970s in terms of there being more female heroes in literature, with "integrated and constructive myths" and "androgynous" women who were "intellectual and sexual, aggressive and nurturing, independent and loving, effective in both the public arena and the home," romance fiction heroines represent ongoing battles over fusing such seemingly paradoxical qualities to this day (10–11). The genre is a witness to the fact that this fusion still has to be fought for—thanks to a society that, even into the twenty-first century, has a reactionary preference for dualistic patterns of gendered action.

Romance fiction is the rare genre that envisions successes for women in those battles, largely by conceiving of a social and political restructuring that enables women to have it all. As the genre has evolved, romance heroines have come to reflect and model women's lives in which they do not forgo selfhood but initiate the action of playing multiple roles in service of a nonromantic goal and are adequately supported by their community (romantic partners and others). These novels can in fact claim to be in line with desirable "integrated and constructive myths" (Pearson and Pope 10). If literary fiction offered some models of female heroes over forty years ago, mass-market romance has been working out the nitty-gritty of that heroism ever since.

ROMANCE FICTION SCHOLARSHIP AND THE HEROINE

While romance scholarship has not developed a cohesive theory of the romance heroine, the character is the fulcrum of most analyses. It is useful here to quickly survey the field's history as a prelude to understanding changing approaches to the genre overall and heroines in particular. The first generation of romance scholarship can be traced to Ann Barr Snitow and Tania Modleski's 1979 and 1980 articles, respectively, on Harlequin novels and romance readers, as well as Kay Mussell's *Women's Gothic and Romantic Fiction* (1981) and *Fantasy and Reconciliation* (1984). Modleski followed up her article with the book *Loving with a Vengeance* (1982), Janice Radway's *Reading the Romance* appeared in 1984, and Jan Cohn's *Romance and the Erotics of Property* in 1988. These works put the genre's scholarship on the map, treating it as a popular literature worthy of study, largely through a feminist lens, with Marxism, discourse analysis, Russian formalism, ethnography, and psychoanalysis as accompanying tools. Snitow began the process of noting the complicated nature of the romance heroine and the appeal she may have for the largely female readership, while Modleski suggested that the heroine was an agent of retribution, allowing women readers to experience the mixed pleasure of masochism and then sadism as the romance hero first exercised patriarchal power and then came to heel by the novel's end. Radway found elements of feminist consciousness and charted the components of a heroine's journey in the single-title historical novels she studied. Additionally, through discussions with her chosen group of readers, she developed a taxonomy for the genre using that data set: romances that either fail or succeed in acknowledging the readers' awareness of patriarchal problems while also offering an ending that assures them of happiness within that structure. Cohn read selected category romances against earlier works like *Pride and Prejudice* and pointed out that a narrative of heroines acquiring economic power lay beneath the one about passion.

For several decades, many of these works served as the dominant perspectives and models in the genre; most new scholars began their engagement with romance by fretting about its associated stigma and countering that either through reader-response studies or literary and discourse analysis about feminist examples. The latter tack, ironically, may only have reinforced a sense that the genre has a reactionary core. By and large, the field seemed to be on the defensive, warily circling the themes of courtship and marriage in the women-focused genre while debates about mass culture, feminism, and pornography raged in the public arena and academia.

Heroines were discussed in these studies but without specific definitions or distinctions. Radway, for instance, presented the genre as the narrative of the heroine's journey from tomboyish adolescence to traditional femininity and motherhood (i.e., becoming a mother and returning to her mother as well). Cohn wrote about heroines grappling with economic insecurity while reassessing the contemporary market value of female chastity and Mussell discussed how only female protagonists who passed a test of domestic competence won Mr. Right and the status of a romance heroine. Romance author Jayne Anne Krentz edited an anthology in 1992 in which best-selling writers distilled their visions of romance heroes and heroines, at least partly as a rebuke to what they perceived to be scholars' negative views on romance readers and writers.

After a somewhat fallow period, 1997 saw a shift, with new scholars entering the field without seeming to dwell solely on which romance novels were worth studying as feminist exceptions.[10] Pamela Regis's seminal 2003 work, *A Natural History of the Romance Novel*, made an argument about the inalienable elements of the genre and the heroine's journey to achieving marital felicity in a defined society, while explicitly rejecting scholarly precedent that limited itself to scoring the genre on its feminist credentials. A harbinger of the second generation of romance scholarship, in which I situate my own work, Regis was followed by numerous essay collections that compiled a variety of new approaches to romance, notably, Sarah S. G. Frantz and Eric Murphy Selinger's aptly named *New Approaches to Popular Romance Fiction* (2012) and William A. Gleason and Eric Murphy Selinger's *Romance Fiction and American Culture* (2016), as well as *From Australia With Love* (2004) by Juliet Flesch on Australian romance writing, *Desert Passions* (2012) by Hsu-Ming Teo about orientalist themes in romance novels, *Happily Ever After* (2016) by Catherine M. Roach, which expanded Regis's primary elements of a romance novel and linked the genre to a secular erotic theology, and *Human in Death* (2017) by Kecia Ali, on ethics in J. D. Robb's female cop *In Death* series.[11] The recent *Black Love Matters* (2022) is a collection compiling the perspectives of Black romance authors as well as academic writers on the features of Black life and love in romance novels. The romance heroine is present to various degrees in many of these works, since the genre often centers her, though she may be a shadow presence in these analyses or described as a technical element or symbol for a myth or ideology. Other salient perspectives on the heroine include essays that study how specific authors choose to construct her (Kate Moore and Eric Murphy Selinger, Veera Mäkelä, and Katherine E. Lynch et al.). While she is frequently discussed in relation (or opposition) to the hero in studies of heterosexual romance, it is her relationship to herself (selves) that I foreground in this work.

Though I trained as a student in the first generation of romance scholarship, this book bears the imprint of the new wave I saw in my post–graduate school years, by which I mean it is not about the rare or potentially feminist examples of an otherwise regressive genre but about a phenomenon at its core. In effect, I spotlight the heroine not only to supplement previous assessments of her role in a romance novel, but to provide this additional perspective: that every romance heroine's journey is a recognition and heroic rejection of the false choices that prevailing ideologies in different spheres force on women and an allegory for the working of the genre itself.[12] In other words, my study is not about exceptional feminist romance heroines; it's a glimpse into how romance heroines always engage in acts of heroic self-definition on multiple fronts, which the genre mirrors through its constant evolution and repudiation of its public pillorying.

Romance heroines enact the dilemma of being "voluntold" into a prescriptive gender role versus a full selfhood, one of the many dichotomies that women face. In these false choices, we see the ideological pressures women encounter that require them to choose between seemingly incompatible elements of their social, political, and economic identities. The pattern has a long, well-documented history. Margery Hourihan reminds us that the persistence of the quest myth in Western culture reinforces binaries such as "men to women, reason to passion, soul (or mind) to body," and also structures them into a good versus evil dichotomy (2). The hero is portrayed as being the superior actor and when he encounters women, they are cast as helpers or opponents; moreover, the story defines good and bad femininity and inscribes the subordinate place of women (Hourihan 3). This tradition explains the presence of such dualism in the romance heroine and how she might expect (and is expected) to be drawn to the "inferior" element (such as physical need or sentiment). By the end of a novel or in the course of a romance series, however, the heroine rejects such judgments and composes her own dialectically formulated self.

Critics have provided some analysis of this trajectory and self-making in the past. In 1979, Snitow pointed out the genre's distillation of the psychological and social experiences of its female readers and its layered appeal to them as she examined the life and behavior of the heroines in a sampling of Harlequin Mills & Boon category romances. She rightly noted that the heroines in her data set "are pliable" and exhibit some paradoxical behavior, with several "scenes of the hero and heroine together in which she does a lot of social lying to save face, pretending to be unaffected by the hero's presence while her body melts or shivers" (145). It is her observation that has sparked this book-length study because I realized that the implications of this phenomenon are worth unpacking: the "social lying" feature is a door to the heroine's ontology, even in those short, somewhat simplistic 1970s romances. In effect, romance heroines experience (and represent) themselves as many selves, but it's the onslaught of demands others make on them that causes their initial fragmentation. How the heroines reconcile some of these (often opposing) demands, spurn others, and construct a new self through a dialectical process is the core narrative of all mass-market romance fiction.

This study, therefore, is not about select outlier feminist characters but about a constitutional trait of the genre. While a great deal of prior scholarship on romance novels has in some way engaged with the question of whether they are feminist or not, this book is an outgrowth of a more recent scholarly wave that feels no pressure to excavate such potential (a tendency that partly stemmed from scholars in the 1980s seeking to justify their own popular culture analyses). It examines the working of a central dynamic, which is visible in some form in *all* romances as I have defined them. In other words, my study is not picking "progressive" novels. It is not my intent to claim that these novels are feminist (or not). My goal here is to analyze how the genre perceives the persistent ideologies and structural inequalities that try to force women into a cul-de-sac, how the plots function around the tension produced by one or more of these binary choices, and how the author writes the heroine out of it.

In some cases, the resolutions to the dilemmas themselves contain paradoxes and go against readers' avowed progressive politics, the most pronounced examples of these novels being termed "problematic faves."[13] In a related vein, Eva Illouz's *Consuming the Romantic Utopia* points to the contradictions of capitalism that infuse romance narratives in many media, such as the simultaneous adoption of leisure and consumption practices as character traits alongside the principles of rational productivity; I see this most clearly in the *In Death* series as well as in other novels where a worker heroine marries into wealth. My focus is on understanding romance heroines within this context and how their actions beyond the love plot reflect changes in women's lives as well as the evolving tensions between political principles and personal desires, whether that be feminist wariness of prescribed sexual/affective bonds, economic independence warring with the promised comfort of being financially stewarded, nuanced ideas of gender presentation competing with traditional feminine culture, or political subversion of, or naturalization into, a community.

Jan Cohn, among others, points out some of the contradictions inherent in and gratifications resulting from romance fiction, both stemming from the fact that women and their literary stand-in, the romance heroine, experience forbidden desire (for and against existing authority/patriarchy). Tracing the origins of romance fiction to socioeconomic changes in the eighteenth and nineteenth centuries, Cohn notes that marriage became the "locus of contradictions" for women in bourgeois patriarchal ideology: the place where the tension of not having opportunities to gain economic power in a new system clashed with being told that love or affective desire needed to guide them to marriage (which had been the older mode of career advancement, so to speak). Cohn sees romance fiction as a genre that rose to provide a fantasy solution to that catch-22—a narrative that provided the heroine a roadmap to economic power without violating the bourgeois rules for being a good woman. But the romance heroine of the mass-market form, per Cohn, also faces the exhortation of second wave feminism to be independent even though economic opportunities for women were still scarce. (Cohn was writing in the 1980s but the point is sadly still relevant.) Consequently, Cohn's argument that mass-market romance represents a woman's journey to power while strategically negotiating the contradictions imposed on her by bourgeois patriarchy is valid.

This book departs, however, from her reading that the genre provides the alibi of love and marriage for the real story—the "aggressive" pursuit of economic unassailability for women—and is a fantasy solution to an insoluble problem of economic precarity (127–30). My analysis sees the romance heroine's journey, in four realms in heterosexual romance, as both revealing the contradictions that hedge women in, and imagining actual solutions to them. The heroine rescripts companionate erotic bonds and seeks nurturing human networks in order to gain economic, sexual, gender, and communal coherence. In other words, while Cohn and others writing in the 1980s saw limited solutions to women's powerlessness in the romances in their data set, the distance from that moment, as well as developments in the genre (reflective of societal change), open up a different reading: instead of seeing the genre as a hero/heroine story, it's productive to see it as a heroine/heroine one. The heroine/heroine story locates the tension between the heroine's internalized false dichotomies and her dawning awareness that she contains multitudes and that society wants her to abandon some of her selves. It is to *this* conflict that romance texts offer the following solution: practice accepting one's desire for sex, love, as well as extra-romantic agency, choose a political ally as your erotic partner, and envision other allies who support policies that are necessary to your future fulfillment and integrated self. This is partly what explains the iterative attraction of romance novels—they stimulate a dopamine response, but one that forges the cognitive pathway to recognizing what a full self looks like rather than the one that causes addictive behavior that prevents revolutionary change.

The central female protagonists of romance often undertake journeys of identity to get to that full self. They struggle to establish who they are amidst a world that seems determined to limit their choices, and become heroes on the way to claiming their right to self-definition. In their journey (whether in a single novel or a series), they enact a dialectic in which they accept some aspects of external definitions of their identity and contest others; this dialectic resonates with romance readers—the genre generates over a billion dollars per annum—because it represents the dichotomies women continue to face in the twenty-first century under late capitalism: native versus outsider, paid professional versus unpaid mother or homemaker, silly femme versus intelligent butch, sexual sophisticate versus chaste virgin, worthy matron versus morally corrupt MILF/cougar, careerist versus welfare queen, and so forth.[14]

The COVID-19 crisis has thrown one such binary into stark relief, with many media pieces on women in 2020–21 structured around the dichotomy of paid and unpaid labor. At the time of writing, even a simple search with the keywords "pandemic" and "women" yields over a dozen articles from the *New York Times* alone that describe how women, especially low-income women of color, have been forced out of paid positions and school to take on the bulk of domestic work and caretaking. This is not a surprise to women, who must often leave jobs and careers when such crises loom. The pandemic of free-market patriarchy depleting women's mental, physical, financial, and communal health is ongoing.

Similarly, the period between 2020–22 has given us examples of women being lambasted in other domains. There has been a peanut gallery criticizing or policing women athletes, for instance, whether it be Megyn Kelly chiding Naomi Osaka after she withdrew from the French Open for mental health reasons, social media users and a loudmouthed British TV host complaining about Simone Biles being weak during the Olympics (without caring that she is a survivor of an era of US gymnastics associated with Larry Nassar), or the European Handball Federation fining the Norwegian women's handball team for refusing to wear their "uniform" of bikini bottoms. Meanwhile, runner Sha'Carri Richardson was given a month's suspension that prevented her from competing in the Olympics because she took the compound THC (in a US state where it was legal) to deal with the stress of her mother's death. It also came to light that athletes who are mothers have to pay for childcare if they go to the Olympics. Women athletes also come under suspicion of not being a woman based on their testosterone levels, as was the case in 2014 with Indian sprinter Dutee Chand and, more recently, South African runner Caster Semenya. You pay if you're too much of a woman or if you're not woman enough.

The political landscape is rife with corresponding equivalents of reining in women. Hillary Clinton's intelligence, experience, and ambition were seen as such a great threat in the 2016 US presidential election that the conspiracy theory generators worked overtime to label her the head of a child-trafficking cabal. Representatives Alexandria Ocasio-Cortez, Rashida Tlaib, and Ilhan Omar are routinely threatened and called un-American for their policies, their ethnicities, their faiths, and their gender. California Congresswoman Katie Hill was forced to resign in 2019 after news outlets published nude photos of her as well as details about her sexual relationships crossing into her professional ones. Hill's bisexuality and her powerful position on the House Oversight Committee likely played a role in what was essentially a revenge porn smear campaign (Factora; Serfaty et al.).

In crisis or in seemingly good times, women are constantly forced into a box and threatened with harm and excommunication. Romance dwells on this problem, sometimes in the realist mode and sometimes in the fantastic or mythic one. The heroines' identity quests often involve them facing two seemingly mutually exclusive choices, with various characters or a community pushing one choice on them as more virtuous or societally acceptable—an ultimatum they question.

Their journeys to negotiate selfhood against this false binary are similar to the genre's relationship to the "literature vs. trashy novels" rhetoric that dominates most references to romance. So in addition to representing the struggles of women under late capitalism, the dialectic in which heroines piece together their true selves from contradictory elements also serves as an allegory of the genre's fight to retain ownership of its identity (in the face of media and scholarly attempts to define what it is and to limit its novelistic potential).[15] In other words, alongside being similar to the struggles of most other novel protagonists in a bildungsroman, the quests undertaken by romance heroines parallel the genre's struggle to control its identity as a specific form of love narrative. In this process, it ignores labels (academic as well as popular) of what it is and is not, and continually recalibrates itself by taking on new elements while shedding ones that no longer fit a contemporary audience's ideas of romance and the erotic. It is congruous that spurning such simplistic binaries by having the heroine question any imposed on her in favor of a dialectical synthesis is the genre's chosen narrative mechanism.

In effect, these are stories of how the romance novel observes itself through others' censorious eyes and how it organizes itself against (often conflicting) public judgments: stereotypical or predictable versus illogical or hysterically unpredictable, seductive versus boring, disabling versus empowering, feminized versus feminist caricature, sexually scandalous versus conservative, consuming versus consumptive, duplicitous versus one-dimensional, revolting

trash versus addictive junk. Its heroines echo its awareness of its public reception and are the primary way in which romance authors tackle not just women's
issues but reveal their experience of academic and popular judgements on romance fiction. When romance fiction heroines fight back against false choices,
they thus enact not just the symbolic function of battling misogyny but embody
the genre's own self-deterministic nature.

In anatomizing this aspect of the genre, my book also steps in a different
direction than earlier romance fiction scholarship that prioritized surveys of
readers, literary genealogies, and narratological structures seen in works like
Radway's and Regis's, respectively, which are often imitated by entrants to the
field. The methodologies in those studies are ethnography and feminist psychoanalysis (Radway) and narrative history and structuralism (Regis). This book
aims to broaden those paradigms by applying the close reading technique from
literary studies to select texts through an intersectional lens, thus bringing the
workings of varied ideologies into focus and historicizing changes in the genre
overall. This tack is more in keeping with my roots as a literary and cultural
studies scholar and provides a template for others.

I have published on readership of romance in prior work but found that the
method can entrench one in the defensive crouch, using reader responses on
romance fiction's worth or virtues to shadowbox the imagined critic of the
genre. This was a default perspective for graduate students like me in the 2000s
and is the knee-jerk reaction of many romance readers to public disdain. Alternately, the ethnographer bestows on themself the ability to see problems that
the average reader seemingly overlooks. Ethnography can be a valuable tool,
of course, particularly in learning about the experiences of writers, as in the
work of Joanna Gregson and Jen Lois, but it is not my strength. I have not been
able to progress from asking readers how and why they read romance to fruitful insights that will deepen my analysis. For that reason, rather than writing
a listicle-like survey of "good" romance novels or developing inferences based
on self-reported data on readership, I elected to foreground the richness and
depth of different kinds of romance novels and use those details to demonstrate
the genre's relevance and appeal to its audience.

For readers who would have liked to see a larger data set, I have included
a short list of suggestions in an appendix but you will find that you can locate
one or more of the patterns I identify in my sample in almost any heterosexual
romance you turn to. For those of you who may not expect as much plot sum-
mary of the included novels as you will find here, that, too, stems from my literary studies background; each of the two novels in a chapter serves as evidence
of an ideological domain that operates in the genre while letting me carry out

in-depth close reading at the level of specific word choices and plot turns. This method felt appropriate because my claim that the genre represents problems such as the virgin/whore dichotomy or the pressures of paid and unpaid labor may seem self-evident, but the workings of that representation deserve unpacking. I also offer the plot summaries because there is no accepted romance canon, and I cannot assume you will be familiar with a specific novel or indeed with the remarkable diversity of plots the genre can contain. Finally, my hope is that this focus on a few texts will act as a corrective to the tendency in both academic and media romance critics to subsume the complexities of an individual romance novel under broad claims that create the impression that the genre is a monolith.[16]

WHY THESE NOVELS

While limited in size, this study includes a wide-ranging sample of ten novels, which span thirty-five-years and many subgenres. The technical term for this methodology is a purposive heterogeneous sampling, and the novels represent variations of the false dichotomy phenomenon that is endemic in the genre: a heroine faces a world that labels her reductively, but she fends off these external attempts of categorization and develops her own integrated self. She thus alludes to and challenges the false dilemmas through which patriarchal culture tries to control women. Moreover, these novels allegorize the high/low binary that detractors use to pan the genre, with their authors' awareness that romance novels are ghettoized and disparaged in a zero-sum game of cultural capital forming a shadow narrative to the heroines' struggles. Nine of these ten authors are American, the exception being a New Zealander, reflecting the outsized role of American romance publishing in the genre after the 1970s.

In selecting my texts, I have aimed for a maximum-variation sampling of subgenres and plots: historical romances set in the nineteenth century (Regency and Victorian espionage stories and an Underground Railroad tale in the antebellum United States), a futuristic sci-fi thriller, an urban fantasy series, a contemporary single-title murder mystery, a contemporary Harlequin category romance, a contemporary single-title paranormal, and a contemporary single-title fairy tale.[17] This selection is meant to help readers see the ubiquity of the abovementioned phenomenon in the genre, and though it may appear in a slightly different form in an individual text, it is not an aberration only found alongside some specific definition of a feminist heroine.

The book's five chapters (each analyzing two novels) lay out four discursive spaces (plus their intersections) in which heroines grapple with a dialectical process of identity formation and self-determination: sexual desire or assertion, gender expression and roles, labor and class, and community/nation. In each sphere, they determine who they are by fusing together options that are often presented to them as mutually exclusive or incompatible, such as ideologies of sexual behavior, versions of womanliness, paid and unpaid work or activities, and multiple citizenships. Additionally, the final chapter brings all these spheres together to demonstrate how they operate simultaneously in the narratives of Black heroines.

The primary romance story in all the novels in the study involves cis, monogamous, heterosexual, allosexual characters, because queer and polyamorous romance, while not devoid of the pressures and inequalities of heteropatriarchy, would steer the analysis in a slightly different direction from the operation of the intra-gender power dynamic I am most invested in unpacking. It therefore felt prudent to constrain the sample to these variables. But romance novels with minoritized identities related to sexuality, the body, and neurodiversity have made significant inroads into the genre in recent years, and I hope future work will examine examples of such. Certainly the evolving genre is worthy of sustained attention from a host of perspectives, including queer studies, fat studies, disability studies, and critical race studies, especially as the romance publishing and writing world grapples with its stated commitment to diversity and inclusion.

CHAPTERS

"Sexuality" demonstrates how romance heroines' bodies are a locus for reframing existing narratives of heterosexual desire through *Love in the Valley* and *Dark Desires after Dusk*. In the former, flirtatious young virgin Julia Fry fights to not be treated as a frivolous sexpot by the reserved, priggish man to whom she is attracted. Battling a series of comic misunderstandings about her sexual experience, she proudly declares her sexual feelings and admits both her virginity and carnal needs. In contrast, the academic heroine in the paranormal romance *Dark Desires after Dusk* is a familiar stereotype—an absent-minded, unworldly scientist who is focused on her work, partly because she is afraid of her sexual needs. Her journey—a literal road trip—overcomes this stereotype of the brainy but physically weak and sexually naive spinster. She synthesizes a new self through the support of a "found family" (of hedonistic, sexually amoral Valkyries) and a freewheeling demon lover, both of whom help her to accept her full powers. Julia and Holly, in their measured and upfront approach to expressing or controlling desire, embody the genre's longstanding resolve to treat female sexual desire as a key narrative element of the human story. The novels also show how the genre's practitioners alter the explicitness of sex scenes as and when appropriate—in express defiance of romance fiction being labeled either reactionary or debauched.

"Gender" explores gender display and its place in maintaining or challenging the normative gender order. The chapter examines how the heroine in the urban fantasy *Fever* series is literally ground into the dirt for her American southern-belle upbringing and cutesy personal style while an ex-cheerleader and entrepreneur in *To Die For* faces murder attempts for her contemporary version of southern US womanhood and confidence. The latter heroine is a sexy blonde seemingly targeted by someone who refuses to believe that a former cheerleader could have worked hard for professional success. While she has to deal with this stalker and two exes who dumped her for flaws related to her femininity, *Fever*'s heroine has to fight for the right to define herself outside of the "ditzy blonde who gets killed / butch survivor" binary with which she is presented by an inhuman heteropatriarchy. In both cases, different antagonists conflate the heroines' bodies, appearance, and actions and treat them as deserving of punishment, while they maintain their resolve and resist the criticisms of others. Their goal, like that of the genre itself, is to reconcile pieces of their past selves and new identities without succumbing to a society's vision of who they should be. This chapter on gender-based identity struggles thus takes on the most common stereotypes imposed on women in general and on romance heroines in particular.

In "Work," I examine labor-based identity in the novels *Dreaming of You* and *Naked in Death*. These heroines' encounters with the hero and other characters involve their self-reconstruction in relation to their worth as productive actors (rather than passive consumers or laborers). While *Dreaming*'s Victorian heroine combats challenges to being accepted as a popular author of social problem novels, *Naked*'s protagonist never considers giving up being a twenty-first-century data-driven cop to become a full-time socialite wife to her rich husband. While the former novel is a direct allegory for romance authors and the misconceptions associated with their profession, the latter poses an interesting feminist intervention in a masculine profession and stages how class mobility and neoliberal policing shape the heroine's work life and self-presentation. Additionally, the heroines show two different approaches to emotional labor (the labor of monitoring one's feelings and affect in professional settings) and emotion work (doing the same in home settings) and their male counterparts play significant roles in helping them build their professional identities and ease their domestic management burdens.

"Citizenship" examines national identity through the historical romance novels *Spymaster's Lady* and *My Beautiful Enemy*. In both, the heroine engages with the public dimension of citizenship, one that is varyingly a source of reassurance or tension to her when she has to deal with other political actors. The Napoleonic era French-Welsh spy in *Spymaster's Lady* and the Anglo-Chinese *wuxia* (warrior) in *My Beautiful Enemy*'s Qing China / Victorian period Britain both grapple with their patriotic loyalty and identity as they fall in love with an Other. Asked by powerful state forces to deprioritize their existing allegiances for another polity, both refuse to choose between lover and patria despite its dangerous consequences—loss of liberty, love, and life. Through this identity conflict about one's place in, and loyalty to, a nation, the heroines' allegiances and actions question the false choice between political selves forced on them. As they encounter contradictory evidence, they reassess what they thought or others told them of their national heritage and duty, eventually rejecting some of that doctrine to make room for a new self-conception. These historical romances serve as a space where the genre enacts its resistance to false dilemmas as a play between its heroines' (and readers') competing territorial identities—the political is made personal.

"Intersections" brings together all the above discursive perspectives to demonstrate how they can operate alongside those of ethnicity and race, most visible in romance novels with Black protagonists and protagonists of African heritage. In Beverly Jenkins's *Indigo*, a romance heroine on the Underground Railroad in antebellum Michigan upends her contemporaries' (and readers') expectations of class, gender, sexuality, and citizenhood as well as racial identity. As a property-owning, straitlaced, anti-slavery activist who takes control of her sexual and political sovereignty, this heroine refuses several false double binds to construct a free Black female selfhood. In the second example, *A Princess in Theory*, a working-class orphan learns to write her own Cinderella story as she configures a place for herself outside the limitations that anti-Black racism, sexism, anti-science ideology, and class impose. In this *Black Panther*–evoking story of a lost princess from an African nation (that is written as having never experienced European colonization), the scientist heroine learns how to accept a retconned heritage, newfound blood relatives, and a chance to apply her public health skills in the service of her new community. Author Alyssa Cole brings to life a classic fairy tale but adds a twist that centers a Black woman's power and worth.

In each of these chapters, I show a different facet of my argument that romance fiction heroines do not just serve a narratological function but also embody the genre's self-determinist nature, and I make a case for why dialectical progression is the natural narrative strategy and perspective in romance fiction. Refusing to cringingly accept the label of pornography or aspire to the classist and sexist conception of what may be termed capital L Literature, the genre has flourished while constantly discarding old ideas of courtship and intimate partnerships and absorbing contemporary ones, thus becoming a dynamic space for the love story. It is a fitting operating principle for a genre whose stories are of heroines controlling their own identity in a world that prevents women from having it all and tells them they must pick one of two options that society gives them in every arena of their lives.

REPLACING JOSEPH CAMPBELL'S MONOMYTH WITH A DUOMYTH

The romance heroine's journey unfolds amid a community she creates through people she encounters—a community that helps her battle forces that want her to pick between two seemingly exclusive choices (such as mother or warrior). That the genre as a whole is on to a female heroism model that has been elusive or marginalized in other fiction might be further proven with one final perspective on heroines. In her discussion of what makes successful heroines in Patricia McKillop's fantasy novels, Christine Mains improves on Pearson and Pope's discussion of a female hero by pointing out the limits of their conception. She notes that their examples show the female hero's journey ending in death or failure, but in fantasy fiction, there are examples of powerful women, ones who can have it all—even independence along with love. She paraphrases Pearson and Pope's argument that "the female hero who seeks fulfilment in all aspects of identity, in selfhood, in work, and in relationships, is unlikely to achieve her goal" (28), but she points out that this and other models of the female hero fail to explain the successful women in McKillop who manage to achieve multiple goals. She therefore proposes what she terms a "duomyth" as a better explanation for the powerful women in her study (29). Mains identifies two key elements of the duomyth: first, these stories have a male character who is an expression of an aspect of the female hero, so the heroine's journey does not necessitate solitude or a choice between love and life, and second, the stories reconceive narrative marriage in a way that shows a couple whose pair-bond lasts across disagreements over time (32). She suggests that such a revamped version of the concepts of love and marriage, with equality possible alongside romance, is a better feminist schema than expecting authors to eschew love and marriage because they allegedly trap all women.

This duomyth is increasingly visible in mass-market romance, especially in the last two decades' heterosexual romance series: the heroine grows into an equitable romantic relationship with a man, the pair may argue but make up, and the heroine isn't forced to choose between career, identity, and love. (While heroines may grapple with these issues in many permutations of romantic bonds, the duomyth is most relevant to straight coupledom, which it extracts from the inequities of patriarchy.) Moreover, in opposition to data that shows that men do less emotion work if their female partners have increased work stress that spills over into home life (Minnotte et al. 789, 790), romance offers examples of the opposite behavior in male heroes when heroines face professional demands, including in the examples in this study. Male romance heroes take on emotion work in the sense of "providing support and encouragement to others, thereby bolstering self-esteem, creating positive outlooks, and enhancing the well-being of others," and they often make financial and domestic contributions to the partnership in a way that allows the heroines to take on other goals (Minnotte et al. 775). This structure aligns with Main's duomyth notion of successful women heroes, who have a male helpmeet who represents an externalized version of some of their own qualities, and with whom they have a long partnership that lasts beyond routine squabbles. In this sense, even if emotion work or other labor might be solely performed by the heroine at the beginning of a romance, over the course of the story it becomes something others do for them, especially their heroes. The pandemic is the latest evidence that real life is trailing behind this ideal, but that the model exists in this genre is worth highlighting—improved societies must be imagined before they can be fought for.

To conclude, in the romance novels in this study, heroines do not accept that women's independence makes long life and strong, loving relationships impossible—they overcome that threat. The romance heroine is thus one who serves to show that the "can't have it all" idea is a central ideological weapon of contemporary patriarchy; she can neutralize it by demanding a supportive community (intimate partner and others) and acting to intervene in her own life—and that this is the path to restoring her atomized parts into one unified, true self whose journey continues beyond the romantic HEA. In the love story, she is heroic in seeking the truth of her sexual needs and gender display as well as her worth as an economic actor under early and late capitalism—with its attendant geopolitical and technological tensions—all while finding and maintaining companionate relationships. These themes are even more prominent in narratives undermining or challenging ideological frameworks that allude to real-world oppressive equivalents, and in these novels the heroine lays claim to the citizenships in political society that speak to her truth. Indeed then, it is in romance fiction that Russ's desire for "fictional myths growing out of [the lives of women] and told by themselves for themselves" is being fulfilled, through novels that "provide myths for dealing with the kinds of experiences we are actually having now, instead of the literary myths we have inherited, which only tell us about the kinds of experiences we think we ought to be having" (92). The love story, in other words, is but the starting point from which heroic action for women can be imagined, one that paves the way for other kinds of female agency and adventures in mass-market romance.

NOTES

1. That first study on heroes was meant to redress the fact that the hero had rarely been examined in detail even though romance novels function through both heroes and heroines, and both can serve to critique the primary ideological forces of the past century.

2. Russ capitalized the words "Love Story" to distinguish it as a genre, but in order to maintain consistency with other uses in this work, all instances have been kept lowercase.

3. Margaret Anne Jensen notes that the number is "an indication that [the novel] is but one in a regularly released series" (59).

4. I understand that statements about women and heroines risk the charge of gender essentialism, so I'd like to again note that the genre has focused on cis women's journeys until recently and this study examines that tradition.

5. *Love in the Valley* is the first in Napier's Marlowe series (for Harlequin Mills & Boon, when there weren't other narratively linked series in category romance in the 1980s). *Dreaming of You* is the second in Kleypas's *Gambler* series. *A Princess in Theory* is the first in the *Reluctant Royals* series, and the heroines in these novels as well as in *Indigo* appear briefly in later ones starring other romantic protagonists.

6. See also Dana Heller on how patriarchal myths deny women the quest story (11).

7. Pearson and Pope also provide other examples of women under the Mistress and Wife stereotypes or archetypes to show how even in these roles women can be heroes if they either highlight how inadequate that category is or demand equality.

8. The other two do so but without as much success, or they role-play to some degree to cope with patriarchal constrictions. To Pearson and Pope, women who escape entrapment in limiting sex role definitions and who can act directly in the world have a greater chance for fulfilment and social effectiveness than women in any other of their categories. The Sage is entrapped by her wisdom; the Artist is restricted by the need to act indirectly. The Warrior may be punished for her violation of the strictures—sexual, religious, or economic—of her society, but

inside she is free and whole, having created and acted upon her own inner voices and having openly confronted the world (251).

9. Pearson and Pope create a further parallel between Campbell's hero's journey and the female Warrior's journey by saying that the woman does not need a man; but just as a man may be aided by a goddess, the woman Warrior gets "strength from the helpful god or the "light" male" (248), reflecting a social change in which men and women believe they can help each other without the loss of either's career (249). This alliance is evident in the romance novels included in my survey (which is limited to heterosexual pair-bond novels). In each, the woman romance hero follows this path of departure and pieces together new knowledge of a self that internalized oppressive ideologies had fractured or appropriated and often does so with the support of the romantic partner.

10. For a thoughtful argument about this first/second generation distinction, see the Introduction to Sarah S. G. Frantz and Eric Murphy Selinger's edited collection *New Approaches to Popular Romance Fiction* (2–8).

11. For a comprehensive review of the most significant scholarship on mass-market romance, see the 2020 collection *The Routledge Research Companion to Popular Romance Fiction* (Kamblé, Selinger, and Teo).

12. Maureen Murdock's *The Heroine's Journey* approaches contemporary women's lives through a mix of psychology, New Age feminist mythology, Campbell's hero's journey, and memoir but doesn't substantially aid a literary or cultural analysis of the ideological forces that a romance heroine contests. Young adult and steampunk romance novelist Gail Carriger's *The Heroine's Journey: For Writers, Readers, and Fans of Popular Culture* tries to create a parallel structure to Campbell's hero's journey for other novelists by using mythological female figures as archetypes for women-centered stories. It is structural/morphological in nature and more of a writer's instructional manual that is useful for identifying or writing certain plot beats in heroine tales. Similarly, Jayne Anne Krentz's 1992 anthology *Dangerous Men and Adventurous Women* has a few essays by romance writers that discuss the heroine as a significant character trope in the genre but are meant partly to defend the genre from feminist critiques and explain the essayist's approach to the trope to other writers.

13. Romances with billionaire or prince heroes, for instance, continue to stage a form of money porn or female acquisition of political privilege through companionate marriage. "Age-gap" romances with older heroes resurrect the desire and fear of the punishing/protective father figure. There are the recently christened "dark romances," where the older theme of unequal sexual power between the protagonists, including scenes of sexual assault, are recast as role play involving dubious consent or consensual kink, with the suggestion that the submissive partner has equal power. Stories that eroticize pregnancy or

romanticize biologically formed families continue to circulate, as do those that erase or marginalize POC or foreground traditionally Western and Christian perspectives and spaces. Readers routinely exclaim over the latest novel they've read that is "bananas"—because it represents one or more contradictions that the reader senses.

14. Twitter user Will Sommer posted about Senator Elizabeth Warren being called a cougar in some alleged "scandal" about having had sex with a man in his 20s. The photo he tweeted showed a press conference being called by "Blundering pro-Trump smear artists Jack Burkman and Jacob Wohl." To Burkman and Wohl, the "scandal" was clearly meant to prove that she is somehow unfit for office (@willsommer).

15. Novelistic texts are those that utilize the novel form's ability to borrow and adapt different narrative forms and structures of narrative in order to keep evolving and staying relevant.

16. I delineate this phenomenon and its repercussions for the genre's public image (and treatment in academic circles) in the essay "Romance in the Media" in the *Routledge Research Companion* (2020).

17. In maximum variation sampling, a small sample is collected but it captures a variety of cases that show the widely differing elements of data possible within that set so as to propose claims about the average case.

ONE

—ᴧᴧᴠ—

SEXUALITY

THE POPULAR PERCEPTION OF THE term *romance fiction* is that it's a synonym for *sex books*. When critics have addressed episodes of sex in romance
novels, they have frequently read them as symptoms of women's internalization
of regressive, confining ideologies. For Jan Cohn, romance limits the heroine's
journey solely to sexual development triggered by a sexually disturbing man,
and she also sees the genre's channeling of female desire into monogamous
marriage as a deterrent to the questioning of hegemonic sexual mores. While
this critical tradition emphasizes what romance fails to achieve, this chapter
scrutinizes romance heroines' sexuality for alternative readings that can tell
us what it accomplishes.

Women's experiences of sex and sexuality, which romance mirrors, are undoubtedly structured by heteropatriarchal double standards into binaries of
virgin / whore, sexual naïf / sexual adventuress, matron / MILF or cougar,
motherly wife / lover, and so on. What has yet to be studied, however, is that
the genre shows writers' uneasiness about these false binary choices and their
attempts to counter them by dialectically synthesizing elements of those oppositional states, which results in a more sexually nuanced heroine. The character
will often change or reaffirm her sexual self-schema—that is, her understanding
of which sexual and romantic desires are a good fit for her, including in novels
that start with the heroine facing a stricture about the "correct" way to feel and
behave in this arena. In general, romances show the heroine's relationship to her
own sexuality evolving. Even if we were to read her desires as eventually being
corralled within her relationship to the hero, it is still worthwhile to acknowledge that she will frequently acquire a more fluid perspective regarding sex and
not remain trapped in the initial "virginity=good / sexuality=bad" dichotomy.

In effect, the heroine starts with a "co-schematic profile": showing avoidance or approach-avoidance behaviors, which are a mix of negative and positive cognitive and affective responses to sexual cues toward the love interest triggered by positive and negative ideas about sexuality that she has internalized (Cyranowski and Andersen 1365). Over the course of the novel, she restructures her profile to a "positive schematic" one, exhibiting attraction behaviors. If hesitant about her sexual desires or made to feel diffident about them at the outset, the heroine eventually expresses a verbal and physical affirmation of her sexual self and her bond with a partner. This shift involves bodily states (including virginity and arousal), emotional awareness (thinking and feeling desire), and actions (receiving sexual overtures, enjoying them, initiating them, and controlling them). The heroine's process of synthesizing a new schema occurs in the face of others' assumptions, actions, and reactions vis-à-vis her sexuality (others such as the hero, rivals, foils, false heroes, family, acquaintances, etc.—essentially, various representatives of sociopolitical ideologies). Romance novels often chart the complex sexual development of heroines along this arc, but this complexity gets overlooked in an environment that often sees sex as oppositional to intellect or literary value, ideologically colonized by the patriarchy, or a stand-in for other discourses. It is not just the perspective of outsiders to the genre but also of those who study it closely that can gain more nuance from a look at this dialectical change in the heroine's sexual schema.

As noted in the introduction, Ann Barr Snitow remarks on the heroine's conflicting reactions to a hero's sexual overtures, especially the fact that she hides her attraction to him. Cohn, too, mentions that the hero's potent and intimidating allure awakens an alien self in the Harlequin heroine that confuses her (25). Cohn attributes the anxiety the heroine feels about this to a discrepancy between the hero's sexual and nonsexual behaviors (168). She's on the right track but proceeds to read this sexual anxiety and its diffusion solely as a sign of the uneasy nature of sexuality for women trapped between a traditional valuation of their sexual innocence and a post–second-wave feminist critique of that innocence. A few decades on, it is time to see if there is more at work here, especially in a broader data set spanning a wider time period.

In their sexual responses and beliefs, as in other discursive spaces, romance heroines do experience (and present) a fragmented self, which results from the paradoxical messaging and judgments that other characters (and other repositories of traditional norms) impose on them. The uneven responses of heroines to sexual cues reflect the real-life struggles of women in a world in which slut-shaming, sexual harassment, and battles over reproductive rights persist despite the 1960s' sexual revolution and feminist gains—a world in which women are still being pigeonholed into the virgin/whore binary, which they may resent but often internalize.

The binary has been around for centuries, certainly all through the Judeo-Christian era, and was consecrated in social, political, and cultural domains during the late eighteenth and nineteenth centuries and exported around the world through European colonization. As Mary Poovey notes in her study of Victorian gender ideology, even the supposed ideal woman, safe in the domestic realm as an "Angel in the House," was always shadowed by an "earlier image of woman as sexualized, susceptible, and fallen" (11). Women began to be cast as being in need of protection and discipline by their wiser (reproductively different) male counterparts, and their bodies were read/represented between the twin (oppositional) poles of the maternal or the sexual: "The contradiction between a sexless, moralized angel and an aggressive, carnal magdalen was therefore written into the domestic ideal as one of its constitutive characteristics" (11). As Poovey notes, this binary was a common thread that ran through the discourse about women, though it was sometimes meant to delineate class differences.

Cohn also sees romance fiction as a discourse on female sexuality rooted in the specific historical conditions of bourgeois society, and she argues that even as the genre recognizes the contradictions facing women in the arena of sexuality, unlike radical feminism, it proposes weak solutions. While she rejects the perception that sex in romance novels is a mere marketing device to increase sales via titillation, she sees romance sexuality as a problem for a different reason. Cohn reads the genre as a story of a girl maturing into a woman but exclusively in the sexual-emotional realm. In other words, the romance heroine's arc into growth is initiated by the hero rather than her career or some other narrative and confined to that realm alone (158, 171). This is the most conservative face of romance according to Cohn, rooting the heroine's growth in retrograde notions of sexuality and gender roles. The heroine achieves the state of womanhood through sexuality under the discourse of love and only after that can she enter a state of knowledge about herself and domesticate passion into love. Cohn attributes this structure to the fact that the contemporary feminist call for sexual independence (separate from marriage or similar consecrated affective bonds) was too risky for most women; the exchange value of a woman as a commodity in the sexual market was still ideologically linked to chastity/virginity, so the genre folded the desire for female sexual expression into a marriage story, which Cohn reads as accepting (and picking one side of) the good/bad woman dichotomy.

While sexuality in romance is more complex than Cohn's reading of the samples available to her, studies routinely bear out the persistence of this binary in actual life well into the twenty-first century. In 1982, Luis Garcia surveyed popular and academic findings showing that women are often perceived as being less interested in sex than men but they are judged poorly if seen as violating this "fact" (873).[1] In 2001, Myra J. Hird and Sue Jackson surveyed teen girls and showed how they categorize themselves as "angels" and "sluts" in response to a media message that sexual activity is a marker of adulthood but within a social environment that critiques them for their sexuality as well. Moreover, as Michael J. Marks and R. Chris Fraley observe, gender stereotypes about sexuality—namely the double standard—seem to get activated in social groups, leading to women being judged more negatively for their perceived sexual experience in those settings, especially in categories such as dominance, intelligence, and success (49). In other words, women are evaluated per long-held gender stereotypes when it comes to sexuality but in an inconsistent manner; it is the effect of these fluctuations on women that is represented in the seemingly erratic sexual values and behaviors of romance heroines.[2]

Essentially, the phenomenon in which others' perceptions affect sexual self-schemas in people is visible in how romance heroines are written (typically by women writers). Just as co-schematic women (those who experience a mix of positive and negative cognitive and affective responses to sexual cues) exhibit approach-avoidance behaviors, so do many romance heroines.[3] This is not to psychologize novel characters but see them as dramatizations of an actual behavioral phenomenon, one that novels resolve in ways that lead to a happier schema for the heroine. In effect, romance fiction represents a type of sexual bildungsroman in which heroines learn to access and piece together their true sexual selves out of the narratives others impose on them, which initially incite a quagmire of desire and anxiety.[4] Their actions that end this confusion show different paths to sexual selfhood.

In Susan Napier's Harlequin Mills & Boon category romance *Love in the Valley* (1985), virgin Julia Fry struggles against the beliefs—of the stodgy hero and of others—that she is a flibbertigibbet sexpot or a naive victim of patriarchy who cannot conceive of sexuality without the mask of love. As she battles a series of screwball comedy–style misunderstandings about her intellectual and social worth and her sexual appetite, she tries not to be defined by virginity or the carnal needs that Snitow sees heroines hiding. In fact, after initial co-schematic behaviors through which she tries to manage her desire for the hero with alternately comical-antagonistic or blasé responses, she later declares her sexual interest in him openly, while he is the one who flees intimacy on learning of her sexual tabula rasa. Although Julia is seemingly an outlier compared to her 1970s–80s novel contemporaries, who feel endlessly torn about their arousal, she is a useful illustration of the full dilemma women face due to the sexual double standard—namely, how to experience sexual desire without shame or self-harm in a patriarchal society that is conflicted about female sexuality and attempts to either demonize or de-sex women.

Love in the Valley is set in New Zealand and has an ensemble cast that includes hero G. B. H. "Hugh" Walton and his adoptive family. While Hugh is a towering man of few words and immense intellect and dignity, Julia is a curvy blonde who admits to the temperament of a chef and a rashness that is more appropriate to her youthful looks than her actual age. (Janice Radway and Cohn have both observed that romances begin with a childish and immature heroine who acquires mature womanhood largely via sexual fulfillment.) Julia is no child, but the world cannot look past the supposed markers she bears of such childlikeness. Her brother points out her teen appearance at the start of the novel, while her mother worries over her single state. Her indulgent father says she is discriminating about men, but it is a label that troubles her because it implies excessive (or even immature) expectations on her part when it comes to men (21). "Was she too discriminating?" she wonders, contemplating how

> her friends all seemed to fall in and out of love at the drop of a hat. She was sure none of *them* were still virgins.
>
> The trouble was that she had never been severely tempted, not even by some of the suave operators she had met in Europe. She had never yet met a man who made her breathless, who made her heart pound, who thrilled her with his touch. . . . Oh, she had had great fun with a number of men—laughed, talked, petted a little, but had never felt any compelling curiosity to carry it further. She couldn't believe that all there was to love was liking someone enough to fall into bed with them. (21–22)

This section highlights the somewhat problematic conflation of sex and love, but it also shows that Julia has not been chaste—it's penetrative sex that has not tempted her yet. Additionally, the passage identifies her as demisexual, someone for whom sexual arousal depends on feeling a powerful emotional connection to another person.[5]

Yet, Julia is dogged by assumptions that people, including Hugh, make about her sexual availability and desires based on her friendliness and her body type. Some of Hugh's judgments are stereotypes of behaviors or body types associated with a woman being sexually active (especially from a "young" age—whatever that means), while others result from Julia leaning into those stereotypes just to needle him. Initially, Hugh treats Julia with a mix of bafflement and wariness edging into contempt for her friendliness toward all men (ranging from his brothers to her friends and even a fishmonger) because he reads it as promiscuity mixed with airheadedness. She soon challenges his perception of her as a sex kitten, arguing with him when he interprets even her responses to food or music as vapidity or unintellectual sensual consumption. As they grow closer, and he is forced to concede that she is intelligent, he persists in seeing her as a woman who needs to sexually enamor every man in her vicinity—a perception she engages with in different ways from their earliest interactions.

Julia first meets Hugh after causing a car accident and reacts to his grimness by behaving like a ditzy flirt. She sees herself through his disapproving gaze as a braless, buxom girl who is testing her sexual boundaries, and she quite enjoys his misreading of her face and body as that of an oversexed teen. He terms her "a little girl, playing at being adult" (30) and concludes that she enjoys being sexualized by the men in whose houses she works as a domestic laborer (30–31). Julia gets a kick out of the fact that he is critical of "her cheeky expression" and looks disapprovingly from "the firm, bouncy outline of her breasts against the tight sweatshirt to the curvaceous thighs encased in black leather" (30). This sets up a dynamic in which he reluctantly finds her attractive but expends considerable effort in suppressing his desire since he thinks her precocious, oversexed, and flighty.

Soon after their car crash interaction, for instance, they meet again when she jokingly throws herself onto what she thinks is his actor brother's sleeping body and discovers that it is Hugh in the bed (35–36). Her campy performance before she learns of his identity includes yelling "Darling Ricky, let me be yours for one night of love" and "Take me, take me, carve your name on my body . . . it's already on my heart!" (35–36). Hugh takes this farcical playacting at face value, painedly calls her a "resident groupie" (40), and, when she denies the charge, he speculates if she is instead the infamous niece of the housekeeper, someone Julia knows is an "irresponsible, promiscuous, high-school drop-out" (41).

They start on this uneven footing, with him barely tolerating her, but his later reactions range from coldness to condescension to sarcasm to sexual overtures, not in any particularly logical sequence. After observing her chatting with a fisherman with the intent of getting a good bargain, he implies that she uses her body for financial benefit (86). When he sees her in the middle of a playful tussle with his brother Richard, he assumes they are canoodling in public. His snide reaction implies that she should stick to her job of being the family's temporary hired help rather than "seducing male members of the household on the hall floor," evoking a stereotype of working-class women with loose morals (63). He is convinced that she has actually had sex with legions, saying, "How [Richard] got the impression that your innocence is a point at issue is beyond me" (113).

Despite his verbal dismissals, his attraction to her starts to become evident in his body language, resulting in mixed signals: "She felt an uncharacteristic surge of self-consciousness as he stared at her and moistened her lips one against the other as if she could hide them from his gaze. The grey eyes rose to meet her startled blue ones and for an instant Julia saw masculine curiosity" (87). Another time, she finds herself sitting with him in a hot spring in their bathing suits, and when his proposal that they start a fake romance to neutralize the rivalry between his two amorous brothers makes Julia laugh, he stops the laughter by kissing her. Startled and aroused, she participates in the kiss; but when he ends it, he implies it was just to teach her a lesson (104). He also resorts to sexualizing her body to win an argument when she asks him to fix his siblings' problems:

> "What a receptive bosom you have, Julia."
> His sarcasm hurt. "There's no need to sneer, just because *you* don't use my bosom to cry on."
> "If I use your breasts at all, Julia, it won't be for crying on," he said softly, in wry-self-derision, his eyes flickering down.
> The blood drummed in Julia's head as she stared at him, her mouth slightly open. She felt instantly hot, her breathing all out of control. Did he know what that sort of comment did to her? Of course he did, he must. She stirred uneasily under his veiled gaze. What was he thinking? And was it as erotic as what she had in mind? No, he was just trying to distract her train of thought. (129)

Hugh's behaviors and judgments of her keep Julia off-balance and constantly defending herself. As a result, while she is increasingly drawn to his grave intelligence and his muscled body, she is unsure of his feelings and somewhat baffled by her own since he insists that they are opposites, and she has always thought her type was "someone who laughs a lot, who can make me laugh. Dark, handsome . . . and, of course, short!" (8–9). Her preconceptions about what she finds attractive and the inconsistency of Hugh's fascination with her kinetic and sexual energy are only two of the many factors that interfere with her feeling and expressing desire for him (i.e., cause her co-schematic cognitive reactions).

Her confused emotions and actions are also warranted if one tracks the many cases of gender and sexual stereotyping that the novel provides. This stereotyping accurately reflects how the social environment privileges the male gaze, shapes women's beliefs about themselves and other women, and sows doubts in women's minds about the way men view them. Early in the novel, it is clear that Julia has encountered a range of male sexism, with some men expecting the "pretty, blonde doll" to be trusting and who assume "small body, small mind," while other men frown on the "mix of innocent face and deliciously adult curves" (30). Later, Hugh's mother (kindly) says she is a "slip of a blonde" who might help Hugh open up (70), evoking associations of a lightweight, fun woman (who will save a dour man). Moreover, Ann, a rival for Hugh's affections, directs her disapproval at Julia's "voluptuous curves" since "on Julia, [even] bedraggled looked sexy" (64). Ann interprets the sight of a drenched Julia—following a prank involving a swimming pool—as evidence that she isn't intelligent, educated, or classy enough for Hugh, who is headed for political office. Her implication that Julia's sexiness comes with qualities that are incompatible with what a man like Hugh needs in a partner makes Julia question if her perception of him is accurate—a suspicion he echoes (150–51, 154).

Men in Hugh's family also seek to limit Julia's identity through sexualization. Two of Hugh's brothers, for instance, briefly fancy themselves in love with her. His brother Richard keeps addressing Julia by evoking female objects of desire from literature (either cold-hearted, unattainable figures or ones overcome with passion). He is a method actor and while he is playing Romeo and doing stage readings of seventeenth-century poetry, he treats her as Shakespeare's nubile Juliet (89, 126), as beautiful Cleopatra (124), and as the sexualized women in the poems of Robert Herrick (59) and Thomas Carew (16). When he finally ends his courtship, it is not because he respects Julia's wishes to be platonic friends but because Hugh is a rival he can't compete with; she is effectively a pretty woman who he considers unavailable only after another man has laid sexual claim to her. Later in the novel, he suspects that she is pregnant and abandoned, and he is astonished when she alludes to her virginity (by mentioning Mary and the Immaculate Conception) because he perceives her as sexually active.

Julia is misread by Richard's rock star twin too. Steve wants a sympathetic ear while he undergoes heroin withdrawal and decides that Julia fits the bill (76). Demanding her attention, he once yells at her and breaks a glass because he thinks she is ignoring him, and though he apologizes, he ends the apology by kissing her without her permission after terming her a "sweet and lovely lady" (82). Worried about his mental health, Julia chooses not to rebuke him, an example of the emotion work that women often do to minimize damaging male egos. (See chap. 3 for more of this discussion.) The twins' interactions with Julia thus range from playful to aggressive, and Hugh misreads both her actions and character without indicting the men (59, 113). He scolds her for pitting the brothers against one another and says, "flirting is as natural to you as breathing," adding that she needs to exercise "active discouragement" (87). Julia rejects the accusation, pointing out that many men need no encouragement for such behavior, but she still worries about his poor opinion of her as "a flighty little piece" (60).

The novel includes other incidents of men sexualizing and assaulting her, though they are related in a comical fashion (such as the story of the owner of an Italian restaurant who kept pinching her when she worked for him) (84–85). Nor is this type of male harassment directed only at Julia. Hugh's sister Ros expresses anger at an older artist whose commune her own twin is in, one that she says is an "artistic dictatorship." Ros, critical of this man's "gigantic ego," says that he will make her sibling "suffer artistically and emotionally" and views him as a "lecher and a hypocrite" who has probably "had it off with every woman in that commune, yet he spouts on about woman's essential purity" (77).

In addition to experiencing and seeing how men directly sexualize women, Julia sees (and echoes) women being labeled and judged in other ways as well. Hugh's adoptive mother dismisses "cool, cerebral" Ann as a "bore" who is "convenient for" Hugh "and available"—in effect, an intellectual uninterested in sex (57). Julia accepts and repeats this critique when fighting with Hugh, asking him if he and Ann "stroke each other's egos" (implying that Ann—a computer scientist—is incapable of any sexual stroking) (152). That she has internalized the social loathing of women's emotions is also evident when she muses that she "hated the thought of being one of those clingy, weepy females" (163). Similarly, her assessment of Hugh's dead birth mother, a battered woman, as someone who "had died for the sake of love, or misguided loyalty, or whatever strange, twisted emotion had bound her to her husband" betrays the contempt with which people view women who stay in an abusive relationship (173).

It is logical in the light of these disparaging messages about women's emotional and sexual selves that Julia's sexual schema is in flux. In other words, she shows a co-schematic profile in her thoughts about Hugh, her sexual awareness of him, and her actions (approach and avoidance) toward him as their encounters increase in frequency and duration. Even during their second interaction, when she's jumped in his bed by mistake, she feels a spark of interest that she suppresses: "His shoulders and chest were massive under the black silk pyjamas, the thick mat of hair she had felt when she had thrown herself on to him revealed by the unbuttoned jacket. What a body! The thought came unbidden and Julia hurriedly qualified it—if you had a liking for all-in wrestlers" (37).

For a while, Julia tells herself she just wants to understand what makes him tick, but her desire for him starts to dominate her thoughts:

Julia's mind drifted into realms of fantasy. What would Hugh be like in bed? Surely he would shed some of that self-restraint along with his clothes? Or perhaps, because of his largeness, he needed it even more. It must be a little like making love with a steam-roller! . . . Her thoughts roamed from fantasy to indecency as she tried to imagine Hugh in the flesh. She had never seen a naked man in reality, but basic knowledge of human biology filled the gaps. He had a magnificent chest, wide and hard and warmly furred, would the rest of him match up? Weren't feet and hands supposed to indicate the size of a man's vital parts? Julia blushed at the involuntary tingling sensation that invaded her as she remembered the large, capable hands on the Maserati's wheel. (57)

Julia's mind becomes preoccupied with Hugh, leading to a desire that puzzles her with its contradictory impulses: "If only she wasn't so confused about her feelings . . . her original dislike all jumbled up with compassion and curiosity, and despair that he seemed to have so little of her beloved laughter in his life" (70).

A little later we learn that "Julia struggled with uncertain emotions. It was difficult to retain your sympathy with a man who could be so effectively nasty with so little effort. . . . Julia hated hurting others, and never before had she pushed herself where she wasn't wanted, but something about Hugh roused an instinct in her, at once aggressive and protective, a curiosity that constantly craved appeasement" (73).

Her thoughts start to spill over into contradictory actions as well. After a public spat, she apologizes to him in private, taking so long over it that her mind recognizes she is stalling so she can spend time with him. She thinks to herself, "Why was it so hard to say? *Because once you've said it he's going to shut the door on you again,* whispered the little know-it-all inside her head, *and you don't want him to shut you out, not ever*" (73). While leaving, her kiss of thanks turns more intimate than she had intended, and she deliberately misdiagnoses her arousal as low blood sugar: "Going up on her tiptoes, she planted a laughing kiss on the highest reachable point—the vulnerable spot where his strong throat curved into his collarbone. The unexpected throb of his pulse against her soft mouth imbued the kiss with a disturbing intimacy and Julia whirled away from his arrested gaze, breathless at her own temerity. Back in the kitchen, she attributed her slight giddiness to her headlong rush down the stairs and had a snack to revive herself" (75).

She convinces herself that they can be friends, but her thoughts reveal a mix of physical attraction and the hope of intellectual compatibility:

His smile was slightly crooked, revealing the fullness of his lower lip and straight, even teeth. It was a beautiful, masculine smile, one that made you want to smile back, and keep on smiling. . . .

She wouldn't be satisfied with a nodding acquaintance with his strange, complex personality. She wanted more, more perhaps than he was willing to offer, but it was unthinkable that she would retreat now to the safe, uncontroversial distance that he kept everyone else at. She had trespassed this far, and now she must cling to her advantage. . . .

They were no longer locked into that circle of challenge and counter challenge, now a new element had entered their relationship. She found herself liking his articulate intelligence. He was talking to her as an equal, and what a difference it made! (85–86)

When she sees him in a bathing suit, however, the sexual attraction she feels is evident in her gaze on his body. She was

aware that her unthinking cry had emanated from her subconscious, that unruly desire to see what Hugh was like underneath his civilised wrappings. . . .

Julia took a deep breath at the sight of him bearing down on her. Steady on, my girl, she told herself, you don't like big men. But she liked the look of this one. . . .

The sleek, clinging, racing briefs in red which seemed to accentuate[,] rather than cloak, his manhood, riding high at the top of the solid columns of muscle that were his legs. Shorn of his clothing he was definitely not shorn of his power! Julia sternly quelled a sudden urge to escape the approaching colossus, and concentrated instead on admiring his symmetry.

No wonder he was so hard to bump into—the flat, broad stomach was rippled with muscle, the high arch of his rib-cage supporting a deep chest and powerful shoulders. Each pace threw a different set of muscles into relief on his body, solid-packed yet beautifully proportioned as a whole. (97–98)

Yet later, when he asks her for a favor to make up for inadvertently injuring him, she hesitates, worried by the pleasure she feels at the request. Even after she becomes his regular typist, she often feels conflicted about her desire and runs away from her mixed emotions:

Hugh leant back in the big chair and Julia felt the strong flex of muscle under her hand as he straightened his legs out in front of him. She was tempted to leave her hand where it was, but suddenly she was aware of the flesh under the cloth, of how much she wanted to run her fingers up that warm, hard thigh. . . .

Julia was heart-crashingly aware of the living, breathing man . . . so big, so strong, so close, and of her own nervous reaction to his nearness.

"Oh goodness, look at the time," she babbled, looking at the grandfather clock by the door. "I'd better go down and get supper for everyone."

She scuttled to the door, barely hearing Hugh's "good night," so anxious was she to get away before she did something stupid, like throw herself at him. (111–14)

Julia frequently thinks about Hugh and often schools herself not to—even after realizing she's in love—or cautions herself against coming on too strong (115, 117, 142). If she backs off during conversations that veer into topics he finds unpleasant, it makes him open up to her, thus rewarding her self-censorship (130). In other words, her feelings occasionally manifest as avoidance behaviors, where she tries to suppress her interest in Hugh, but also in approach behaviors.

Both types of behavior can be seen in the hot spring episode above as well as in other sexual encounters. After an incident where he gets sprayed with a marinade she is making, he kisses her to stop her giggles and she fully participates: "Julia melted into him, sliding her arms under his jacket, around to his back where her hands spread across the hard-packed flesh, nails burrowing into the warmth, urging him closer" (120–21). Though she is mainly described as being the recipient of his actions, her point of view tells us about her pleasure: "It felt so good, even better than it had before. . . . [His hands] making [her breasts] tauten and sending a lick of heat plunging to her belly. . . . [His] urgency which startled and excited Julia" (121). With Hugh touching her breasts,

> Julia shuddered against him, her back arching further as the cupping, massaging motion of his fingers took effect. She groaned his name, glad she had worn no bra, glad that she fitted so perfectly into his hands. She had never felt such an urgent need for assuagement, a need which overrode inhibition and common sense, and stripped away all her preconceptions of what naked passion could be. . . . Her legs, hanging over the side of the table, were trapped by the crowding strength of his and Julia twitched them helplessly, aching to wrap them licentiously around him, to draw him even closer than was physically possible. (121–22)

While Hugh directs this kiss, it is she who initiates their first lengthy sexual interaction in his attic apartment, where she coaxes him to strip off his shirt and show her some bodybuilding poses. He concedes but mocks her with "Usually-so-honest-Julia. Why so coy?" (suggesting hypocrisy in a sexually experienced woman) and also labels her childlike, telling her she's "Like a baby, so fresh and sweet" (134). When he kisses her after giving her these contradictory cues, she verbally rejects his infantilization of her but responds with a mix of shyness and desire (132–37). That desire grows steadily, though she is not always able to express it clearly to him or herself because of his noted inconsistency (and possibly because everyone expects her to be a cheerful woman of shallow

passions). In considering Hugh's opinion of her, "she couldn't blame him for
what he thought—that she was as free and easy with her favours as she was with
her words. She wondered at her own reluctance to enlighten him, sensing that
it had its roots in the growing attraction she felt towards him. Hugh would run
a mile from a virgin . . . too much of an emotional risk . . . but an experienced
woman he might be prepared to meet on equal ground" (113).

Julia also shows her interest in Hugh by engaging in sharp banter, often rejecting his characterization of her as superficial (84), scolding him into taking
a compliment (110), and reassuring him of her true admiration while touching
him (111). She does criticize him for his phlegmatic nature and ponderousness,
leading him to accuse her of finding him boring or ridiculous, but he is aware
that she is drawn to him (as evidenced by a remark he makes before their abovementioned first [unfinished] attempt to have sex). During this encounter, she
revels in his muscled contours and obvious arousal, insisting that he proceed
with alacrity and thus rejecting the binary of the scared virgin and the sexually
experienced jezebel: "She wasn't afraid of what was to come, she wanted it so;
she didn't feel like a virgin, she felt all woman, limbs heavy, languid, and she
had no intention of breaking the spell of sexual urgency by revealing the truth
of her inexperience" (135–36).

But her mumbled confession that she is finally ready to have sex for the first
time because she loves him stops him cold. (He reads her desire as demisexual,
which is undesirable to him—a preference she has suspected.) Her wishes are
not in doubt—she wants him—but his reluctant desire for her (among other
factors noted earlier) seems to compel her co-schematic tendency. In other
instances, especially before this scene, she has admitted her desire for him to
other family members. Even after she and Hugh reach détente, she continues
to be open about it—to his mother no less, who encourages her not to give up
on him. But his denial and criticism of her in and outside the bedroom (such
as when he is pretending to be interested in her in front of his family while pri-
vately terming his loving performance "revolting sentimentality") is a powerful
barrier to her free expression:

> Oh, how she longed for him to mean every single sentimental word of his
> wooing. It gave her the shivers, imagining what it would be like to have Hugh
> so completely and utterly in love with her that he laid his heart at her feet with
> delicious phrases. . . .
>
> How could she blurt out that to her it was no joke, that the lesson was more
> painful than he could possibly have conceived. For the first time in her life
> she had to control her instinct to tell the truth, holding back the words until
> she was almost bursting with the frustration of it. (126–28)

Admittedly, unlike many earlier Harlequin Mills & Boon heroines, Julia is erratic but not in denial about her feelings; yet, analyzing her behavior and internal life can also elucidate the behavior of these other heroines because they are on the same spectrum as far as cognitive/affective confusion is concerned, one called forth by the hero's and others' attempts to push them into one of the virgin/whore categories. In trying to overcome Hugh's rigid beliefs about sexuality and concomitant traits, Julia challenges his thinking repeatedly, insisting that while she is not a "naturally controlled personality," that trait isn't equivalent to uselessness (110). She notes that she loves her job as a chef and that cooking "requires discipline and knowledge as well as flair" since "it can be tough—long hours and hard physical labour, especially restaurant work. I've studied and worked for years to get where I am today, I reckon I'm entitled to enjoy myself. Can't you accept that I like to laugh when I can because there are too many reasons in this cruel and unfair world to cry!" (110–11). Hugh does change his mind in the face of evidence that he is wrong about this dichotomy—sexually and emotionally open=undisciplined layabout / sexually controlled=thoughtful achiever—that he was pushing her into, but his erroneous belief that she is a sexual epicurean changes only after learning of her virginity and hearing her declaration of love.

Unfortunately, Hugh then replaces one misconception with another, recasting her as a sexual naïf, incapable of separating lust and love. Despite her frustration (sexual and emotional) with his new assessment, she sticks to her declaration of love, thinking, "in the midst of joy and passion she had been true to herself" (141). In retaliation, Hugh invites Ann back to the house, parading her around Julia as his true soulmate (an intellectual companion rather than someone confusing carnal attraction for compatibility). In this instance, Julia first stays quiet because she's worried "she would shriek like a fishwife"; the self-silencing is an attempt to avoid another gendered stereotype (145). So she waits to confront him and then accuses him of class snobbery and elitism, asking, "Are you ashamed to have sunk to the level of seducing servants?"—a charge with which she evokes, and forces him to refute, a sordid cliché of male employers and the women they use sexually and discard (146). She batters down his barriers in this conversation, forcing him to acknowledge their mutual attraction and even provoking him into a passionate kiss, but he still flees from her demands (155). The episode leaves her worrying that he thinks someone as passionate as her cannot be a cerebral match for a lawyer on track to be the country's prime minister someday. Her co-schematic profile thus persists in the presence of both his and her doubts.

Julia refuses to give up on their relationship despite these false binary misjudgments about her body and her mind (ones variously echoed by Ann,

Hugh's well-meaning but dramatic family, and other acquaintances). Instead, convinced that Hugh is fleeing from some other fear, she figures it out with his mother's help. She learns that his birth mother and he were both victims of domestic violence and that he is afraid of his own potential to be violent. To disabuse him of the notion, she provokes a confrontation by implying that she has been having sex with other men, channeling a seductress despite her lack of sexual experience: "Virgin though she was, her body seemed to have taken on an instinctive voluptuousness of its own—flaunting, seducing, draining his physical resistance" (180). Again, the scene is a pointed refutation of how virgins or sexually active women are supposed to be fundamentally different. She then grabs his fist and puts it against her face, tricking him into an epiphany of the baselessness of his fear that he might hit her if he's angered. But on realizing that she was playing shrink, he prefaces their eventual sexual consummation with a hint of erotic asphyxiation by grabbing her throat. Julia is described as being both trepidatious and aroused by this action, unlike the fearfulness typically associated with virgins, and she welcomes his move of laying her on the floor and initiating penetrative sex. They both orgasm during this episode, with his breeching of her hymen causing minor pain that is soon replaced by "fierce, groaning satisfaction" (184). Despite this moment of sexual compatibility, when Hugh proposes afterward, he is somewhat pessimistic about a match between himself as an older, gray-haired, priggish legal scholar and a woman who is spontaneous and who he thinks will be bored by him soon. But Julia is determined to see their relationship consecrated and accepts the proposal with all haste, insisting that their differences are complementary. When he finally declares his love, she experiences something resembling an orgasm, suggesting the fulfillment of her demisexuality in a fusion of her body and emotions: "'Oh!' Her head fell back and she shuddered with a kind of ecstasy that transcended the intense physical satisfaction they had shared" (188).

Love in the Valley is thus about Julia's perceived sexual self—precocious teen, flirtatious young woman, femme fatale who can bring brothers to blows, sexpot who is all body and no brains, virgin who is interpellated by conservative sexual ideology, and even a sad, seemingly abandoned pregnant woman— and how she counters some of those perceptions and adapts others into her sexual self-schema. While she wonders at the nature of her seemingly inexplicable attraction to Hugh, who is her opposite in expressing emotion or feeling sensations, she refuses to treat herself like a freak for wanting him or to be treated as one by him or others; she is co-schematic, to use the above sexual schema model, but moves toward positive schematic over the course of the novel. She is neither ashamed nor proud of her virginity, knowing only that sexual arousal has never manifested itself in her as strongly for any man before Hugh. On finding herself intellectually and erotically aroused by him, she invites his response but hotly contests his attempt to downplay the value of her feelings, paint her as a sexpot, or treat her as a child who does not know her own mind and body. She views him as sexually desirable and someone who she could make happy, and she wants him to see her in the same light. While lacking sexual experience, she owns her sexual needs, and while she has anxieties about their relationship, she is able to overcome the fears she feels and bring the courtship to a sexually and emotionally satisfying close.

The focus on Julia's sexual desire reflects the genre's commitment to being unashamed about its sexual content, even if those unfamiliar with romance novels misunderstand them. Julia can thus serve as a case study of how romance heroines enact not just a structural or narratological function but also demonstrate the genre's self-deterministic nature. The quests undertaken by romance heroines are not about their lives and destinies alone (or of their readers) but they also serve as an allegory of the genre's struggle to determine its identity as a form of love narrative and to resist academic as well as populist attempts to define it and limit its potential. The genre, I would suggest (only half-jokingly), has a co-schematic sexual self schema; it has a positive attitude toward sexuality but knows that it is seen as hypersexual and worthless from time to time. It's still working out how to be happy with its own sexual nature—a process that will continue till women can be sexual without being sexualized and celebrated without being celibate.

While Julia's sexual journey represents one common approach to sexual desire in romance, another approach involves heroines who are pursued by the hero (rather than pursuing him) and who are often negative schematic in their sexual schemas. The issue can be traced to the double standard and to the strain of having to choose between different identities and roles. In Kresley Cole's paranormal romance *Dark Desires after Dusk* (2008), the academic heroine who is negative schematic is a familiar stereotype—an unworldly and celibate scientist focused on her work to the exclusion of all other aspects of herself, which results in phobias and neurosis.

Academia, if one were to consult romance fiction, can be limiting, forcing one to choose between safety and self-fulfillment, between a sickly elitist world and a healthy, populist reality. *Dark Desires after Dusk* is based on this idea and also gestures to a concern about women and the demands that are placed on them, especially ones that seem to put their intimate and public selves into conflict. Holly Ashwin is a young lecturer at Tulane who is working on a mathematics PhD in cyber cryptology. She also struggles with an obsessive-compulsive disorder. It manifests itself as a desire to clean and organize objects into sets of threes, an inability to eat food that has touched something (including her own bare hands), and "sidewalk crack avoidance" (*Dark Desires* Epigraph unpaginated). So what we have here is a female academic with a seriously high IQ and some serious oddities. Her focus on her professional life—teach, grade, read, write—is represented as problematic and coterminous with behavioral disorders or breakdowns.

Holly's own musings tell us that she uses the walls of academia to keep her anxieties at bay. She values the regimented nature of her academic life, with its divisions of the year into semesters, and semesters into weekly lectures. She plans to stay close to campus for the rest of her life while her boyfriend Tim travels to conferences to present their joint work. As Cole draws her, she is something of a cliché of the Ivory Tower academic and math nerd. She even dresses the part: curly hair confined in a bun, knee-length pencil skirt, twinset sweater, unobtrusive pearls, as well as 1950s-style glasses to help with her hyperopia or longsightedness (a metaphor for not being able to see what's nearest, i.e., herself). Oh, and she is a virgin (because she's afraid to have sex, and she and Tim have agreed to wait till after marriage).

But we quickly find out that she has a whole side to her that she has sensed but not understood, an absence that is linked to her sex life (or lack thereof). She is a Valkyrie (with a mixed Valkyrie-Greek Fury/Erinyes heritage) but doesn't know it. Having been adopted by humans, she has no knowledge of her genetic heritage (and accompanying powers or magical sorority-cum-family) till the events of the book begin. She is aware of this part of herself but has buried it in her subconscious because she isn't able to reconcile it with her otherwise normal-seeming (human) self. For most of her life, she has treated that part of herself—physically strong and sexually demanding—as dangerous to her ordinary life and in need of suppression. Her OCD can thus be read as a side effect of being born with dual, seemingly oppositional roles—cerebral human and fleshly Valkyrie.

Psychologists term this "role strain"—the effort of satisfying the demands made by different roles. In fact, at first glance, Holly seems to represent the findings of role strain research that suggest that positive indicators of mental health in women are inversely related to the number of roles they play. For example, Angela McBride in her 1990 article "Mental Health Effects Of Women's Multiple Roles" notes that "there is ample literature demonstrating that multiple roles are associated with competing demands, which can lead to role overload and resulting strain. Measures of role strain include somatization, depression, anxiety, obsessive-compulsiveness, discomfort, anger/hostility, and dissatisfaction"

(381–82). Holly exhibits many of these symptoms. But McBride also surveys literature on the role enhancement hypothesis that suggests that under certain circumstances, multiple roles can have a positive effect: "Problems can accumulate across roles, but so can rewards; participation in multiple roles may cancel some of the negative events generated by a particular role. Involvement in multiple roles has been found to offer certain benefits. Some women with multiple identities have reported superior health . . . ; some employed women have a more autonomous sense of self as a result of working . . . , and a number of dual-career families rate their life-styles positively. . . . Verbrugge and Madans (1985) found that the healthiest women have multiple roles—a job, husband, and often children" (381). In other words, more roles don't necessarily mean mental distress.

McBride also notes factors that can increase or decrease the stress of multiple roles, such as a helpful community:

> The sheer number of burdensome events associated with a particular role may not stress women as much as whether they feel able to choose that role and to organize their resources to meet demands (Verbrugge, 1986). Social support has been thought both to build stress resistance and to serve as a buffer when stress is present. . . . The needs of persons under stress can include emotional support, informational support, and instrumental support. The presence of a spouse may be equated with social support, but the number of socially supportive relationships in one's network may make more of a difference than having a spouse. The benefits of social support may depend on the degree of the individual's integration into a large social network. (382)

So women may in fact be healthier if they have the freedom to take on many roles, a choice that is influenced by whether they have a network of acquaintances that have their backs.[6]

In this light, Holly's oddities are not a symptom of facing two roles but of having to turn away from the Valkyrie-self because she didn't have anyone in her life to tell her that both roles—human academic with intellectual prowess and Valkyrie fighter with sexual needs—were okay to take on. As a result, she has spent her teen and adult years avoiding anything that can trigger strong physical and emotional responses (by avoiding sex and sexually suggestive situations), and she has sublimated her sexual needs into regimented activities such as a nightly swim (81, 195). In other words, the unfulfilled desire to inhabit both roles is one that she tries to manage through repetitive actions and medications. By suppressing part of who she wants to be—a woman of intelligence who also has a strong sex drive and physical strength—she has become neurotic. In a broader sense, however, the novel suggests that women become neurotic when they feel bad that they cannot do/have it all—be superwomen—but they don't realize that it's because they lack support in managing the multiple roles they desire. In other words, Holly's tics and anxieties result from the dearth of a professional and personal community network, one that would have helped her grow into aspects of herself that run counter to patriarchal notions of what a woman should be. That this suppressed self just happens to be an actual superwoman who likes sex alludes to the superwoman complex and women's sexual liberation.

After Holly's hidden self pushes up into her consciousness as a defense mechanism when she is attacked by demons, she soon comes to grips with the paranormal universe (called the "Lore") she is thrust into, but she is not so willing to accept her newly discovered role. She does not want to play a superhero in the genre she has found herself forced into but Cole deliberately immerses her in it. The situation requires the protagonist to accept the new (or hidden) self for the greater good of the community and provides a way out of the problem of the heroine-in-identity-crisis brought on by her being asked to choose between seemingly mutually exclusive selves. Cole's resolution is two-fold: one, having her heroine reject the false binary (human academic / dangerous Valkyrie) in favor of synthesizing elements of that seeming dualism; and two, supplying her with a social network that supports her becoming someone who can do it all—in Holly's case, quite literally becoming a superwoman. It is a resolution to the problem of reconciling the divided self that romance heroines have to tackle at some point, which matches McBride's suggestion of how role strain can be alleviated through community help.

Holly as a human academic is mostly solitary, afraid of shadows, dirt, disorder, and spontaneity. She even shuns swear words, speedy driving, and masturbation (sublimating the last into long swim sessions). Even after the initial incident that triggers her full Valkyrie side, when she kills the demons that intended to rape and impregnate her, she is frantic to go back to "normal" (i.e., her half-self). It is unsurprising. Nothing in her world up to that point has suggested that these two selves are compatible or has helped her cope with their dual demands; her biological mother and adopted parents are dead, her boyfriend wants her to focus on writing programming code so he can publish it under his own name, and she has few close friends. During one of the two times she loosened her control and indulged her Valkyrie side as a teen, she frightened a lover with her carnal enthusiasm; he fled and later bad-mouthed her at school, resulting in social ostracism (92–93).

The teenage lover's reaction is one of many reminders that she exists in a world that tries to control and sexually stereotype women in general and her in particular, a process that ranges from lethal violence to verbal labels. The novel alludes to the former by including the story of a serial killer who kidnapped and tortured young women to death while insisting that they laugh through their pain (evoking the common catcall of "smile" that men direct at women) (180). Two songs that Holly hears in a bar also bring up women's objectification: Jimmy Buffet's "Let's Get Drunk and Screw," which invites a woman to a sexual encounter while saying others think she is a "snuff queen" (i.e., sex worker), and Stevie Ray Vaughn's "Pride and Joy," which terms the (presumably female) lover a "sweet baby" (153, 163). Holly is also aware of instances when people see her through a sexual lens (either terming her "goody two-shoes, a prude" [99] or "Hotty Ashwin" [9]). The demon hero Cade makes sexual judgments about her (initially terming her "definitely a virgin" who is *Starving-for-it*" [99], and "a skirt" [188]—the last a sexist metonymic slang term that reduces women to a piece of women's clothing—but also encourages her to be a "bad girl" [193]). Most people in the Lore universe initially only see her as the foretold "Vessel" who will birth a super being (35), and term her as either "bred or dead," a phrase she objects to (220).[7]

The lack of a supportive community that could explain and nurture all aspects of Holly's identity, compounded by her constant awareness of the world's judgments, are at the root of her role strain, OCD, and negative/co-schematic personality. This is most clearly visible in her confused reactions to sexual cues, especially Cade's seductiveness. Early in their acquaintance, she is with him in a hotel room where she battles her desire for him:

> Her mind was wracked with ideas and images that shouldn't be in there. She was unable to stop seeing that golden hair leading down to his navel. The more she endeavored not to think about it, the more the picture flashed in her head.
> What would it be like to nuzzle that trail? To clutch his hips as she lowered her face to it . . . ?
> Her heart thundered in fear of what she might do if she lost control.
> The last time had been eight years ago. She'd terrified a young man, even . . . *hurting* him.
> And he hadn't been the first. (68–69)

This fear of her own paradoxical desires and of hurting or repelling men is a running theme. She shies away from Cade and as noted earlier, even from sex with her long-term boyfriend, Tim, no matter how much she tries to talk herself into imagining a life with him: "But a full, abiding relationship between [Tim and her] would work only if she were normal sexually. Otherwise, how could he survive her strength? And how could they deal with her weird conflicting needs? At once, she had the instinctive drive to overpower, and the instinctive need to be overpowered" (102). As a result of this fear of her own needs, she keeps claiming that she feels no sexual attraction to Cade even while she experiences desire—"She was furious, as much at his actions as at her own reaction—the mere site [sic] of his privates made her feel hot and flustered.... Unable to help herself, she let her gaze flit to [his penis] again" (129). Without considering the context, such passages could be misinterpreted as duplicity or hypocrisy (100, 165–66).

The gradual end of her solitariness through her forced acquaintance with Cade and the world of the Lore, and their acceptance of her different aspects, free her to be a Valkyrie, both in terms of her physical powers and her sexual needs. As she goes on a road trip with Cade to search for a cure for her Valkyrie "condition," his assurance that she doesn't have any disorders, his regular lessons to help her manage her strength, and his largely amoral attitude to sexuality start helping her disparate selves align.

She experiences her first orgasm with him when he seduces her into accepting his caresses, but only after he convinces her that he is too strong to be hurt by her sexual wants (unlike the boys in her past): "Every second of every day in the past, she'd fought not to think about the needs of her body. Now it seemed there was no fight, there *could* be no fight" and as she is "*losing control . . . those impulses arose.*" Cade then asks permission to penetrate her with his fingers, and "with a moan, she accepted defeat. This was too delicious, too overwhelming for her to resist. . . . Her climax overtook her. Her eyes flashed open in shock at the almost frightening intensity—stronger than anything she'd ever felt before" (201–2). She reflects on this experience later in wonderment, grasping that she need not be afraid to express herself sexually as long as her partner is strong enough to match her (207).

Initially Cade makes the sexual moves but midway through the novel, he bargains with her to take the lead, which she first worries about, wondering, "Would he be inwardly laughing at her inexperience? Comparing her to [another]?" and wishing "she were a better kisser than" a demoness they have met (209). After listening to his instructions to start an open-mouthed kiss, she begins, though she is "unable to tell if she was giddy or nervous or both," and he lets her "explore him with tentative licks" and "allow[s] her to slowly control the pace," and she "couldn't seem to stop herself from deepening it—" (210). Interestingly, it is right after she has taken this step that she realizes her hearing has become superhuman, so the narrative establishes a link between her sexual agency and her Valkyrie powers (211).

As their journey continues, she gives in to the thrill of driving above the speed limit when coaxed by Cade, an experience that both gives her a new sense of herself and incites her sexual desires:

> Holly felt like a different person—a boots-wearing, seafood-eating, thong-clad driver of million-dollar cars. . . . Her heart was racing, her adrenaline pumping. But she felt something she never expected.
>
> She was getting really aroused.
>
> By the time she was flirting with two hundred miles per hour, there was no ignoring it. Her breaths grew shallow, and she wriggled in the seat. *Still getting worse.*
>
> *Two hundred ten.* She licked her lips. Speed. Seductive. *Sexy.* (225–26)

Cade responds to her restlessness by performing oral sex on her, which is also the first time she touches her own breasts and the self-stimulation contributes to her next orgasm. Again, accepting and reveling in her need for reckless speed loosens her inhibitions around sexual propriety and pleasure.

While Holly continues to have doubts about her place in the world of the Lore, thinking and saying that she needs normalcy (257, 268), she starts to realize that Tim was not as supportive as she had imagined in comparison to Cade, and in fact, he expects her to give up her job to be a stay-at-home mother, an expectation he justifies with her OCD-related fear of travel (218, 258). When a female colleague calls to tell her about Tim taking public credit for her research, she confronts him and then dumps him when he tries to gaslight her. She grasps that he has cultivated her fears for his own benefit and does not want her to have a job while she raises their family (which would make it easier for him to steal her ideas) (277). Following the breakup, she chooses a sexual relationship with Cade, initiating fellatio (which she decides she likes) that becomes mutual oral sex and signaling that "The shy virgin was gone, replaced by a hungry, demanding Valkyrie who expected to give and get pleasure" (281). Eventually, she even overrides Cade's hesitation about penetrative penis-in-vagina sex, first using a martial arts move to press him to the floor and then caressing his sexual organs till he cannot resist their collective desires anymore (290–93).

Unlike Tim, Cade accepts her fully and even tries to understand her cerebral passions, and it is an idea he mentions when he is training her in armed combat that leads to a eureka moment about how she can write code to destroy malware. When she is later forced to defend herself against a super villain and then slaughters a church full of zombies, followed by a stretch alone in the Alaskan wilderness to deal with her temporarily broken heart, she survives because of the training he gave her. She then starts to embrace her destiny, conquering her aversion to dirt and chaos along the way.

She starts this process midway through the novel when she wonders how she could be normal, a question prompted by the entrance of Cade in her life as well as her Valkyrie-soothsayer aunt, Nix:

> "Normal for a Valkyrie or for a human?" she asked, sniffling. "I don't quite have a grasp on either, since I've never been fully one or the other."
>
> The truth of that sunk in at that moment. This meant Holly had to reevaluate everything. What was her personality truly like? She didn't recognize herself. (117)

But eventually, she understands that not being "fully one or the other" is not a flaw, and that she can be better if she's both. The novel makes clear that part of Holly's enhanced confidence comes from the tutoring that Nix gives her through pep talks and guidebooks, encouraging her to embrace her powers (as well as from Cade's support).

Her acceptance of her Valkyrie powers of strength and super-healing is cemented when her eccentric Valkyrie cousins welcome her into their ancestral family residence. After this homecoming, and then the final reconciliation with Cade, she finally understands that her cerebral and sensory sides are not incompatible and accepts her super-heroine status as well as her impending motherhood.

> All she'd ever wanted was to feel normal. In the Lore, she did. Even with her lingering quirks and compulsions, Holly fit in.
>
> Nix had told her that she would finally get a sense of herself on her journey, and in fact, Holly had discovered who she was: Holly the Bright.
>
> It was her new Valkyrie name. (354–55)

In other words, a slow building of community makes her happier in her personal life and better at performing both her academic and Valkyrie roles. (In addition to Cade and her aunts, even the ghosts of the women murdered by the serial killer in the story mentioned earlier help her when they think she is under attack, reinforcing the theme of community assistance [231].) Role strain is thus alleviated, leading to her happiness. As a Valkyrie, Holly learns to do all the things that she was afraid to do as a human woman—have vigorous sex with a strong partner, defend herself from assault, continue to write anti-hacking cyber code without sharing credit with her reactionary and unethical male colleague, and go to war alongside Cade. One transformation opens the doors to all elements of her personality that had hitherto been fragmented and subsequently damaged, resulting in a repressed academic.

Dialectical progression through synthesis, instead of choosing one role over another, is thus the only solution to cure the neurotic heroine, a process that requires community aid. Again, this is compatible with role strain research that suggests stress and illness result less from women having multiple roles and tasks and more from a lack of systemic and familial support in tackling these roles. This lack is exacerbated by others' beliefs that women's multiple roles are conflicting or mutually exclusive and by the paucity of choices regarding what they can do and when; romance novels tap into this problem, one created by neoliberalism (which hacked away at social services and communities as Second Wave feminism began arguing that women deserve better professional opportunities). In romance novels, authors provide a solution to this stress by having heroines reject the imposed binary and embrace multiple roles after encountering or creating a system that will support them—this is often the hero, and in paranormal romance novels, an entire world of odd creatures who see multiple selves and roles as normal and advantageous.

Through Holly, Cole is tackling what is a central concern of the genre—the damage done when women are forced to set aside certain elements of themselves because they are deemed incompatible or socially undesirable. Over the course of the novel, events and characters force Holly to reject this false dichotomy and help her reconcile her dueling halves—the superwoman and the quirky human. By accepting the dangerousness and sexuality in her nature, she grows into a powerful Valkyrie who is not afraid or in need of rescue and who still likes doing intellectual work involving math and following routines in her daily habits.

To recap, Holly is a human professor with potential lethal abilities, ones she does not comprehend herself. Her mousy persona is a way to cope with her fear of them but also prevents her from coming into her full powers. To be happy, Holly has to accept that her seemingly divergent selves are all necessary to achieve different goals. She also has to learn that as long as she has the opportunity to be a teacher and a fighter, a lover and a mother (an opportunity that is possible if she has a family and a society that sees these multiple roles as normal and nonexclusive), she is not a liability to others or to herself. In this take on the identity conflict that is central to the journey of romance heroines, Cole rejuvenates the trope of the workaday academic and turns it into an origin story of a super-heroine—someone who can truly have it all.

So to return to where we began, Snitow says heroines are practicing "social lying"—that is, they feel desire but pretend not to. If heroines can be seen as mirroring women, the question is, do women behave this way? Research suggests that women internalize misogynistic ideologies about their sexuality.

Research also suggests that there are "co-schematic" sexual profiles, women who have both positive and negative sexual thoughts and who react with approach-avoidance to sexual cues. Romance novels dramatize the idea that the former causes the latter confusion in thought and behavior and they try to narrate the heroine out of the problem. As a result, the character seems to lack coherence in her sexual responses. We often see this structure in Harlequin Mills & Boon romances after the 1970s and to some extent even in *Love in the Valley*, where the heroine is openly attracted to a man who reads and reacts to her in traditionally illogical ways, prompting her own sexual journey. Nevertheless she persists in her desire, which is what all romance heroines find the courage to do. Unlike Julia, Holly in *Dark Desires* is initially fearful of her own sexual needs and works hard to sublimate them, consequently showing severe role strain. Her avoidance behaviors dominate her interactions with the hero (and other men, including her boyfriend, who is an intellectual convenience). She exhibits approach behaviors only episodically at first. It is after she starts to accept all her selves that her negative self-image changes permanently when it comes to her sexual schema and she becomes sex positive, nay enthusiastic. This sexual confidence comes on the heels of her newfound community and lover, who accept and encourage her powers and quirks as normal and desirable and her needs as worth fulfilling.

NOTES

1. Garcia suggests that people follow different "scripts" in sexual and social interaction.

2. Hird and Jackson sum up their study stating that

heterosexual intimacy presents a myriad of conflicts and dilemmas for girls. Construction of the "good girl / bad girl" dichotomy mitigates against control of their own sexuality. Indeed, the girls' accounts suggest a system of gender relations largely dominated by male need and initiation. The cost of acquiescence is high, pushing a girl from virginal "gatekeeper" to violated "whore." The potential consequences extend beyond reputation, however, to pregnancy, STDs and HIV (Kippax et al., 1990; Waldby et al., 1991). Although girls did construct a sexuality suggestive of their own needs, there was again a dichotomous split between sex "for fun" on the one hand and sex as "special love making" on the other.

3. A positive schematic person would show positive cognitive and affective behavior alone.

4. While early research on sexual self-schemas proposed a bipolar model (in which respondents were seen as being in the middle or in positive/negative

extremes of a spectrum when it came to sexual attitudes and behaviors),
Cyranowski and Andersen propose a "bivariate" model that includes more
"topologies," including that of the "co-schematic group: individuals with a
schematic representation of their sexuality that includes both positive and
negative aspects" (1365). They write, "We theorized that the conflicting self-
views of these women would be disruptive for them, as manifested in affective
and behavioral approach–avoidance responses to sexual cues. As such, co-
schematic women may display moderately restricted levels of sexual behavior
(which appear similar to those of the aschematic women), yet they should
report larger discrepancies in their sexual affects. Specifically, we hypothesized
that co-schematic women would endorse positive sexual affects, such as
desire and arousal, as well as negative affects, such as sexual anxiety" (1365).
In their Sexual Self-Schema Scale, they note that "Factor analyses indicated
that women's sexual self-views are composed of three factors: two positive
aspects (romantic/passionate and open/direct self-views) and a negative aspect
(embarrassment/conservatism)" (1366). Speaking further of the results of their
data, they explain that "the profile for the co-schematic group is the product
of salient but conflicting positive and negative schemas. Co-schematic women
were preoccupied with sexual thoughts and reported a greater desire for sexual
activities. These sexual activities, however, activated strong negative as well as
positive affective responses; they reported high levels of sexual anxiety as well as
sexual arousal in response to sexual interactions. Behaviorally, this cognitive–
affective coactivation may lead to a pattern of sexual approach–avoidance
responses, with the net result being a moderately restricted pattern of sexual
behaviors that outwardly matched that of the aschematic group" (1371). When
it came to discussing romantic attachments, they claim that "both positive
and co-schematic groups indicated high levels of passionate feelings for their
romantic partners, and both sought emotionally close relationships. However,
the co-schematics also hold negative sexual self-views, which may permeate their
romantic attachments and lead to insecurities about romantic relationships.
Compared with positive schema women, co-schematic women reported more
anxieties about being abandoned or unloved by their mates, yet the co-schematic
women in current relationships reported the most relationship satisfaction and
were of all groups the most likely to be living with their romantic partners"
(1374). Moreover, a comparison between co-schematics and aschematics on this
dimension suggests

> the co-schematic women reported strong positive responses to romantic partners
> and a desire for close relationships. At the same time, however, the negative aspects
> of the co-schematic group's sexual self-view may undermine their attachment
> efforts. For example, lack of self-confidence and fears of rejection may inhibit
> co-schematic individuals' initiation of romantic contacts. Alternatively, their

conflicting self-views may promote feelings of insecurity and an anxious need
for emotional intimacy, which may produce behaviors or responses that strain
or sabotage romantic relationship efforts. Specifically, for co-schematic women,
high levels of passionate love and a desire for emotional intimacy were paired with
negative views of the sexual self and anxieties of being abandoned or unloved by
their mates. This conflictual cognitive–affective pattern may lead to a strong (or
even a "dependent") need for close, committed romantic relationships. (1375)

Finally, "The simultaneous activation of strong positive and negative sexual
self-views was manifest in the response patterns of the co-schematic group. The
coactivation of this group's positive and negative self-structures was reflected
in their conflicting responses to sexual cues, that is, co-schematic women
experienced elevated levels of both positive sexual responses (e.g., sexual desire,
preoccupation, and arousal) and negative sexual responses (e.g., sexual anxiety
and self-consciousness)" (1375).

   5. For a history of romance heroine virginity and compulsory demisexuality,
see McAlister's *The Consummate Virgin* (2020).

   6. For more on the role enhancement hypothesis, see Quinn M. Pearson's
"Role Overload, Job Satisfaction, Leisure Satisfaction, and Psychological Health
among Employed Women." See also Linda Beth Tiedje's "Women with Multiple
Roles: Role Compatibility Perceptions, Satisfaction, and Mental Health" and
Laura M. Hecht's "Role Conflict and Role Overload: Different Concepts,
Different Consequences" for discussions of role enhancement as well as the
role conflict phenomenon (including the depression that results when a woman
believes that the multiple roles she is playing are conflicting).

   7. Even the women who are on her side come up with comical titles for
her after she gets pregnant and has broken up with Cade. These titles evoke a
sociosexual category, such as Holly the Preggers, Holly the Spawner, Holly the
Plucky Single Mother, and Holly Crocker (echoing Betty Crocker, the asexual
motherly baker figure invented by a flour company. For more on Crocker, see
Tori Avey's "Who Was Betty Crocker?").

TWO

GENDER

WHILE SUSAN NAPIER'S JULIA FRY and Kresley Cole's Holly Ashwin show us visions of a female heroism that seeks and synthesizes a self in the face of a prescriptive discourse of sexual behavior, another variation of romance heroism plays out in the realm of female gender identity and display/expression as well as associated sexual schemas relating to affect and actions. In this chapter, heroines MacKayla Lane in Karen Marie Moning's *Fever* series (2006–) and Blair Mallory in Linda Howard's *To Die For* (2005) exemplify this heroic journey of maneuvering with or against stereotypes linked to female appearance and femininity, the former in an urban fantasy / paranormal romance and the latter in a murder dramedy. In their stories, we see all the elements of a heroine discussed in earlier sections: Sandra J. Lindow's point about the heroine being a woman who starts discovering herself (by affirming her own definition of femininity in this case) after danger disrupts her home, Russ's thoughts on a heroine solving an intellectual puzzle (tracking down a murderer in the face of skeptics who doubt whether someone with her gender presentation has the intelligence to do so), and Pearson and Pope's conception of the female Warrior hero being an independent actor who battles danger. Both novels also testify to Christine Mains's argument that heroines on quests need not give up marriage or love but can have a successful romantic partnership with a man who becomes an ally, a partnership that is resilient and survives crises and lasts beyond easy happy-ever-afters.

Gender, particularly how heroines express it and others read it, is central to MacKayla and Blair's struggles in these novels. Gender as a collection of socioculturally scripted stereotypes, and what Erving Goffman describes as "conventionalized portrayals" of "culturally established co-relates of sex," is a pressing problem in many romances, forcing heroines to fight their way out of narrative cul-de-sacs they are backed into (1). Gender conventions persist in various areas in romance as in life, such as in expectations of women's bodies, which, as Claudia Malacrida and Tiffany Boulton note, "are subject to a wide range of competing discourses about ideal feminine embodiment" and scripts that demand women be simultaneously childlike and sexual (751).

These expectations are tied to what Judith Lorber calls "gendered imagery," which suffuses our sociocultural landscape in language, media, and other arts and encompasses behavior, body types, clothing, and self-adornment (30–31). Candace West and Don H. Zimmerman also explain gender in terms of people looking at others' behavior through normative conceptions within a binary paradigm that upholds men's dominance and women's deference (146). But additionally, they consider it "an achieved property of situated conduct"— behaviors that people exhibit to access and maintain a place in society, particularly membership in sex categories (126). Rather than intrinsic traits that are inalienable and congruent with reproductive organs, gender is a "product of social doings of some sort," something people *do* routinely "in light of normative conceptions of attitudes and activities appropriate for one's sex category" (129, 127). Gender is iterative, something one performs on repeat, and is both the enactment and reinforcement of social rules about expressing one's "natural" sexual assignment.

In acting out a female gender, heroines enact or respond to external expectations of a gender display that is associated with their perceived gender. Gender display is a subset of how we do gender, a collection of nonverbal behaviors that enact and simultaneously construct gender. This display enacts a "kind of gendered norm through dress, cosmetics, adornments, and permanent and reversible body marks" (Lorber 31), and includes "physical markers such as hairstyle, body language (i.e., way of walking), mannerisms (i.e., way of talking)" (Mignon R. Moore 114), "body display" or how a female body is clothed or revealed (Mee-Eun Kang 985), and gestures, movements, and expressions (Cara Wallis 165).[1] Gender display is a schema that people learn socially, but in social interactions, they read others' displays as if masculinity and femininity are innate (Wallis 161–62). One might imagine gender display as analogous to *différance* in language but in the realm of behavior—an artificially constructed system that poses as natural and in which the gender binary is hegemonic.[2]

Romance heroines also dramatize how gender is part of a power dynamic in which everyone is forced to participate, whether through submission or subversion. Raewyn Connell, writing about Western cultures in the 1980s, identifies "emphasized femininities" that cope with the "global dominance of heterosexual men" through compliance and, in exchange, receive the "most cultural and ideological support" (187). This pattern of femininity includes a "display of sociability rather than technical competence, fragility in mating scenes, compliance with men's desire for titillation and ego-stroking in office relationships, acceptance of marriage and childcare as a response to labour-market discrimination against women. At the mass level, these are organized around themes of sexual receptivity in relation to younger women and motherhood in relation to older women" (187). In effect, "emphasized femininity" is the display of behaviors by women that show that they accept men as stronger, more valuable, and more capable in every realm, public and private. These behaviors endorse the pigeonholing of women into a sex object and child bearer. Connell considers it an ideology that frames "compliance, nurturance, and empathy as womanly virtues" while "power, authority, aggression, technology" are ceded to masculinity (188, 187). Our heroines have to contend with these allocations and decide if they want to play along or reject them. Connell also adds that this "emphasized femininity" is "performed femininity," with men as the default viewers of the performance, and it is very public and culturally constructed, with the mass media offering tips on how to perform it (187–88).

Mimi Schippers, however, argues that a "hegemonic femininity" does exist, and "consists of characteristics defined as womanly that establish and legitimate a hierarchical and complementary relationship to hegemonic masculinity" ("Recovering the Feminine Other" 94). In other words, Schippers contends that certain feminine gender displays don't just submit to gender inequality but profit from a derived power gained through supporting the narrow version of normative masculinity that occupies the highest status in society. These displays may participate in sanctioning or punishing the femininities of women who enact the hegemonically masculine qualities of "desire for the feminine object (lesbian), authority (bitch), being physically violent ('badass' girl), taking charge and not being compliant (bitch, but also 'cock-teaser' and slut)" (95). This hegemonic femininity is on display in romance when we see multiple female characters jostling for proximity to male power but also when characters disapprove of "misbehaving" women, as they do in both novels in this chapter. Schippers also emphasizes that such disfavored femininities *are* femininities; not borrowed masculinities as much as a refusal to be ladylike or to have one's sexuality controlled by or channeled toward men alone.[3]

In addition to studying behaviors and mannerisms, scholars like Mignon R. Moore have provided a useful taxonomy for women's gender display in terms of clothing and other adornments of their bodies. In a study of lesbian gender presentation (and self-awareness) in Black communities (mentioned earlier), Moore categorizes "physical style" into three groups (124):

1. Femme: women whose views about their own gender display suggest their presentation is traditionally feminine (124).
2. Gender-blender: women who report weaving together masculine and feminine elements. (Moore also notes that some community members term this as "femme aggressive," in which "clothes are worn in a masculine style and presentation" while "hips, hair, and breasts often signal that these are women's bodies" [125].)
3. Transgressive: women who self-report their masculine presentation as high, with clothing and other accessories traditionally associated with men and close-cropped hair (125–26).

Moore's classification provides a more granular vocabulary for gender display that involves a nonverbal, extra-bodily aspect of a woman's self-presentation, which is useful for understanding romance heroines. While Moore's use of "gender-blender" applies mainly to a lesbian space, I use it here in the context of two straight characters because the mixed style it connotes applies to them as well (125).

When looking at these heroines through this perspective, it is also valuable to note a possible cause and effect that Holly Devor sees in some who exhibit a "gender blender" mode (women who consider themselves female but are misgendered due to a combination of bodily appearance, gestures, voice, and/or a nonfemme style of dressing [25]).[4] While this misgendering can cause distress to some, they also receive some level of social approval or value for their seeming masculinity; this social reception functions as "a powerful reinforcer of masculinity" and teaches these women to prize it because being read as male provides "social advantages" (28). These advantages primarily have to do with freedom of movement and being able to feel safe at all times because of a "masculine appearance," as well as getting respect (28). Additionally, Devor traces some of the "gender blender" subject's positive relationships and feelings towards male friends and fathers, who include them in traditionally male trades and activities when they are young, to this perception of getting approving signals from them (20). Devor thus infers that these subjects are socialized to suppress traditional femininity by male companions and family members, and they internalize an ideology that sees men as more competent and something to aspire to.[5] This phenomenon finds expression in many romance novels, including the ones in this chapter, with the heroine being regarded as less capable and more vulnerable when associated with a traditionally feminine self-presentation. In several cases, she then takes on or is told to take on a masculine persona and/or appearance to prove her worthiness in a quest.

We also know that people's "vestimentary" behavior has often been regulated and legislated because appearance provides or hampers access to certain statuses and related material resources, as Marjorie Garber has documented in her study of European sumptuary laws (22). She notes that when gender was involved in dress code debates, it was usually related to women's subordinate status (to men or to women of another class) or treatment as a commodity (23).[6] In general, the sumptuary laws' intent was to clarify who was or was not entitled to certain privileges (of class and gender), and thus make it easy for an onlooker to identify someone's status based on their appearance (29). Variations of these rules exist now, too, and those who wish to be "low and inside" a hierarchy conform to them while those who flout them prefer to be "high and outside" (22). The heroines of this chapter have to grapple with such vestimentary protocols as they get hemmed in by how others read their appearance as a measure of their abilities and withhold or provide them with resources that can aid in their missions as a result. This grappling can range widely from what Schippers terms "gender maneuvering," or manipulating one's gender performance to change the existing gender structure ("Rockin' Out of the Box" xiii), to achieving goals through a "gender display" that the patriarchal system rewards, to acting in ways that echo hegemonic masculinity (the last if one is from an oppressed group that wants more than the system deems appropriate) (Jedidiah McClean 21).[7]

When it comes to women, gender and gender display are often associated with fragile femininity that needs to be protected and guided by a strong male, while certain occupations (and quests) are gendered male from the get-go (and their culture makes particular demands on women entrants to these bastions, as chap. 3 details). This is the "normative conception" whose subversion, while possible, is often met with a range of negative consequences. The reason for such retaliation, as Wallis says, is "that a woman who demonstrates masculine nonverbal behavior may be considered offensive because she threatens power relations" (162). MacKayla Lane, the protagonist of Karen Marie Moning's urban fantasy romance series doesn't start out this way. But her heroic potential is initially dismissed based on her gender display of "emphasized femininity" (including elements of "femme" style and "ladylike" phrasing) and because she wants something that some consider impossible without abandoning that femininity.[8]

In *Darkfever* (book 1, 2006), MacKayla, who has grown up in the American state of Georgia as a carefree, middle-class southern belle, complete with

matching accessories, is ripped from that self and from her belief in a traditionally gendered life after she looks into her sister's mysterious death in Ireland;
along the way, she enters a dangerous world that demands aggressive action,
but she is told that her femininity makes her unfit for such a mission. In effect,
since her gender is "well-routinized and accredited" at the start of the series,
and because she can "do gender appropriately," various actors tell her that this
femininity makes her a cute weakling (West and Zimmerman 131, 146). Her
dilemma is that changing her behavior might make her appear masculine and
violate how her southern mother raised her (which is in line with Allan and
Coltrane's observation that "a woman pictured in a 'male' occupation . . .
tends to be perceived as more assertive and 'masculine' than is traditionally
expected" [200]).

When we meet MacKayla in the prologue of *Darkfever*, she is already a
woman divided. (The main text is a flashback to the above conflict between
southern womanhood and her mission, and the prologue is a spoiler of how it
impacted her by the novel's end.) She knows she's a sidhe-seer (a human who
can look past the beautiful facades of faeries to their monstrous selves), a Null
(someone who can temporarily erase a faerie's magical powers), and a diviner
of magical objects. It is an identity that she confesses she "accepted only recently and very reluctantly" since it is dangerous and allegedly incompatible
with her emphasized femininity (3). The rest of the novel and series narrates
how she is dealing with this identity crisis. Her struggle is further complicated
by a potential shift from singlehood towards coupledom amidst men whose
desires are suspect and who often reduce her to a conventional understanding
of her sex category. They, among others, evaluate her feminine appearance and
behaviors as a symptom of physical and mental limitations. This is in keeping
with Goffman's observation that gender displays are treated as indicators of
something essential in a person, rather than just performative shortcuts signaling a role or positionality in a specific social event (7). Accordingly, people
around her read MacKayla's "identificatory stylings" (a term Goffman uses for
"hair style, clothing, and tone of voice") as proof of weak womanhood (2). To
them, her "incumbency" in the "woman" sex category undermines her ability
to seek out justice for her sister (West and Zimmerman 136).

Consequently, MacKayla must not only fight for her life against monsters
(of the human and faerie variety), but also for the right to self-determination,
rejecting the "imperiled idiot blonde femme / butch badass" gender binary that
she is presented with by both antagonists and allies, who ask her to choose between her version of emphasized femininity and death.[9] Her hero journey is to
learn to "gender maneuver" (socially reconstruct or negotiate the relationship

between masculinity and femininity in a specific setting, per Schippers), balance between disfavored femininity and emphasized femininity, and build toward a form of "alternative femininity" (displaying nondominant *and* non-submissive behaviors) to get the results that are otherwise reserved for male heroes (*Rockin' Out of the Box* 37–38; "Recovering the Feminine Other" 97).[10]

Unlike the novels in other chapters of this study, the *Fever* series is told in the first person, a commonplace in the urban fantasy sub-genre. As such, we know only what our heroine knows and experience events from her limited perspective (including her awareness of her personality and self-presentation). However, while the bulk of the first novel is a flashback in which we see the feminine heroine mocked and manipulated by different actors while she struggles toward self-construction and self-knowledge, the framing device of the novel's prologue shows us a wiser MacKayla who has synthesized her old and new selves. She tells us that before her sister was killed, she was sure of her own identity as a daughter, a younger sister, and an unambitious bartender. The first chapter contains a snapshot of her pretty, all-American girl self, spending the Georgia summer swimming, tanning, and listening to cheery music: "I was lounging by the pool in the backyard of my parents' house, wearing my favorite pink polka-dotted bikini],] which went perfectly with my new I'm-Not-Really-a-Waitress-Pink manicure and pedicure. I was sprawled in a cushion-topped chaise soaking up the sun, my long blonde hair twisted up in a spiky knot on top of my head" (4–5).

When the older MacKayla in the prologue looks back at this woman, she seems wistfully critical of this indolent self who was comfortable with normative gender display and identity and her position in a social structure:

> I thought I knew who I was, where I fit, and exactly what my future
> would bring.
> Before, I thought I knew I *had* a future.
> After, I began to discover that I'd never really known anything at all. (7)

The voiceover is a stark foretelling of the crisis of self that will arise when she goes to Dublin to find her sister's killer and is told that her laidback, pink-wearing, manicured self is incompatible with her genetic legacy and subsequent quest. The Georgia MacKayla, her older self tells us, believed she was a genteel woman whose destiny was to become a wife and mother and continue a southern female tradition, (i.e., subscribe to a normative female gender role): "I used to think my sister and I were just two nice southern girls who would get married in a few years, have babies, and settle down to a life of sipping sweet tea on a porch swing under the shade of waxy-blossomed magnolias, raising our children together near Mom and Dad and each other" (*Bloodfever* 2). In *Dark-fever*, where we first see this MacKayla, she is presented as someone who is poles apart from the person she has to become if she is to save herself and the world. The older, savvier self even calls the former self Mac 1.0 (a debut version) or Pink Mac (a childish one). But younger MacKayla doesn't immediately realize in the first book that she will be required to choose between these incompatible selves and that her body, her clothing, and her personality are going to be regarded by others as liabilities when it comes to her goal of finding her sister's killer. Fighting faeries apparently comes with a uniform, and it isn't pink.

Others' mockery of her appearance is a subset of the critique of the female sex. Numerous characters categorize her (and women in general) in reductive and demeaning ways, especially early in the series. In *Faefever* (book 3, 2008), for instance, a criminal named O'Bannion calls her a cunt, while another man says, "A woman who's having sex with a man is a compromised source of information at best. At worst, she's a traitor" (189, 210).[11] Moreover, Mac 1.0's emphasized femininity, in terms of behavior and appearance, is also viewed misogynistically by many beings that she encounters in Dublin. Even her series-long partner, the mysterious bookstore owner Jericho Barrons, initially criticizes her appearance and attitude as unfit for the demands her quest will place on her. His is an essentialist reading of her gender display, which she resents:

> "Go home, Ms. Lane. Be young. Be pretty. Get married. Have babies. Grow old with your pretty husband."
>
> His comment stung like acid on my skin. Because I was blonde, easy on the eyes, and guys had been snapping my bra strap since seventh grade, I'd been putting up with the Barbie stereotype for years. That pink was my favorite color, that I liked matching accessories and eye-catching heels, didn't help much. But I'd never been turned on by the Ken doll.... I wasn't jonesing for a white picket fence and an SUV in the driveway, and I resented the Barbie implications—*Go procreate and die, I'm sure that's all someone like you can do.* (*Darkfever* 48)

Her thoughts underline a distinction here between her own gender display and her prescribed sexual identity as well as mate preference and life goals.

Barrons also associates her (blonde) hairstyle, her clothing, her accessories, and her love of pink with girlishness, incompetence, and an emotional idealism that spells fatal vulnerability (*Darkfever* 105). When they first meet, he terms her "a victim, a lamb in a city of wolves," and he predicts that she will die if she doesn't leave Dublin (53). At another time, he dismisses all beautiful women as lacking grit, saying that they "rarely possess sufficient depth of character to survive without their pretty feathers. Strip them down and they crumble" (91).

The narrative universe seems to agree with his belief. By the end of the first book, she has been tricked twice by a sexually powerful faerie into giving up control of her own body. She has stripped naked under its spell and almost had sex with it in public. Though it is equivalent to being roofied, Moning frames the episode to highlight how others read MacKayla's actions through stereotypes of women's sexual susceptibility and judge her as lacking physical and mental fortitude. In one case, she is chided fiercely for this flaw by a stranger, an older woman who she discovers is the head of an all-female order that kills evil faeries. The woman's wrath at MacKayla's lack of street smarts and perceived sexual vulnerability toward the enemy is another voice in the chorus that criticizes her for being too weak to face the challenges of a war—a weakness that is portrayed as related to her biological sex (frail female body) and her gender (feminine naivete and sexual passivity). MacKayla is thus told to choose between a femme aesthetic and personality on the one hand and life (including productive action and mature sexuality) on the other.[12]

At the end of the first book, she is tortured and nearly killed by a powerful enemy, making her poor skills in this war evident. She survives after she ingests an evil faerie's flesh but loses some of her old self while temporarily becoming stronger and less human. It is a mix of communion, rebirth, and the transubstantiation of Mac 1.0 to 2.0. She describes her changed gender display in the next book's prologue almost as a side effect of that milestone: "Nothing in my sheltered, pampered life prepared me for the past few weeks. Gone is my long blond hair, chopped short for the sake of anonymity and dyed dark. Gone are my pretty pastel outfits, replaced by drab colors that don't show blood. I've learned to cuss, steal, lie, and kill. I've been assaulted by a death-by-sex Fae and made to strip, not once but twice, in public. I discovered that I was adopted. I nearly died" (*Bloodfever* 4–5). She has also begun engaging her foes in fights by the end of book one, becoming more "badass" and less femme. In the opening chapter of *Bloodfever*, she lists the results of her latest battle on her body—a "splinted arm and fingers, the stitches in my lip, and the fading purple and yellow bruises that began around my right eye and extended to the base of my jaw" (7)—as physical evidence of her transformation from a weak pretty girl to a scarred fighter.

As circumstances and people insist that emphasized femininity equals death, MacKayla starts displaying disfavored femininity in appearance and actions. But while lying to a police inspector about her bruises, she still thinks about the parts of herself that she is giving up. She imagines the pastimes enjoyed by her peers who abide by the traditional female gender role in her hometown: "In a few hours my girlfriends would be heading up to one of our favorite lakes where they would soak up the sun, scope out datable guys, and flip through the latest fashion magazines" (8–9). But she seems resigned to the idea that for her (someone hunting down her sister's supernatural killer and lying to a cop while trying to accept the knowledge that she is a fairie-seer), there was to be "no sun. No datable guys. And my only fashion concern was making sure my clothes were baggy enough to accommodate weapons concealed beneath them. Even in the relative security of the bookstore, I was carrying two flashlights, a pair of scissors, and a lethal, foot-long spearhead, tip neatly cased in a ball of foil" (9). The contrast between this MacKayla and the MacKayla of *Darkfever* couldn't be clearer. Instead of cute bikinis, her clothes now have a "concealed carry" functionality, a purposefulness without which survival is doubtful. The spear-carrying MacKayla—and it is unavoidable to see that spear as a phallic substitute signaling masculine strength—is different from the trusting one who was attached to her phone, to pretty clothes, nail polish, and flirting. (She's different even from the MacKayla who "disguised" herself by foregoing makeup, wearing a ponytail with a baseball cap, jeans, baggy T-shirt, tennis shoes, and no accessories except for "hideous" magnifying spectacles [*Darkfever* 151]. That episode was a deliberate "gender blender" display that she believed would make her unattractive—and thus invisible—to a world that only notices femme women.)

In the conflict against supernatural evil, "glamor girl" Pink Mac was a liability, one she says she only overcame because Barrons "taught me who and what I am, opened my eyes, and helped me survive" (*Bloodfever* 4). Under his tutelage and through her own battles, she notes that "I've shed *years* of polished southern civilities" (4). A great deal of MacKayla's earlier self is attributed to her mother's teachings about what makes a proper southern lady, exposing some of the ideological processes through which normative gender is constructed and perpetuated in society. In the early books in the series, for example, MacKayla explains the reason she uses nonsense words in place of curses: "Born and raised in the Bible Belt, Mom had taken a strong position about cussing when we were growing up—*A pretty woman doesn't have an ugly mouth*, she would say" (*Darkfever* 57). Women's outer beauty is thus linked to an inner self that follows biblical rules of women's appropriate behavior. When she later uses the epithet "dickhead," she apologizes silently to her mother for going against her lessons on polite language (91). Similarly, she is uncomfortable when she sits in a way her mother would disapprove of (69). Other mentions of her mother always reference feminine rules, such as her gift of a cosmetic pack of "basics no proper southern belle would ever be without" (88). The mother represents MacKayla's socialization into traditional femininity and gender display, and the novels show a pattern in which she feels torn between it and the male attire and male battle tactics she thinks she must adopt to survive.

We often see real-world analogies to this dilemma women face. In 2018, a *New York Times* article on a seminar meant to professionalize women trying to run for political office reminded readers that "The female political candidate's uniform developed largely as a feminized version of the men's suit, chosen to demonstrate that women could fit into what was a male-dominated world" (Vanessa Friedman). Similarly, hair length has always had gender implications. A moral panic resulted in the US and elsewhere when teen boys began growing their hair in the 1970s, and polls showed that hair length was another gendered form of presentation that affected workplace life, with men being regarded as less employable if their hair exceeded a certain length (Hillman 8, 158). On the other side, 1970s' women activists cut their hair as a rejection of traditional femininity (Hillman 61). But women politicians in the US have also been negotiating the insistence that they must look like a typical male candidate, showing vulnerability in their stories and diverging from the traditional "uniform" instead (Kate Zernike).

Female celebrities provide more examples of this discourse. In 2020, Rachel Reiderer did a survey of Dolly Parton's career from "walking, talking boob joke with a hillbilly accent," to a savvy businesswoman and philanthropist, the opening phrase epitomizing how Parton was often disrespected for her appearance and speech. Reiderer also recounts bringing up the singer's "ditzy talk-show giggle and surgical enhancements" to a queer friend who was a Parton fan, only to have them propose a feminist reading of Parton's gender performance. Parton is just one striking example of how femme-presenting people have often been subject to such dismissive attitudes about their competence. I myself recall being advised by graduate school professors to dress in pantsuits rather than skirts when on the academic job market; the ostensible reason is to avoid flashing your underwear at someone during interviews (which are often done during the MLA convention in hotel rooms while sitting on a bed), but echoes of femininity being a liability are not far off. Women athletes are almost always paid less than men for their alleged comparatively low sports skill or ability to draw an audience but viewed with suspicion as soon as they discard markers of a traditional female body and performance.[13]

Mirroring these real-world pressures, MacKayla is also told that her femme self is useless. But she resists succumbing to this rhetoric wholesale and holds on to the old MacKayla even into book three of the series, *Faefever* (2008). Her every subsequent attempt to express that self by wearing feminine garb for a few hours ends in disaster, however, as if the universe is punishing her for performing femininity and thwarting her in her mission because she isn't being masculine enough. There are scenes in which her colorful, "glamor girl," Juicy-Coutured body collapses weakly in mud and filth when she encounters paranormal enemies. Take the beginning of *Faefever*. In keeping with the series' typical structure, it begins with a prologue in which MacKayla frames the upcoming chapters as the story of her recent past, in this case with an image of her heading out on a date a few weeks earlier:

> It's me. Pretty in pink and gold. . . .
> There's a sparkle in my eyes and a spring in my step. I'm wearing a killer pink dress with my favorite heels, and I'm accessorized to the hilt, in gold and rose amethyst. I've taken extra care with my hair and makeup. I'm on my way to meet Christian MacKeltar, a sexy, mysterious young Scotsman who knew my sister. I feel *good* for a change.
> Well, at least for a short time I do.
> Fast-forward a few moments.
> Now I'm clutching my head and stumbling from the sidewalk, into the gutter. Falling to all fours. I've just gotten closer to the *Sinsar Dubh* [*Black Book*] than I've ever been before, and it's having its usual effect on me. Pain. Debilitating.
> I no longer look so pretty. In fact, I look positively wretched.
> On my hands and knees in a puddle that smells of beer and urine, I'm iced to the bone. My hair is in a tangle, my amethyst hair clip bobs against my nose, and I'm crying. I push the hair from my face with a filthy hand and watch the tableau playing out in front of me with wide, horrified eyes.
> (*Faefever* 7–8)

At this point, the older, harder, wiser narrator MacKayla stages a dialogue with her younger, softer self about toughening up. This narrative device, in which pronouns shift from first person to third person to second person and back ("I," "you," "me," "my," and "her"), shows MacKayla's psyche in the process of splintering between contradictory ideas of what she should be. Her older self is urging her to become something (strong, unfeminine, hardened) that is fundamentally unsustainable; the call to change is premised on a binary (weak femininity versus strong butchness) that is self-alienating:

> I remember that moment. Who I was. What I wasn't. I capture it in freeze-frame. There are so many things I would say to her.
> Head up, Mac. Brace yourself. A storm is coming. Don't you hear the thunderclap of sharp hooves on the wind? Can't you feel the soul-numbing frost? Don't you smell spice and blood on the breeze?

Run, I would tell her. Hide.

But I wouldn't listen to me.

On my knees, watching that ... *thing* ... do what it's doing, I'm in the stranglehold of a killing undertow.

Reluctantly, I merge with the memory, slip into her skin. (*Faefever* 8)

The MacKayla narrating the prologue has informed us that this MacKayla will soon lose more of who she was when she first came to Dublin fresh from Georgia. At this point, the first chapter begins, and the narrative voice shifts to the MacKayla of a few weeks ago, who starts recounting the event in the first person. By the end of her confrontation with the ancient book of spells that has brought her to her knees, her pretty appearance has been lost, and that's just the start of her losses:

I pushed to my feet, dragged the back of my hand across my mouth, and stared at my reflection in a pub window. I was stained, I was soaked, and I smelled. My hair was a soppy mess of beer.... I plucked the clip from my hair, scraped it back, and secured it at my nape where it couldn't touch much of my face.

My dress was torn, I was missing two buttons down the front of it, I'd broken the heel off my right shoe, and my knees were scraped and bleeding.... I looked around for my missing heel. It was nowhere to be seen. I'd *loved* those shoes, darn it! I'd saved for months to buy them.

I sighed inwardly and told myself to get over it. At the moment, I had bigger problems on my mind.

I hadn't passed out.

I'd been within fifty yards of the *Sinsar Dubh*, and I'd stayed conscious the entire time.

It appeared recent events had "diluted" me, and I was now more like the Book. Evil. (*Faefever* 15–16)

She recognizes that the loss of her pretty appearance is also symbolic of an internal transformation toward something powerful and destructive, which is what (almost homeopathically) enabled her to survive this recent skirmish with the object that epitomizes that evil tradition. Her new strength comes from no longer being a good southern woman. In other words, her newfound survival skills come from internalizing the evil she is fighting, and they work in inverse ratio to her prettily dressed, traditional (innocent/weak) womanhood. At this point then, the series still positions the two states as mutually exclusive and MacKayla faces the following binaries: strength versus femininity, survival versus beauty, practical knowledge of evil versus ignorant optimism. Her struggle with these false distinctions becomes a motif.

As she tries to clean up after the above incident, she recalls that in the past she would have reapplied cosmetics at the first sign of dishevelment but that is no longer the case: "A month ago, I would have immediately fixed my face. Now, I was just happy I had good skin and glad to be out of the rain" (29). Instead of looking pretty, she craves being self-reliant and physically strong, like she became after eating pieces of faerie flesh (something that would have been anathema to Mac 1.0): "The only time I'd ever felt like I could take care of myself, since I'd come to Dublin, was the night Mallucé had nearly killed me, and I'd eaten Unseelie to survive. . . . I'd felt like I finally had an edge that night and hadn't needed anyone else to protect me. I'd been able to kick ass just like all the other big, bad men around me. . . . It had been exhilarating. It had been freeing" (*Faefever* 39). The realization is followed by her acceptance of other changes, such as in her interior décor preferences and habits. As she observes, "Genteel southern Mac was shamed by my lack of china and silver. Spear-toting Mac cared only that there might be leftovers and food should never be wasted" (*Faefever* 40).

But while she is choosing functionality when it comes to possessions, she tries to fuse her earlier ideas of traditionally feminine presentation with a deadlier (literally darker) side. The image calls up both Moore's femme style and hints of Schippers's "badass" disfavored femininity, with its potential for violence:

> I'd dressed up again tonight, wound a brilliant silk scarf through my hair and tied it, letting the brightly colored ends trail over my shoulder, and drape softly in my cleavage. I was nothing if not determined; at least twice a week I would wear bright, pretty clothes. I was afraid if I didn't, I'd forget who I was. I'd turn into what I felt like: a grungy, weapon-bearing, pissy, resentful, vengeance-hungry bitch. The girl with long blond hair, perfect makeup, and nails might be gone, but I was still pretty. My shoulder-length Arabian night hair curled flatteringly around my face, complementing my green eyes and clear skin. Coupling red lipstick with my darker do made me look older, sexier than I used to.
>
> I'd chosen clothes tonight that hugged my curves and showed them to their best advantage. I was wearing a cream skirt, with a snug yellow sweater in honor of Alina (beneath a short, stylish, cream raincoat that concealed eight flashlights, two knives, and a spear), high heels, and pearls. (*Faefever* 52–53)

The darkened hair, tools, and weapons are reminders of her transformation, and the novels' prologues show the gradual replacement of femininity with hegemonic masculinity by a female character in order to enter into the public realm. When she mentions a female role model, however, she alludes to fellow southerner Scarlett O'Hara's use of femininity, saying "It's just that in the Deep South, women learn at a young age that when the world is falling apart around you, it's time to take down the drapes and make a new dress" (*Faefever* 129). Like Scarlett, MacKayla believes that feminine presentation is not just frippery but can play a life-saving role. So it is more accurate to say that she starts thinking of both femme and transgressive gender display as performances with expedient utility, rather than natural or mutually exclusive states.

But Barrons, as noted earlier, initially pressures her to choose between these states, accusing her of immaturity, passivity, and stupidity. He insists that she be more aggressive, less sentimental, and less femme if she wants to win fights. When he takes her into spaces that are meant to hold up hegemonic masculinity, on the other hand, he requires a gender display of compliant, emphasized femininity, such as tight, minimal clothing and heels, which messages sexual readiness, terming it more "womanly" (*Darkfever* 117). This requirement aligns with traditional gender roles and institutionalized sexism in Western cultures, including the virgin/whore binary and the reiteration of women as subordinate sex objects via draping their bodies in provocative clothing (Wallis 168–69). The messages Barrons gives MacKayla are thus mixed, though the first set of instructions is meant to train her into becoming a warrior. His paradoxical behavior shows up at other times, too. Though he apologizes after an argument in book 3 by buying her the kind of youthful, branded clothing she likes, in the scene that follows, he uses a compulsion spell to freeze her in place to demonstrate her continuing powerlessness. Then he demands that she verbalize who she is but rejects answers like "daughter," "sister," "girl," or "twenty-two" (her age) with the intent of forcing her to tap into a libidinal anger and recognize an identity outside a socially constructed one (*Faefever* 227).

> "You exist only inside yourself," he said. "No one sees you. You see no one. You are without censure, beyond judgment. There is no law. No right or wrong. How did you feel when you saw your sister's body?"
>
> Rage filled me. Rage at what had been done to her. Rage at him for bringing it up. The thought that no one could see or judge me was liberating. I swelled with grief and anger.
>
> "Now tell me who you are."
>
> "Vengeance," I said in a cold voice. (*Faefever* 227)

It's a demonstration to show her that she wears a polite façade, which she uses to gain familial and social approval but that limits her to others' definitions of what a woman should be.

Not satisfied with critiquing her clothes or her tendency to think of herself in relational identities, he acts like an army drill sergeant thwarting a script of feminine nurturing and social rituals to make her a tough guy. Later in the same novel, he throws away a birthday cake she makes for him, telling her, "You have no business looking forward to pink cakes. That's not your world anymore. Your world is hunting the Book and staying alive. They're mutually exclusive, you bloody fool" (*Faefever* 273). His training to be cutthroat comes in handy when she is attacked and manages to defend herself, and these episodes make her more determined to develop a fiercer side. His method is a form of socializing her away from feminine gender display but not toward an alternative femininity as much as hegemonic masculinity, with its echoes of a primitive self. She names this new risk-taking self "Savage Mac," an animalistic creature who can be "powerful, predatory, padding on certain paws" (*Faefever* 287).

Yet the narrative demands even more of her than ceding some pieces of herself; at the end of *Faefever*, three faerie princes gang-rape her and reduce her to a mindless, animalistic body under a magic spell (again evoking date-rape drugs). In the stream of her thoughts during the rape, recounted in the next book, memory and reality suffer erasure while her past self is annihilated, as is her ability to think or use language:

> If my thoughts were coherent enough to form sentences, I would tell you that I used to think life unfolded in a linear fashion. That people were born and went to . . . what's that human word? I dressed up for it every day. There were boys. Lots of cute boys. I thought the world revolved around them.
> *His tongue is in my mouth, and it's tearing apart my soul.*
> *Helpmesomeonepleasehelpmemakehimstopmakethemgoaway.*
> School. That's the word I'm looking for. After that, you get a job. Marry. Have . . . what are they? Fae can't have them. Don't understand them. Precious little lives. Babies! If you're lucky, you live a good, full life and grow old with someone you love. Caskets then. Wood gleams. I weep. A sister? Bad! Memory hurts! Let it go! (*Dreamfever* 4)

What is also undergoing annihilation in this excerpt is the road map of the gender normative life she had been raised to expect, as well as her grief over her sister's death—everything that was the foundation of the previous MacKayla's young, loving self.

The rape is doubly horrific because the spell makes her body undergo orgasms even as her mind withholds consent and the trauma of that division fractures her sense of self completely. Before it is erased, she has the realization

that the MacKayla who is disappearing is a feminine self that was molded by
media culture into a social mimic and consumer:

> *The more they fill me the emptier I am. It's slipping, all slipping, but before it goes,*
> *before it's gone completely, I get a hateful moment of clarity and see that*
>
> Most of what I believed about myself, and life, I derived from modern
> media, without questioning any of it. If I wasn't sure how to behave in a
> certain situation, I'd search my mind for a movie or TV show I'd seen, with a
> similar setup, and do whatever the actors had done. A sponge, I absorbed my
> environment, became a by-product of it.
>
> I don't think I ever once looked up at the sky and wondered if there was
> sentient life in the universe besides the human race. I *know* I never looked
> down at the earth beneath my feet and contemplated my own mortality.
> I tunneled blithely through magnolia-drenched days, blind as a mole to
> everything but guys, fashion, power, sex, whatever would make me feel good
> right then. (*Dreamfever* 4–5)

The excerpt documents her insight into the cultural programming of women—
"the institutional arrangements that are based on sex category"—and how they
are trained to seek specific pleasures (West and Zimmerman 146).

The dissociated first-person narrator then adds something that shows how
her speech and self-recognition fade away during the rape and the accompanying shame that victims are socialized to feel:

> But these are confessions I would make if I could speak, and I can't. I'm
> ashamed. I'm so ashamed.
>
> *Who the fuck are you?* Someone shouted that question at me recently—his
> name eludes me. (*Dreamfever* 5)

That question—"Who the fuck are you?"—repeats itself through her fugue
state, her rambling thoughts a chronicle of lost hope and willpower as well
as despair that women are taught the wrong fairy tales about being rescued
instead of learning how to defend themselves:

> How could I have been such a fool to believe that at the critical moment,
> when my world fell apart, some knight in shining armor was going to come
> thundering in on a white stallion, or arrive sleek and dark on an eerily
> silent Harley, or appear in a flash of golden salvation, summoned by a name
> embedded in my tongue, and rescue me? What was I raised on—fairy tales?
>
> Not this kind. These are the fairy tales we were *supposed* to be teaching
> our daughters. A few thousand years ago, we did. But we got sloppy and
> complacent, and when the Old Ones seemed to go quietly, we allowed

ourselves to forget the Old Ways. Enjoyed the distractions of modern technology and forgot the most important question of all.

Who the fuck are you?

Here on the floor, in my final moments—MacKayla Lane's last grand hurrah—I see that the answer is all I've ever been.

I'm nobody. (*Dreamfever* 6–7)

Her last clear thoughts—that her culture has failed to teach women the correct lessons and the correct questions—are a scathing indictment of the values that she holds responsible for leading her to her current abject state. She was too feminized and didn't learn to be strong enough on her own, and the result is her complete reduction to a sex object. The episode is the nadir of her hero journey, one from which she is rescued by a teenage female comrade and eventually by Barrons, who assists her new self-construction.

The narrative later reveals that he's repeating the phrase "Who the fuck are you?" to her in her catatonic state after he has brought her home; as we saw in an earlier passage in *Faefever* (227), it is a phrase he's used during her training to make her discover an asocialized self, and he uses it after her assault in an attempt to recover her mind out of the objectified nonentity that the rapists made of her. The question is also part of his unorthodox, two-pronged trauma management strategy. One, since she had been placed under an aphrodisiac spell and wants sexual fulfillment, he has sex with her; his actions facilitate her reclaiming sexual agency because she eventually takes control and this leads to her overcoming the trauma of being a *passive* object during the rape. Two, he surrounds her with material reminders of the woman she used to be—the one who was fusing parts of her southern belle identity with a tougher faerie-hunter self. Since the rape has robbed her of that nascent identity, Barrons provokes her into fighting that loss despite his prior disapproval of her femme presentation. She resists his attempts even as she uses his body, but he refuses to let her stay a languageless, memoryless sexual being, a woman who is nothing more than her biology. He plays the music she used to love ("peppy, happy songs"), surrounds her with photos of her family and her personal possessions (pink nail polish and clothes, fashion magazines, purses, shoes, candles, lamps), and prompts her to remember her history and take control of language (a marked reversal of the training episode where he used a spell to silence her) (*Dreamfever* 44, 74–75).

Barrons insists that she recognize her name and his (a key step in acknowledging one's status as a thinking human), and he even makes her join him in decorating a Christmas tree (thus inching her closer to her familial, cultural, and religious identity). He brings her a birthday cake, even reminding her that she had brought him a pink one. In other words, he accepts and helps her reclaim the feminine self that he had mocked and that she had been giving up for a hegemonic masculinity-based one.[14] He functions as the helpmate that Christine Mains sees in fantasy novels starring female heroes—the man who is essentially a projection of the heroine's male aspects (and thus one of the selves she has initially been alienated from by the normative gender binary) and with whom she is subsequently able to construct a long partnership.

Barrons's actions may not have shown that he valued the woman she was, but he knows that she did, and he assists her in recovering that self. His therapy slowly works, and her recovery starts with a change in her language. From a purely carnal creature who uses crude, monosyllabic expressions of lust, she starts to swing back on the pendulum, confusing herself by using polite euphemisms (like "petunia" for "buttocks" when she and Barron are having sex)—a habit that belonged to the traditionally sanctioned feminine vocabulary and sensibility of the Georgia MacKayla (45). Her return from her fugue state moves her a step closer toward a synthesis of those selves that she had previously experienced as discordant—a combination of Mac 1.0, Pink Mac, and Savage Mac. As she reflects, "The animal I'd been recently hadn't left me. She was still in me and would be forever. I was glad. I welcomed her feral nature. Pink Mac had needed a good dose of savagery. It was a savage world out there" (*Dreamfever* 68).

She names this synthesized self "Black Mac," noting "I still liked pink, I would always like pink. But there wasn't anything pink inside me anymore" (75). The implication of no longer being pink on the inside is that her tribulations have irrevocably altered her raw state, and while her aesthetic tastes may have elements of youthfulness, they don't reflect her mental toughness. Her outside is also restructured because the sexual marathon with Barrons leaves her with the "useful new shape" of a muscled body; the idea that repeated sex made her stronger is a striking departure from the misogynist equating of sexual women with moral and physical fragility (70). The journey to accepting all her selves progresses further after she has an angry confrontation with Barrons about her recent trauma and his part in it: "'What was I supposed to learn Barrons? . . . How about this: The more weapons, knowledge, and power you can get your hands on, *any way you can*, the better. Lie, cheat, or steal, it all comes out in the wash. Isn't that what you think? That emotion is weakness and cunning priceless? Wasn't I supposed to become like you? Wasn't that the point?' I was shouting, but I didn't care. I was furious" (*Dreamfever* 157). She's angry that he had wanted her to take on hegemonic masculinity in lieu of femme gender display but is now critical of her for doing so, like the fathers of Devor's gender blenders (20–21). This is when he admits that he no longer wants her to be remade in his own image, devoid of her own blend of femininities; the narrative makes room here for the suggestion that an alternative femininity may be desirable after all, with a gender display that a woman hero manages as she wishes and a mix of nonsubmissive and nondominant behaviors.

Despite MacKayla's wariness toward Barrons after her recovery, she works with him to save the world using all her latent powers and regained strengths. Her divided selves finally come together after she ends up in a different universe in *Shadowfever* (2011), the last book in this arc of the series, where she believes she has accidentally killed Barrons; only then does she admit she desired and loved him for helping her reconcile all that she was and was becoming:

> I had to be ripped in half to stop feeling so torn in two. Divided, never knowing who to trust.
> I'm now a woman with a single ambition.
> I know exactly what I'm going to do.
> And I know how I'm going to do it. (23)

From here on out, she feels no shame or hesitation about strategically using all her selves to achieve what she wants—vengeance for her sister and herself and the resurrection of Barrons from the dead. She is to be both avenger and rescuer, with no gender display restrictions.

The one instance where *Shadowfever* mentions her appearance shows a complete blend of different styles. She notes, "I was wearing distressed black leather pants with a tattooed gray grunge element and my favorite baby-doll pink tee that said *I'm a JUICY girl* across the front and had chiffon cap sleeves. I'd tied a Goth scarf around my blond curls and had on a pair of Alina's dangling heart earrings. My fingernails had grown out and I'd done a French manicure on my hands, but I'd painted my toenails black. The dichotomy didn't end there. I had on a black lace thong and a pink-and-white striped cotton bra. I was having issues" (368). She is aware of the seeming incompatibility of her presentation (black/blonde/pink, leather/chiffon/manicured) and accepts what it represents about her complex inner life and impulses. A resurrected Barrons mockingly asks if she's having an identity crisis, but she dismisses his teasing and calls it her "little *personality* crisis," content to see where the chips fall in the future (368, emphasis mine).

While she started her journey being told that her pink-wearing, sentimental self could not be a warrior, by book five's end, she managed to figure out how to be both, with identity (an internal truth) no longer tied to expression (which itself need not comply with social perceptions and expectations of women). In the moment before she and Barrons eventually have sex with her full awareness and willingness and become equal partners, she finally admits to herself that she has a desiring self (that wants romantic and sexual fulfillment) and a violent self (that wants independence and revenge) and they are not mutually exclusive, nor do they need to line up with a dark or light or butch or femme presentation. She gives both selves free rein and eventually manages to punish those who unraveled her life and killed her sister (with help from Barrons, his fellow soldiers, and the coven of women sidhe-seers).

This plot arc serves to exemplify how romance fiction—after all, the series is about MacKayla's HEA with Barrons—stages the heroine's identity quest as a dialectic. It's a progression in which the persistent conflict between sex (a seemingly fixed biological construction) and gender (a mutating sociolinguistic construction) is played out, often on the heroine's body. Serving as the battlefield for that conflict, MacKayla, who is variously called "Mac," "Ms. Lane," "Rainbow Girl," and "cunt," is both feminized and masculinized in the process, constructing her own alternative femininity of strategic violence, blended gender display, and nurturing attitude toward her chosen community. The core of the *Fever* series is thus less about the fantasy of defeating powerful faeries who seek to annihilate humanity and more about the fantasy that female heroes (and romance fiction) can imagine a reconciliation between the divergent and seemingly homicidal demands that social and political discourses make on them.

MacKayla's gyre-like journey around southern-belle-hood in an urban fantasy romance series might appear quite different from that of the next heroine, gym owner and former cheerleader Blair Mallory in Linda Howard's *To Die For* (2005) (book one of two detailing Blair's HEA). At face value, Blair is far more like the heroines in realistic contemporary romance. Yet there are similarities in hers and MacKayla's journeys to taking ownership of their gender display and asserting who they are in the face of external expectations about their gender. Like MacKayla, Blair is also a pretty blonde from the southern United States (North Carolina) whose life is in peril. The novel is narrated in her first-person voice, and she is aware that the world thinks little of women who look like her. The tenets of Blair's life (especially of managing sexual dynamics within a heteronormative gender binary) come from her southern mother. Unlike MacKayla however, Blair has already built a life, a business, and a strong sense of self, partly because she has been raised amid strong women and has a supportive father. She takes satisfaction in running her thriving gym—that is, until she gets a client who wants to copy her physical style and who is shot and killed by someone in the gym parking lot. Worse, the killer appears to have done so in error, with Blair being his real target. Also unlike MacKayla,

Blair's gender display is less about clothing and accessory-related changes and more about overcoming critiques of her confidence to reclaim her sexual and romantic worth.

Our heroine's journey is interspersed with multiple attacks, literal recurrences of what Pamela Regis terms the "point of ritual death" (an episode that threatens a potential happy ending) (*A Natural History* 35). Blair faces actual death at the hands of someone who resents what she represents: a woman who is financially savvy, independent, confident, and stereotypically beautiful (blonde, with a gymnast's body). As police detective (and old flame) Wyatt Bloodsworth says during his investigation into possible suspects, "You're a cheerleader; there must be hundreds of people who'd like to kill you," using "cheerleader" as shorthand for a woman both desired and resented (250). What's more, that same combination of characteristics might be responsible for her rocky romantic life. Her ex-husband cheated on her (and put the moves on her younger, prettier, less ambitious sister), and Wyatt ghosted her a few years ago after just two dates; their actions are linked to her gender display (including her self-confident and take-charge attitude), and the downsides each man associates with it. In addition to the literal points of ritual death then, Blair has experienced its symbolic equivalent through her rejection by two men (one of whom is the putative romance hero). A key theme in the novel is therefore the social sanctioning of a woman like her, whose gender display is partly Barbie-like but who does not act compliant, sexually passive, or stupid. In other words, her particular configuration of characteristics "constitute[s] a refusal to complement hegemonic masculinity in a relation of subordination" and poses a threat to both hegemonic masculinity and complicit femininity; it is a disfavored femininity that the normative gender order is quick to punish (Schippers, "Recovering the Feminine Other" 95).

Over the course of the novel, Blair tries to survive these murder attempts and fend off Wyatt, who had dumped her for being too high-maintenance and has now realized he wants to be with her after the scare of her near murder. But despite her bafflement at why someone wants her dead, and her attraction to Wyatt (mixed with hurt and anger at his previous rejection), Blair refuses to believe that either situation is her fault. In other words, she rejects the victim-blaming narratives that often surround physical and symbolic violence against women. This is not to say that she is unwilling to change; through a dialectical progression that is integral to the bildungsroman of the romance novel heroine, Blair gives up some of parts of her self in the course of the novel—specifically, the part that is angry at her ex-husband and at Wyatt for fleeing because of her "demanding" nature, and which she has replaced with a veneer of breezy indifference—but she doesn't concede elements integral to her. For one, she forces Wyatt to admit that he was wrong to think that a woman should be meek and pleasant. Moreover, she susses out the killer of her copycat and saves herself from her attacker, thus proving that a cheerleader with a body like "a walking wet dream" is capable of both logic and self-defense (224).

To Die For thus charts the heroine's triumph over two false binaries: one, that she can't be a former cheerleader and a good romantic partner, and two, that she cannot be both an attractive blonde and an intelligent, accomplished businesswoman. The novel's route to this end is two-fold: first, through the use of two doubles or foils who represent extreme versions of the negative trait configuration associated with Blair's gender display and who are eliminated over the course of the novel (plus another double who is a positive representation), and second, through having Wyatt recognize the error of his previous prejudices toward her gender display and become her ally. Since he symbolizes the hegemonic masculinity visible in all of Howard's heroes, his apology also exposes masculinity's dependence on emphasized femininity to shore itself up.

To begin with, let's look at the primary double, Nicole, the copycat who began imitating Blair's physical style after joining her gym. Blair describes the mimicry as follows:

> Her natural color was kind of blondish, but within two weeks of joining Great Bods she went golden blond, with pale streaks. Like mine, in fact. . . . Then she started pulling it into a ponytail on top of her head to keep it out of the way while she worked out. Guess who also pulled up her hair like that while working out? . . . Nicole asked me what kind of lotion I used. . . . The next day, Nicole's skin had a sheen. . . . Her workout clothes began to look like mine: leotards and leg warmers while I'm actually in the gym, with yoga pants pulled on while I was cruising around overseeing operations. (10)

She later tells the police that Nicole "got the . . . same style earrings. She even bought a white convertible because I have one" (44).

While these elements paint a picture of Nicole wanting to look like Blair, others show her deep loathing, arguably a projection of the heroine's own conflicted sense of self and representative of women's conflicted relationships to the display demanded by emphasized femininity. In listing Nicole's behavior, Blair mentions her "false sweetness" and fake compliments, noting that by saying, "'Oh, honey, that's just the greatest pair of earrings!' Nicole really meant 'I want to rip them out of your ears and leave bleeding stumps, you bitch'" (11). Other women corroborate this reading of Nicole as a competitive woman who hid her animosity behind a saccharine facade. Blair quotes another gym user telling her that Nicole would "like to slit your throat, pour gasoline over you, set you on fire, and leave you lying in the gutter. Then she'd come back and dance on your ashes after the fire was out" (11).[15]

Blair also critiques her double's self-sexualization by telling the reader that Nicole, who liked to be called by the diminutive "Nikki," spoke in "one of those breathy little voices that make strong men melt" and had "that fake Marilyn Monroe coo that men seem to like." She mentions Nicole's "syrupy sex-kitten act" and her constant flirtatious behavior around men, and adds that she "was the type who'd play the jealousy game" (46–47). This assessment of Nicole's adoption of a hypersexual, unscrupulous persona is seconded by Blair's gym manager Lynne, who thinks that Nicole was having an affair with a married man because "She always wanted what some other woman had. She wouldn't have been interested in some single guy, other than as a temporary boost to her ego" (182). Lynne also speculates that Nicole was a selfish lover when describing a suspicious incident between her and a man in the gym bathrooms, noting: "Maybe she was giving him a blow job, but that wasn't her style, either. At a guess, I'd say she did all the taking and none of the giving" (185).

These descriptions, which are a combination of hegemonic and disfavored femininity, are noteworthy because Blair herself is described as exhibiting some of these traits of the dumb, sexually promiscuous blonde. Wyatt terms her "fluffy" and links the empty-headed impression she allegedly gives off to her appearance: "Everything about you is fluffy, from that Pebbles hair-do to your fancy little flip-flops with the shells on them. You wear an anklet all the time, your toenails are hot pink, and your bras match your panties. You look like an ice-cream cone" (203–4). When he declares this image as antithetical to her being a smart businesswoman, it is similar to Blair's assessment of Nicole as "Cunning, but not bright" (44).

Despite Wyatt's wry admission that he doesn't actually think Blair is stupid, he argues that it is the logical interpretation of her appearance, and both are linked to his judgment of her as flirtatious. He tells her, "You can't help [flirting]. It's in your genes" (288), suggesting that this sexual behavior is an innate part of her, and even half-jokingly warns her against flirting with his colleagues: "There are some guys here who have high cholesterol, so try not to smile at them and give them heart attacks. Don't flirt with anyone who's over forty, or overweight, or married, or under forty, or single" (354–55). He also claims that her beauty and coquetry have given her a sense of entitlement, of getting anything she wants from men, which is why he had decided two years ago that she was too much work to be an ideal girlfriend. This depiction of Blair is reminiscent of how Nicole is portrayed. We learn that Nicole's married lover killed her because of her demands, just as Blair underwent a symbolic death when Wyatt abandoned her for being sexually attractive and high-maintenance. Moreover, the idea that Nicole was a taker when it came to sex is recast as Blair's reluctant (though passionate) desire for Wyatt, such as in intimate situations where he initiates all sexual contact and stimulates both their orgasms—she does not play an active role to do the same for him.

The similarities between Blair and Nicole suggest that they are twinned women; the Nicole half serves the function of a narrative fall guy/gal on whom deeply feared female gender stereotypes can be projected and exorcised (through the murder), while Blair showcases the competent and clever woman that she is alongside her "fluffy" display. She admits, for instance, that she uses the dumb blonde routine when it's convenient, such as when she is trying to get the cops to finish their inquiry into her possible role in Nicole's murder. She asks them to do a "thingie" test (i.e., a test for gunpowder residue) and tells us that the cops "were trying hard not to laugh at me, but sometimes the dumb-blond stereotype has its uses. The less threatening I could appear, the better" (30). She thus performs emphasized femininity to play up to the men's condescension toward the "subordinate" gender so she can get what she wants. Over the course of the novel, Wyatt recognizes that he was hasty in interpreting her gender display. He admits his error in extrapolating from her body and style and pigeonholing her as a diva based on two dates, and he apologizes for dumping her because he thought her sexual attractiveness did not compensate for her assertiveness. In other words, he acknowledges that he wanted her to be a sexually available undemanding blonde doll who fit into normative gender hegemony, and he expresses admiration that she has made her business a success despite her "fluffy" exterior. It is worth noting that Blair gets to contest the charge of flirtatiousness while Nicole is killed for her sexual promiscuity, another example of Schippers's concepts of alternate femininity versus disfavored femininity. Interestingly, while Blair rejects Wyatt's characterization of her as a flirt, only the reader is privy to her mental argument "Yes, I flirt occasionally, but that doesn't make me a flirt" (288). Blair's defense is thus aimed at us and challenges the essentialist tendency of gender normativity, where an element of gender display is read as a reflection of some "natural" essence and used to reinforce gender norms.

The novel supplements this reappraisal of traditional femininity through other characters as well. Apart from the competitive Nicole double, Blair is being hunted by another woman who wants to be her—her ex-husband Jason's current wife, Debra. We are not told anything else about Debra's appearance or profession, just that she is "clingy and insecure" and homicidally jealous because Jason made her think he still had positive feelings for Blair (363). Enraged by Jason comparing her to Blair during marital spats, not to mention his insistence that Debra live in the house he once shared with Blair, Debra sets out to kill her perceived rival, who seemed to have an unfair share of male attention and assets. So while Nicole is an extreme version of sex-kitten femininity that must be destroyed, Debra is the unsexy, irrational feminine that needs elimination. Her jealous streak is faintly visible in Blair when she hounds Wyatt about who he was dating recently, ostensibly in an attempt to find her attacker, but also to annoy him. When Wyatt refuses to answer her questions, she gets her mother, Tina, to ask him, counting on his inability to be rude to her.

Finally, Tina is the third and most interesting double for Blair because the character provides proof that it is possible to challenge the false binaries of beauty versus intelligence and assertiveness versus a happy marriage (something the other two doubles have failed to achieve). In other words, this double foretells a successful stage in the dialectical development of a romance heroine like Blair. Tina, described as a "former Miss North Carolina, tall and slender, blond, and gorgeous," who makes men lose their train of thought, and who is a steamroller when she wants something, is also a capable real estate agent who runs her business and her personal life with finesse. Her husband loves her, and her three daughters look to her as a guide, especially when it comes to dealing with men and gender dynamics. She has raised them on what Blair calls the Southern Woman's Code, whose rules Blair follows in her skirmishes with Wyatt. (An example of the Code is to "never let a man take something back on the first attempt" because "Section three, paragraph ten" of the Code is that "if one [meaning a man] is going to be a shithead, one must pay for it"; other rules include planning a man's punishments for future infractions ahead of time and never cutting him any slack when he makes a mistake [250]). Though Blair fails to stick to her mother's philosophy of not living with a man before a wedding, her mother's Code powers her pugnacious responses to Wyatt's dominating hegemonic masculinity. Blair's tactics involve showily writing down a list of his transgressions, delivering sharp admonishments when he tries to tell her how to run her business, and executing guerrilla moves that keep him off-balance, such as hiding his TV remote and giving him a hard time about his attempts to style her hair when her arm is injured.

Moreover, Tina has violent tendencies, seen when she smashes a malfunctioning computer monitor with a sledgehammer—a trait Blair also possesses; the scene is foreshadowed by Blair's declaration to Wyatt that she is a capable woman who has home repair tools, including a pink hammer. Blair's strength and fighting instinct come from Tina, which, combined with her own cheerleading training, helps her save herself in her climactic physical confrontation with Debra. When the jealous woman tries to shoot her, Blair evades the shot by instinctively going into a backflip (learned as a cheerleader) and accidentally kicks Debra on the chin. The shot goes wild, grazing Jason, who has also been trying to kill Blair to pacify his wife's jealousy, and the police burst in during the chaos to find the would-be killers in hysterics. When Wyatt anxiously asks about injuries, Blair complains about a possibly bruised sandal-clad toe, and he simultaneously commiserates with her over it and compliments her physical skill at disarming the culprit, in a tacit admission that she can be highly competent even while playacting female fragility. He praises Blair's "karate kick," which he says has earned her the SWAT team's respect, and she chooses not to enlighten him that she hadn't planned on disarming Debra (371–75). It's a mix of elements of emphasized femininity, badass femininity, and alternate femininity (since she doesn't kill anyone and doesn't aspire to hegemonic masculinity). By this point, Blair and Wyatt are already engaged and the HEA is fully achieved.

In sum, Blair is initially someone who has been trapped by two binaries: the idea that a former cheerleader won't make a good girlfriend or wife because she would always be a narcissistic drama queen and the notion that as a pretty blonde, she is too stupid to take care of herself personally and professionally (332). The novel provides two resolutions to the problem: first, projecting the most extreme of those negative qualities onto two other women, followed by killing one off and imprisoning the other; second, getting Wyatt to admit that his labels were reductive and he loves all of who Blair is and wants to be with her. The admission comes toward the end, after numerous arguments where she has set him straight about her professional and personal capabilities and refuted his characterization of her as fluffy by stating, "I own a business, and I'm good at what I do! Fluffs don't do that; fluffs let other people take care of them" and "If I'm high maintenance, you don't have to worry about it! . . . Because I don't depend on anyone; I take care of myself and do my own maintenance! I'll get out of your hair and you can go back to your nice peaceful life," to which his succinct response is "Fuck that" (203, 329). He adds later, "I love you just the way you are. I guess I faced the fact that no matter how much trouble you are, to me you're worth it. . . . You're hell on wheels, honey, and [my colleagues] figure I'm going to spend the rest of my life scrambling to put out your forest fires. . . . But I'll never be bored" (332–33). His statement is still rooted in the gender norm that a headstrong woman is treading on the rightful territory of men, but the novel imagines that it no longer diminishes her attractiveness in his eyes.

In the novel's last scene, after Wyatt has witnessed the third double (his prospective mother-in-law) smash her computer with the sledgehammer, Blair notes that he "had the weirdest expression in his eyes, as if he didn't know whether to laugh or run for the hills" (378). But he gamely listens to her father's parting advice to "Just keep a regular check on your list of transgressions so you'll know if there are any major problems you need to handle" (378). The scene normalizes women's anger and nonnormative expressions of it, putting the onus for inciting it (and apologizing) on men. Ultimately, Blair, whose husband cheated on her, and whom Wyatt left because he saw her as too much work, gets to have the man she desires and keep her strong personality too. He declares that he'd never swap her out for the "most even-tempered, uncompli-cated, low-maintenance woman in the world" and when she tells him that he shouldn't expect a Stepford wife, he scoffs at the "snowball's chance in hell of that happening" (332–33). The novel makes it clear that Blair's HEA will not include meekness, self-effacement, or shame about her blonde beauty.

By the end, the novel's tagline "She was a dead ringer. Now she's just dead," and the title, *To Die For*, have a new resonance: the problematic doubles are no longer a threat and with them go all the negative tags attached to Blair, leaving much of the self that she values intact, even as she gives up her anger (and facade of indifference) toward Wyatt. Her resolve of sexual autonomy (in deciding when she'd sleep with Wyatt) bites the dust quickly as well since she is helpless against their combined sexual desire. But she sticks to her rule about requiring a man's repentance: "Walk out, crawl back" (57). Despite his domineering at-titude, Wyatt has to expend a lot of effort to regain her trust before she commits to a life with him. Moreover, she's alive not because of anyone else's help but because of her cheerleading skill, making her say, "This proves beyond a doubt, however, that you never know when you'll need to do a backflip" (375). It is a clear claim that being a cheerleader, one of the most iconically female Ameri-can gender displays, can go hand in hand (or feet, in this case) with physical strength, self-defense, and intelligent action.

Blair's hero journey is thus different from MacKayla's since she never changes her physical display or her personality in any marked way. (Her inju-ries following different attacks leave bruises and broken bones, but she insists on dressing in her usual cute style and even shows off a one-handed handstand while partly incapacitated, not to mention that she keeps running her business and saves herself from her stalkers.) But both MacKayla and Blair represent a heroine who is under attack for her perceived femininity and its attendant con-notations of simplemindedness and fragility. They both have to solve the mur-der of another woman, even as killers come after them, and while they acquire male helpmeets and other supportive women on this quest, their successes are rooted in acquiring control of their preferred gender display and identity. In each case, they fuse seemingly opposing elements of their bodily presentation and personality in defiance of gender stereotypes about women and engage in physical battles that end with their victories, making room for romantic HEAs.

NOTES

1. In addition to Goffman's categories of relative size, feminine touch, function ranking, ritualization of subordination, and licensed withdrawal, Kang added body display, independence, and self-assertiveness when studying stereotypes (984–86).

2. Others have also noted that gender display involves typified gender behavior, which often establishes and reinforces notions of the "normal." As Kenneth Allan and Scott Coltrane note, these typifications construct gender and gender display to socially establish and enforce boundaries between genders and naturalize alleged differences between them (201). Allan and Coltrane draw from sex role inventories to list a variety of stereotypical traits that are associated with masculinity and femininity. In the latter group, they examined the depiction of five traits: Follower, Deferential, Dependent, Passive, and Emotional (190). Their list reminds us that femininity is the gender display expected of those assumed or assigned to fall in the category of female (though this is contingent on place and time period).

3. Schippers uses a specific term for these femininities that I have chosen to omit here because it is the name for an oppressed caste in Southern India. While it has long been used as a synonym in English for an outsider rather than as a casteist slur, I refuse to use it and thus endorse its usage. Hence my use of "disfavored" femininities.

4. In her trademark dry and deadpan style, the comedian Tig Notaro relates how this often happens to her.

5. Though the fathers seemed to change their minds and insist on traditional female behavior when their children reached puberty, which resulted in some dissonance for the subjects, this was not always the case among the subjects' male buddies, who continued to discourage femininity (20–21).

6. While women were not to don certain kinds of dress reserved for men during the Renaissance, Garber lists the notable exception of Queen Elizabeth I, who is said to have cross-dressed as a "martial maiden" to rouse British troops against the Spanish Armada (28).

7. As McClean notes, "Through a gender display individuals are able to secure their gender's allocation of social resources. In the quest for resources, power, and prestige beyond the patriarchally determined level of one's gender status[,] those who have historically been denied equal rights in society will often adopt behaviors ascribed to hegemonic masculinity, in order to access the power of masculine cultural capital" (McLean 21).

8. MacKayla's primary arc was the first five books in the *Fever* series. Even though Moning appears to have returned to her from book eight onwards, this chapter focuses on this arc since it sufficiently illustrates the primary conflict that this book analyzes; the later books only further prove my point that there is a trend in romance publishing for extending a single heroine's role as a central protagonist across many novels.

9. The series uses the spelling "blond" as well as "blonde" for MacKayla. Outside of the quotations, whenever I have used "blonde," it is to stick to the gendered spelling of "blonde" for women. I have chosen the inconsistency partly as a comment about the constructed and gendered nature of the English language.

10. As Schippers puts it in her study of rock music culture, in gender maneuvering, the "meanings and rules [for gender] themselves are constantly volleyed back and forth as individuals and groups try to control the meaning of their activities, their relationships to others, and their place in power relations" (37).

11. See chapter 4 on how women are framed in relational terms and cast as loyal and disloyal to a group based on their sexual relations with a man.

12. This is a recurring theme in many woman-warrior narratives in popular culture, such as *Buffy the Vampire Slayer*.

13. The US women's national soccer team won a six-year-long legal battle to get pay parity in 2022.

14. Readers expressed their resistance to that masculine self too. An Amazon reviewer named Christine was irritated with what they perceived as an overkill description of that change: "Mac has gone from perfectly matched, polished, beautiful, and blonde in pink and rainbows to lean, jagged, scruffy, rough and now Mac in black. . . . got it already, can we move on now."

15. Whether intentional or not, the remark conjures up another famous madwoman who tries to commit arson because of her hatred of the heroine—Bertha Mason Rochester, who Sandra M. Gilbert and Susan Gubar so convincingly read as Jane Eyre's suppressed self.

THREE

—₥—

WORK

SO FAR WE HAVE LOOKED through the lenses of sexuality and gender at heroines who engage in a dialectical process to fuse together their discordant selves. This chapter builds on those perspectives while focusing on class, labor, and the gendered discourse of a profession/vocation. Romance scholars have written on romance heroines' access to economic security, like Jan Cohn in *The Erotics of Property* (1988), as well as on the heroine's triumph in blending the corporate workspace with home and the erotic life, like Erin S. Young in "Escaping the Time Bind." While these readings explore how the genre grapples with the financial contingencies of women's lives, including the demands of evolving capitalism, it is the heroine's own relationship to her labor and professional identity that takes center stage in this chapter. Examining how the genre frames the conflicts that she encounters in this arena shifts the focus from the hero's—or someone else's—money to the complexity of how women determine their domestic and wage lives, including how they conform to or negotiate expectations of the gendered performance of a work self.

Cohn and Young both tease out the contradictions of capitalist patriarchy as experienced by heroines, especially working-woman heroines, though in slightly different ways and with samples from the 1980s and 1990s respectively. To Cohn, the heroine's agency in a career or workplace is a feint, an alibi for her true work: gaining the resources possessed by the economically and sexually powerful hero. This is a way to escape the bind in which she is trapped, the solution that romance offers to the "cultural paralysis" where women have limited economic options and their bodies are their primary bargaining chips, but they are not supposed to be mercenary in marriage or be too regressively chaste before it (Cohn 132). There are certainly numerous examples that lend themselves to this reading.

Writing more than two decades later, Young invites a Marxist and intersectional reading of the same bind but in a subset of corporate romances published in the 1990s by Jayne Anne Krentz, where the heroine's corporate family inheritance nullifies the seeming opposition between domestic and work spheres from the get-go. Young observes that corporate romances neatly skirt the problem of choosing between work or home that women face by granting the heroine both class and racial privilege—the former owes much to the latter, of course—and a businessman love interest who "recognize[s] a lucrative partnership" with her as more valuable than traditional gender inequality (93). Young is right to note that "the corporate romance's resolution to the home/work binary, however, is limited in its availability, particularly to working women. The heroine's ability to achieve a satisfactory balance between home and work hinges on her significant socioeconomic status and her inheritance of a family-owned company" (93). In other words, the escape from the time bind offered here is via inherited wealth, an option that mainly applies to white heroines born into a family that owns a firm. But the solution, despite its clear limitations, is valuable in that these novels show the genre's awareness of a different stage of capitalism (and how it shapes affective relationships) compared to the one in Cohn's sample. The eventual romantic union in the Krentz novels is a narrative of the heroine's emotional and sexual journey existing in tandem with that of her career (as shaped by late capitalism) rather than being an alibi for it.

Both Cohn's and Young's observations on how the genre tackles the relationship between the heroine and the public/private or work/domestic spheres resonate with my previous analyses of the contradictions of capitalism visible in romance and how authors imagine different resolutions to the heroine's livelihood dilemma *and* to the negative connotations of extreme wealth (*Making Meaning*). I have written about the genre's tendency to recast the Cinderella tale within a capitalist utopia that facilitates the HEA through financially powerful heroes, whether aristocrats and *nouveau riche* industrialists in historical romance or corporate heads in contemporary romance (such as Roarke in the *In Death* series). Additionally, authors reframe the hero's wealth as romantic since it eases the heroine's life (by reducing the visible and invisible labor traditionally demanded from women) and in some cases supports noble causes. I continue that analysis of the *In Death* series and the contradictions of capitalism here (and in the discussion of Black romance heroines' economic lives in chap. 5). But my focus is on an issue I touched on briefly in chap. 1 while discussing "role strain" in Kresley Cole's *Dark Desires*: a heroine's labor practices and experiences, her relationship to class and career, and how she faces the binary of the professional and personal self as well as choosing between different professional personas.

One of the heroines in this chapter is a best-selling nineteenth-century British novelist and the other is a police detective in 2058 New York. Both characters reflect contemporary debates about women, work, and the potential to "have it all," and they can be read alongside a commonplace of the so-called "postfeminist" sensibility: criticizing second-wave feminism for allegedly shaming women into desiring professional success and thus putting the burden of employment on an already full domestic plate. These postfeminist critiques rest on the implicit belief that employment and the private sphere are inherently oppositional, each is solely an individual (rather than structural) issue, and it is unfair and unnatural to expect women to get success and happiness in both.

Commenting on this rhetoric, Rosalind Barnett in her 2004 essay "Women and Multiple Roles: Myths and Reality" notes that "as more and more women establish distinguished careers, they are confronted with a . . . variant of the myths surrounding women and multiple roles; namely, that high-level professional women (in contrast to high-level professional men) are incapable of combining their careers with marriage and children without doing irreparable harm to their careers" (159). She also observes that while women are increasingly entering the workforce and men are claiming to support them and even doing more housework, the media keeps claiming that "the current 'experiment' in nontraditional lifestyles for women is causing havoc for women themselves, their partners, and their children. Headlines scream out the *Time Bind*, the *Time Squeeze*, and the *Time Famine*. The *Decline of the American Family* is another media staple" (160). While refuting media misrepresentation of working women and the propagation of the myth that multiple roles equal stress, Barnett says that such articles are full of warnings that men will feel emasculated and children will develop psychological problems because of working wives/ mothers, though studies don't support such media panic.[1]

In Barnett's field of mental health, "discussions . . . about women and work continue to focus on the potential negative effects while ignoring the benefits that employment confers to women," and the "maternal role is seen as the core of women's identity," which is not stressful because it is "natural" (161, 158). This naturalization of motherhood is a phenomenon Mary Poovey traces back to the Victorians, one rooted in nineteenth-century scientific claims that created a "binary model of difference articulated upon sex," with women being shunted into domesticity based on their alleged biological inclinations (8). Regardless of the fact that many women enjoy non-domestic work for intellectual, emotional, and financial reasons and can do it successfully as long as their networks at home and elsewhere support them, the ideology of domestic space being women's "natural" place persists. This problem operates on at least two fronts: first, as and when it suits the culture, women are forced to pick between an identity based either on free labor within the home (wife, mother, etc.) or paid labor outside of it (employee or self-employed professional / entrepreneur), and second, between the kinds of wage labor deemed either acceptable or anathema.

Women's labor is rarely recognized, let alone respected or fairly remunerated. Their career aspirations are placed on the chopping block in periods that demand more unpaid labor in the family, even if wage labor is expected at other times (in addition to domestic labor). The simultaneous demands for, and disrespect of, women's work is linked to what Eve Rodsky sees as a tendency in a gendered culture to treat women's time as infinite and therefore of less value while men's time is regarded as finite and precious and thus in need of veneration and protection (Stynes). Unsurprisingly, the years of the COVID-19 pandemic have seen a slew of articles on how women have been forced to drop out of the labor force, overwhelmed by juggling the demands of paid work, invisible but mounting domestic labor, and health care (for themselves or relatives). The crisis has only thrown into starker relief the fact that women do a disproportionate amount of unpaid labor, but media discourse rarely offers structural or community-based solutions to fix this imbalance. Small wonder then that romance novels, which try to do so (and typically get dismissed as fantasies), resonate so deeply with their readers, a large proportion of whom identify as women.

Heroines in romance fiction are always performing labor of some sort: those in contemporary romance, paranormal romance, or sci-fi/fantasy romance have jobs ranging from private investigator to corporate executive and spacecraft captain to witch; in historical romance, they may run a household or their own businesses. Romance heroines' paid and unpaid work may or may not have much to do with the romantic plot but reflects the author's awareness of the demands of labor in contemporary culture and the pressure on women to ally themselves with the home or the outside world, as well as to conform to social expectations of paid work that is appropriate for women.

Moreover, representations of work in romance go beyond physical and intellectual labor, capturing another key aspect of women's lives—the mental load that accompanies gendered expectations directed at them in all spheres. In discussing this kind of work, Krista Lynn Minnotte et al. distinguish between emotional labor (managing one's emotions and affect in the workplace for a wage) and "emotion work" (the same kind of management but in private life, i.e., not for wages). They note that emotion work involves "the provision of emotional support" (775) and is a part of domestic work but distinct from practical domestic tasks. Rebecca J. Erickson defines emotion work as the "enhancement of others' emotional well-being and the provision of emotional support" ("Reconceptualizing" 888). She says this conceptualization "captures people's attempts to effectively manage the emotional climate within a relationship" ("Why Emotion Work" 338) and notes that "offering encouragement, showing your appreciation, listening closely to what someone has to say, and expressing empathy with another person's feelings (even when they are not shared)—day after day, year after year—represent emotion work of the highest order" (338–39).[2]

Romance novels involve numerous examples of women doing (or being asked to do) physically demanding work, emotional labor, and emotion work, and the genre offers various models of heroines composing a life that involves the kind of labor they value in themselves and that their partners and community support. This chapter shows heroines engaged in all kinds of work while detractors and loved ones at home and in professional circles try to have a say in their professional and personal identity. While J. D. Robb's *In Death* (1995–) series allows for a fruitful exploration of class identity, sex typing, and sex roles associated with paid work, as well as expectations of emotional labor and emotion work, Lisa Kleypas's *Dreaming of You* (1994) foregrounds the issue of the traditional work/home division and what work is appropriate for women.

The heroine of *Dreaming of You*, Sara Fielding, also most overtly exemplifies the genre's efforts at self-definition in the face of misreading or incomprehension. Sara is a writer whose first novel has made her a household name in Victorian Britain. As a young and unmarried woman who is a successful published novelist and who has written about prostitution, she is an oddity in her society. In the face of numerous parties that wish her to conform to a specific image of a country gentlewoman, Sara is quietly resistant, holding on to a sense of self that centers on her work as a novelist. Though she undergoes a period of self-doubt, thinking she may have to give up that part of her identity to achieve domestic felicity with the hero manqué, Perry, she wins her battle over that uncertainty and the proffered false binary.

From the start of the novel, Kleypas makes it evident that Perry cannot see or accept Sara's whole self. He drags his feet in formally proposing marriage, partly because his possessive mother dislikes Sara intensely and doesn't think she is devoted enough to be a good wife to her son. She considers Sara's writing a disgrace and terms her research trips "gallivanting." Perry himself appears to believe that Sara will give up her "daydreaming and scribbling" to become solely a wife and daughter-in-law (and unpaid drudge) after marriage (173). The ghost of Nathaniel Hawthorne, with his scornful dismissal of "scribbling women," seems to be lurking in Perry. Before we hear any of these views about

Sara, however, we encounter her doing research for her third novel in a seedy part of London because "her first two novels, *Mathilda* and *The Beggar*, had both been praised for their attention to detail. She would not want her third, as yet untitled, to be faulted for inaccuracies" (3). This commitment to verisimilitude aside, the scene shows that writing is not a casual hobby for her. She is determined to have her own way when it comes to maintaining the identity she sees herself as having established in her past work: she is an author of social problem novels that she researches scrupulously.

Authorship as a key element of identity is *Dreaming of You*'s chief concern, especially female authorship of popular but somewhat scandalous novels, such as ones that describe a woman's sexual encounters (Sara's first best-selling novel having been about a sex worker). This theme is an unsurprising preoccupation for a romance novelist like Kleypas and the genre; romance authorship is a highly embattled identity, one often under siege on various fronts.[3] Kleypas writes of Sara's professional choices and of the reactions that greet them by having Sara's authorship be the driver of the plot. It is that theme that initiates the romance arc after Sara bargains her way into hero Derek Craven's club to research the social problem of gambling, the subject of her next novel. She earns this concession from the initially surly owner because she rescues him from a street fight in the novel's first scene.

From this moment on, Sara inhabits two physical and psychological spaces: the one in London, where people admire her as an author and regard her writing and research with awe, and the one in the country, where locals like Perry regard her writing as an odd, possibly unsavory hobby and expect her to fit their ideas of being "decent, God-fearing people" (201). After Sara returns to her village from her first foray to London, Perry says "I'll be glad when you stop writing. It makes you emotional, and that won't do for our children, or me, for that matter" (201). He even breaks off their engagement when she asks him to show her some passion, blaming her new sexual demands on her research trip to London and comparing her to the prostitute she has authored in her first novel. Sara briefly experiences a dissociative state in the face of his tirade, "as if she were standing outside herself" (202). In his eyes, her writing and research have led to a sexual deviancy that she must abandon and return to being the "modest, innocent girl" he fell in love with if she still hopes to marry a good man like him (202). She even internalizes some of Perry's judgment (cut off as she is from London and those who admire her writing) for a time; she attributes her unhappiness to her visit to London, which showed her other possibilities of how she could live as a writer, and regretfully thinks, "Why didn't I stay in the village and earn money some other way than writing?" (192). Even her parents, who are kindly and indulgent toward her, don't see her primary self. They appear to confuse her work as a writer of social issues with the sort of charitable, do-gooder role that gentlewomen traditionally played rather than recognizing that she is a professional novelist.

At Derek Craven's London gambling club, however, she finds a community that sees her primarily in her author identity. The sex workers and staff are delighted to provide her source material and are deferential about her writing time, taking special care to be quiet when she is at her desk. In fact, early in the novel, the hero ill-temperedly compares their behavior to the kind of reverence given to the performance of a "holy sacrament" (73). But he, too, understands that she is an author first and foremost, especially after she makes it clear that she cannot contemplate marriage to just any man because most men would become impatient with her writing and even forbid her to do it, a possibility she cannot risk. After he proposes marriage, he visits her parents to ask for their permission, and in that conversation he reveals his understanding of her professional self as her primary self when he assures her father that he would "never interfere with her writing" (302). It is a curious line since such assurance from a man can hardly be a realistic depiction of a nineteenth-century conversation with a fiancée's parent; its true function is to underscore the idea that Sara's happiness is contingent on replacing people from her former circle of acquaintances with those who see (and acknowledge) that her professional identity as a novelist is integral to her and worthy of respect. In other words, in Derek Craven and his gambling club staff, as well as the wealthy readers Sara encounters through him, she finds a community that recognizes her as an author and admires her for it—a new experience but one to which she has a right.

The mental load she carries and the emotion work she performs decrease over the novel as well. With Perry and his mother, she has always put on a cheerful, smiling face despite their condescension and admonishments. He has frequently brushed aside his mother treating Sara as an interloper, saying, "Remember not to take anything she says personally," and Sara has given in, even speaking in a hush, not insisting on physical affection while visiting him lest the mother be offended, and "shrug[ing] prosaically" when her every action is criticized (170, 172). When she and Derek have disagreements before and after their wedding, however, she doesn't have to coddle or serve him. Not only does his wealth take some of the burdens of domestic labor out of the equation, such as the mental load of meal planning and the work of cooking, he delights in teasing and cossetting her. His friends and associates help her in picking the furnishings of their new home, and she is able to control her writing time and space (316–17). Having done thankless emotion work, such as being patient and de-escalating conflict when it came to handling her former fiancé and his mother's judgments about her, it is logical that Sara flourishes with a new partner and a new community who support her self-definition as an author and demand less emotion work or routine chores.

Even among those who recognize her author self, however, Sara frequently encounters inaccurate preconceptions of her and her work. In many cases, the errors reveal ontological confusion regarding authorship, particularly popular fiction authorship, even among those with a reverential appreciation of it. Midway through the novel, for instance, when Derek is trying to convince her to marry another man rather than pine for a scoundrel like him, he threatens to shut down her publisher if she doesn't listen to him; the threat reveals his belief that she writes for financial reasons rather than from a creative impulse. (There are echoes here of the belief that romance authors write for money alone.) She corrects him, explaining that writing novels is what she does and would do irrespective of monetary returns; if she couldn't make a living off it, she would find another job and write on the side.

Variations of such misconceptions about her work mark her interactions with others as well. The sex workers who ply their trade in Derek's club are pleased with Sara for having written about one of them in *Mathilda*, but they do not grasp the concept of fiction; some keep insisting that her book is a true-life narrative about a real prostitute named Mathilda that they think is either Sara herself or someone they might know in person.

> "Is she the one?" [Tabitha] asked [the butler at Craven's club], "That's Mathilda?"
> "Oh, no," Sara said. "I wrote the *novel* entitled *Mathilda*."
> "Then ye knows 'er? She's a friend of yers?"
> Sara was nonplussed. "Not really. You see, Mathilda is a fictional character. She's not real."
> The comment earned a chiding glance from Tabitha. "Not real? I read all about 'er. An' I knows a girl who met 'er. They worked the same street after Mathilda was ravished by Lord Aversley." (40)

At another time (before Sara and Derek get romantically involved), the club staff even suggest that Sara set Derek up with Mathilda, and when she tries to explain why that's impossible by saying, "You see, I created the character of Mathilda as the result of detailed research and discussions. She's really a composite of many women I encountered" they tune her out and begin speculating on whether Mathilda has joined a convent or found a rich man to keep her as his mistress (64). Even Sara's wealthy and better-educated readers commit the error of regarding her fiction as a biography. At a country estate where Sara is a guest at a party, rich aristocratic women are excited to meet the writer that they think is acquainted with the infamous Mathilda and they ask for an update on how the prostitute continues to fare.

Sara is thus repeatedly faced with others' belief that she writes about real people in a documentary style, and she has to do emotion work to correct them politely. Despite the admiration readers express for her, they fail to grasp what it means for her to be the author of a novel. At other times, people are unable to separate the author from her character, reading her fiction as if it is an auto-biography. When she goes to a masquerade ball dressed in a manner suggesting a rich courtesan, for instance, both the staff and the rich dandies who overhear her asking leave to enter assume that she *is* Mathilda. Perry, as I noted above, also accuses her of becoming sexually sinful like her character, as if an author and her creations are barely separate entities and the conflation simultaneously serves to erase her author self.

After Sara and Derek marry, they become something of a celebrity couple, and while Sara sees a new fervor in her public reception after the press finds out she is *Mathilda*'s author, it only underlines this problem of the author being confused with her work. When the husband and wife pair go to social events, gawkers outside want to catch a glimpse of Sara's face, and they call her "Mathilda," thinking she might herself be the prostitute in the eponymous novel. Derek is annoyed at their hailing her, partly because he thinks they see her as public property, but his annoyance also points out the problem of her being mistaken for her character, (i.e., of not being recognized as her author self) (328). Additionally, the press coverage of the mobs that greet her everywhere is far from complimentary, with journalists calling her a "country maid" who has somehow managed to arouse public interest, referring to her and Derek's popularity as the arrival of the day "when pigs fly," and completely ignoring her professional identity in the process (328). Through it all, Sara maintains a genial face while continuing to write, thanks to the continuing support of Derek and others.

Dreaming of You is thus preoccupied with the complicated experience of female authorship, especially of popular novels. Like Sara, romance authors occupy the paradoxical space of hypervisibility and invisibility in our media-determined society. When there is press coverage of the genre, it invariably focuses on the writers—their appearance, their upbringing and personal life, and the monetary associations of the genre—but rarely shows any serious, sustained engagement with their craft and oeuvre. At best, the coverage might be a simplistic sketch of the person as someone who cranks out romance novels; at worst, it is an excuse to drag out old clichés of the genre as the land of Fabio and half-naked women, clichés that the coverage alleges are put together by the romance writer (not author) per some formula. Across this spectrum, the knowledge of the romance genre's sales figures seems to haunt the discourse; romance supporters point to the sales as proof of the genre's value while detractors see it as evidence of the assembly-line production of a standardized commodity. Paradoxically, therefore, finding success as a published writer, an achievement that typically awards one the badge of authorship, works against the romance author, creating the kind of notoriety that Sara experiences when she goes out but rendering her activities as a creative artist somewhat invisible. Though she specializes in fictional narratives about social ills and pays anthropological attention to a specific subculture, the work itself is dismissed by the press. This pattern persists in popular coverage of romance authors. An example of this practice at the time of writing was a profile of author Sherrilyn Kenyon by Lila Shapiro, who discussed Kenyon's contentious divorce, age, mental health, childhood abuse, and declining book sales in more depth than her novels.

In other words, romance writers are visible primarily as symbols of the genre and marked by its alleged salaciousness or goofiness or commercialism in a way that makes authorship elusive as an identity. So while Foucault tells us that authorship in literary texts is like a genre (marked by a writer's particular style and thematic preoccupations), for romance writers, the genre they write appears to prevent their own author-genre from being conceived as real outside their reader community—it nullifies their "author-function" (139). The romance genre makes romance authorship an oxymoron to someone who is not an informed romance reader and even where informed readers are concerned, their awareness of the author seems to be almost as much about the extensional (biological/flesh-and-blood person) concept as about the author-as-genre. In other words, let's think of authorship as a triangulated identity whose three vertices are the writer, the reader, and the episteme that allows the work to be treated as worthy of the questions one might ask in a postauthor world (the list Foucault offers in lieu of the "typical questions" [139]); a romance writer like Kleypas is thus in a nebulous space because her corpus is obscured by the romance genre, where it cannot achieve the third vertex, and uninformed people can't see her as anything other than the bio-author who repeats formulas.

Even when writers like Kleypas are acknowledged to be writing fiction, some coverage of them shows a careless ignorance—lumping Nora Roberts with Danielle Steele or Nicholas Sparks, for instance—while other coverage is more militant in its condemnation, convinced that the romance writer is herself treading the path to iniquity and dragging others down with her by narrating her fictionalized version of it; this writer is always under suspicion for being a sexual deviant or a blowsy joke.[4] At the other end of the spectrum, romance writers are not thought of as fiction writers at all but as fantasists jotting down personal sexual fantasies with no thought to craft or realism, or diarists, documenting actual sexual encounters; in either case, their ability to invent characters and plots is misunderstood or dismissed as irrelevant, and there are subtle and not-too-subtle mentions made of their likely "research" activities (see note 3). Kleypas weaves these concerns into *Dreaming of You* through the way Sara's authorship is either rejected or misunderstood by her informed readers and by those who have only heard of her in the press in her bio-author identity.

While informed romance readers are not as oblivious to the author function as uninformed outsiders, even their remarks can betray the fact that the bio-author is a seductive idea. Current romance fiction marketing, such as through Facebook and Twitter, further encourages this conflation of the bio-author and author function; as a result, a reader who appreciates a Lisa Kleypas romance novel for her particular interpretation of the genre, for instance, and enjoys other novels that are "Kleypasian"—such as Eloisa James's or Susanne Lord's work—may still be inclined to use social media to ask about Kleypas's family and how her personal life is affecting her latest novel.

Despite this simplistic understanding of the craft of writing a romance novel, informed readers are far more benign and appreciative than those to whom Kleypas may only be a pseudonym for another hack who is reiterating a tired formula (and has no special stylistic or conceptual traits of her own and therefore no author function at all). Perhaps from necessity then, the romance author seeks informed readers who at least vaguely sense the author function (an FAQ on Kleypas's site responds to reader questions like "Why [do you write] historicals [and why the specific period of history]?"). This kind of interest from her readers is better than the incomprehension or ridicule of the uninformed, even if the informed readers also conflate her bio-self and her author function. (This conflation is visible in other questions on the FAQ page, such as "do you like writing the love scenes for your books?") The informed reader's misguided or naive understanding of authorship (where the bio-author and the author function are ineluctably fused, partly as a result of deliberate social media marketing) may still be preferable to a romance author, as the admiration of the Craven club's sex workers is to Sara Fielding. It diminishes the pressure of emotion work demanded by a hostile world and celebrates the nontraditional labor the author herself values.

The romance author (including Kleypas) is thus the referent of the allegory that is Sara Fielding; Sara's hypervisibility among a group of admirers, while not devoid of problems, is a valuable alternative to the symbolic annihilation or diminishment that romance authors often face, either through ignorance or concerted ridicule. Sara (as a fictional nineteenth-century author) also serves as the bridge between her twentieth- and twenty-first-century scribbling women descendants (like Kleypas herself) and her eighteenth-century predecessor, the novelist Sarah (with an *h*) Fielding, whose authorship now receives less attention than that of her brother, Henry. (Incidentally, he parodied *Pamela*, a best-selling romance.)[5] This Sarah Fielding was a respected author but has faded into relative obscurity, remembered more perhaps as the extensional (biological/flesh-and-blood person) concept than the author-as-genre; certainly, she does not appear on college curricula with the regularity that her brother still does.

Kleypas's Sara Fielding thus represents a search to affirm one's author self, or at least not let others decide if you are an author or not. Virginia Woolf famously argued that women need a room of their own to write, and Pamela Regis has claimed that a variant of this is needed by readers and exists in online reader community forums; I would add that romance authors and readers appear to need a room of their own (together) where readers can affirm that authorship.[6] Today, novelists' websites, Facebook pages, virtual events, and Twitter feeds are functioning in this capacity, a variant of what *Dreaming of You* allows Sara to have as well. She leaves her country home and provincial acquaintances in order to join a community whose members recognize her authorship in somewhat flawed but well-meaning ways.

This dialectical progression is the way out of a problematic binary. Due to it, Sara does not have to give up her self-definition as an author, though it is an identity that is initially posed as one of two mutually exclusive choices— the other being social integration through marriage to a traditional man (and shrinking into the pre-scripted role of wife, daughter-in-law, and mother). By the end of the novel, Sara has been able to sidestep this binary: she has published a novel about poverty to much acclaim and has thus been firmly established as a "social problem" author; she is a nursing mother, a beloved wife, and a society matron with well-to-do friends; she has survived a sexual assault by someone who thought she was easy prey as a country bumpkin, and a murder attempt by someone who was jealous of her matrimonial happiness. She is also being invited to address community meetings on problems like poverty and termed a "radical" by the papers for her ideas on social reform. She is finally an author in both the bio-author sense and the author-genre sense, neither of which she had to give up in order to find a happy ending as a wife and mother, thanks to her move to London and the community she formed there. It is a move that presages the huge expansion of the online romance community, where authors have found a way to be acknowledged on their own terms—as has the genre itself.

More than most romance novels, *Dreaming of You* is an allegory for the genre's right to control its image as a form of storytelling, nurture the spaces where its readers and writers dialog about its operation, and rebuff anyone else's attempt to encroach on that right. For Rodsky, all people, but especially women, need a "unicorn space," where they pursue an activity that allows them to be interesting to themselves and replaces some of the mental load they bear in a traditional culture; this activity can reverse or forestall the erosion of the unique self that women undergo when identities such as wife, mother, and daughter take over and consume all their time. Women usually feel guilty about the unicorn space, however, and Rodsky suggests that they, their partners, and the culture at large need to understand the worth of the unicorn space in improving women's lives and their romantic partnerships, a transformation that romance novels like this one stage (Stynes).

Dreaming of You shows us the problems encountered by a woman laboring outside the norm of unpaid domestic work in a culture that insists that women not neglect their "natural" inclinations for wifedom and motherhood to pursue unworthy passions. An equally prevalent issue in women's labor has been its ghettoization into low-status and low-paying jobs, as Harriet Bradley has demonstrated in her compelling study on gender in British work history. Moreover, she identifies a "double bind" forced on women who enter male-dominated workplaces: either act like one of the guys and risk losing worth in terms of a personal female identity or become labeled as too female and, by extension, an inferior worker (230). Bradley's argument that "many individual women succeed conspicuously in such jobs by outplaying the men at their own game of toughness and competitiveness" applies strikingly to the character of Eve Dallas, J. D. Robb's protagonist in the *In Death* novels (230). This sci-fi romantic suspense series shows the operation of sex-typing and the gendered nature of professions, especially ones traditionally male or "androcentric," and the romance heroine's journey toward an authentic work and domestic self in opposition to that double bind (Bradley 231). (While a few characters address this heroine as Eve, a pointed evocation of one of the most iconic women in Judeo-Christian discourse, most use Dallas or Lieutenant [Dallas]; I'm going to use "Dallas" throughout the chapter for both consistency and as a reminder of the series' approach to gender roles and their markers, but I once again highlight the multiple names as indicators of the romance heroine's multiple selves.)

Before examining the operation of women's labor in the masculine sphere of police work, let's start with how Robb's homicide detective inhabits a class-conscious narrative that pulls her between two class identities (since paid work in this police procedural series prominently involves the axis of class as well as gender). Dallas has been forging her heroine identity along these two lines over more than fifty books while encountering sexist, homophobic, classist attitudes in the course of both her work and personal life. In the first book, *Naked in Death* (set in 2058 New York and published in 1995), our heroine is established as a personification of 1980s New York—a working-class, indomitable city struggling to curb crime.[7] A decade-old veteran of the force, Dallas is driven, gutsy, and used to violence (though not blasé about it). She also displays unexpected bouts of kindness, which is another evocation of New York's reputation for urban ruthlessness peppered with rare moments of softness.

But a more significant expression of this mirroring of the city in Dallas is her evolving economic and social identity, which is intriguingly dualistic. The gritty world she first represents comes face-to-face with a powerful capitalist New York when she encounters her eventual romantic partner, Roarke, the billionaire libertarian-leaning head of a multi-terrestrial corporation. It seems like a Cinderella tale, bearing at least a superficial resemblance to the theme of upward mobility through marriage. A mid-level professional in a working-class profession (with roots in the criminal working class), Dallas can become one of the 1 percent through this lover (and later, husband).

As noted earlier, I have written about how her personal life becomes smoother following her relationship with a capitalist, though she is an unwilling participant in this ritzy world, a familiar portrayal of romance heroines that Cohn thinks is meant to forestall the charge of mercenariness. What I'm more keen on is unpacking how Dallas ends up grappling with two class positions almost from the first novel in the long-running series. As a police officer, she sees herself as blue collar and her professional life unfolds in that milieu regularly; but by getting involved with (and marrying) a billionaire industrialist, she becomes part of the city's obscenely wealthy class. Yet her job shows her that class's criminal proclivities and extravagances as well, heightening her seemingly innate distaste for that life. The final twist, however, is that while she doesn't embrace bourgeois values in her personal life, she slowly adopts the work strategies of its corporate czars, thus traveling from one class identity to another both spatially and mentally.

Robb positions Dallas as belonging to an unglamorous world partly through the personal history and habitus she gives her. Dallas has had a terrifying childhood with a deadbeat, sexually abusive, criminal father, followed by orphanhood in an indifferent foster care system. In fact, her last name derives from the city in which she was found as a wounded orphan, making her a true urban refugee and street native. Dallas recounts that she received a basic public school education and came to New York to be a police officer as soon as she could. She has been a functional workaholic for years, with little time or inclination for socializing outside of her job. When we meet her in *Naked in Death* (1995), she is living alone and her apartment is no more than a bare-bones space in which to sleep between exhausting shifts at work. She doesn't cook, snacks on junk food, and often survives on coffee. Her clothing is utilitarian, and she seems to have neither time nor money to spend on self-care beyond showering and trimming her own hair. She knows nothing about classical music but enjoys action-packed narratives, views haute cuisine with apprehension, and is comfortable with physical and verbal altercations. (More on this last part later.) She has a working-class existence by profession and by lifestyle choice—and one devoid of emotional labor and emotion work, as well as domestic labor, thanks to automation.

When Dallas starts a sexual relationship with a billionaire she meets in *Naked in Death*, the gap between her inherited (and chosen) class identity and his world is sharply drawn. Several scenes establish how she is made aware of her class (or lack thereof). For instance, take this confrontation with Roarke's British butler / father-figure in which she tells him to "pull the stick out of [his] ass" and explain why he treats her like "some sort of embarrassing rodent":

> Shock turned Summerset's face paper white. "I'm not comfortable with crude manners, Lieutenant Dallas. Obviously you are."
> "They fit me like old slippers."
> "Indeed." Summerset drew himself up. "Roarke is a man of taste, of style, of influence. He has the ear of presidents and kings. He has escorted women of unimpeachable breeding and pedigree."
> "And I've got lousy breeding and no pedigree." She would have laughed if the barb hadn't stuck so close to the heart. (290–91)

Dallas's working-class identity (as located in her speech, physical vigor, and general unkemptness) is thus an inalienable part of how Robb portrays her. Like a significant portion of the city's population, she is a salaried worker with little by way of upper-class sophistication and a great deal of the city's street smarts and attitude, which includes refusing emotion work. But the passage also hints at how friction with Summerset pushes her in the direction of emotion work, where she feels hurt at his class appraisal but seems compelled or unable to express that hurt openly.

Robb also paints Dallas as blue-collar through her professional life of cleaning up the city's dirt, often literally. Here's another encounter with the butler Summerset when she has arrived at Roarke's mansion after a violent store robbery:

> "May I take your coat?"
> She . . . thought she caught a flicker of smug condescension in those inscrutable eyes. Eve shrugged out of her jacket, watched him take the leather somewhat gingerly between his manicured fingers.
> Hell, she'd gotten most of the blood off it. (68–69)

As the blood on her jacket demonstrates, Dallas is marked by the streets and the lowlifes she meets on a routine basis: drug dealers, con artists, flashers, petty thieves, sex workers, and murderers. And again, Summerset's behavior is meant to incite her discomfort, adding to her potential emotion work, since she has to decide whether to ignore or confront his class and gendered judgment.

It is through Dallas's professional topos that Robb further develops her working-class identity. Robb's construction of New York City as a backdrop to her heroine's work in the series, including *Naked in Death*, is particularly worth comment in the context of the crime wave narrative that writers like Pete Hamill crafted around 1990. Specifically, Robb cements the plebeian nature of Dallas's existence by placing her in a New York that reflects the late 1980s and early 1990s. These were the decades of the so-called "crime wave," when numerous media outlets lamented a New York filled with violent crime and diminishing quality of life, the apple that had rotted to the core. In other words, Dallas's New York is often grungy and raving, like the dangerous city described in the 1990 *Time* article "Decline of New York."[8] Robb evokes this 1990 city through Dallas's cases and in descriptions of New York's neighborhoods, all of which reinforce the heroine's identity as someone connected to the underclass. *Naked in Death*, for instance, begins with a recounting of a domestic violence altercation in which Dallas has killed a man who had battered his wife, then locked himself in with their daughter and murdered her while high on drugs. The incident resembles a real one that made headlines in 1990.[9] Apart from this gory tale of an innocent's murder, Dallas's primary case in *Naked in Death* involves violence against sex workers committed in a manner that harks back to the murderous environment of late 1980s run-down New York as reported in the *Time* article, among other sources, and conjures up the specter of working-class crime.[10]

Much of the 2058 urban environment that Dallas encounters during her work hours resembles the media representations of early 1990s New York too: cacophonous and dirty. For instance, Attinger wrote that when New York seemed to be booming economically over the 1980s, another side of it was undergoing decay, leading to the eventual chaos of 1990: "Most brutally hit have been basic social services. . . . Even the basic rudiments of civil behavior seemed to evaporate along with the glitter of the boom times. . . . The streets have become public rest rooms for both people and animals, even though failure to clean up after a pet dog carries fines of up to $100. What was once the bustle of a hyperkinetic city has become a demented frenzy" (39–40). Compare this to the description of a stretch of Broadway Avenue called Prostitute's Walk in *Naked in Death*, where two of the murdered sex workers lived: "Broadway was noisy and crowded, a party where rowdy guests never left. Street, pedestrian, and sky traffic were miserable, choking the air with bodies and vehicles. . . . Even at this hour there was steam rising from the stationary and portable food stands that offered everything from rice noodles to soydogs for the teeming crowds. . . . Eve double-parked and, skirting a man who smelled worse than his bottle of brew, stepped onto the sidewalk. . . . She was propositioned twice before she reached the door" (3–4). This is a New York on the verge of a breakdown caused by the decline of civic services—stinky, irrational, predatory. Repeatedly, the novel creates a mise-en-scène of crime-wave New York, with its attendant social and economic depredation. Dallas is employed in trying to hold back this tide and does so through tactics that mark her as one of the masses she polices. She routinely engages in scuffles on the street with petty criminals, swears at cabbies who get in her way, and physically intimidates witnesses.[11]

But though Dallas is completely mired in this run-down New York when *Naked in Death* begins and continues to be so throughout the series, her move toward coupledom opens the window to a world of bourgeois privilege that exists in the same city. Dallas's job takes her back and forth between these two New Yorks. She works in downtown Manhattan and all over the city, including the outer boroughs, but moves into Roarke's Upper West side mansion. The places and people Dallas encounters because of him represent a very different New York than that of her workaday life (though she expresses more bafflement at the glossier city and its upper class when she encounters them than she does toward the dirty city of honest criminals). Robb has Dallas's feet planted in both worlds personally and professionally, resulting in a divided class identity that is a running thread in the series. Though an extreme portrayal of crossing class, it is echoed in all novels that include a class divide between the hero and heroine where the latter is on a lower socioeconomic rung than the former at the start of the novel; by the end, she is usually represented as holding on to her uncorrupted values even when established in a darker, more luxurious world— a proletariat Persephone.

It is unsurprising then that Dallas is not a speaker for a specific class position. While wary of Roarke's wealth and compassionate and tolerant of petty criminals (unlike 1990s' representatives of the state, like Mayor Giuliani, Commissioner Bratton, and his successor, Howard Safir, with their "zero tolerance" and "broken window" policies), she is also data-driven in her policing, calling to mind Bratton and Giuliani's adoption of a set of statistics-focused business management strategies that are now termed "COMPSTAT."[12] Andrew Karmen notes that COMPSTAT numbers became the department's equivalent of a corporation's fixation on profit and loss statistics and methods meant to rapidly raise the former and minimize the latter through data-management and data-sharing. Dallas embodies this neoliberal model to a great extent, practicing its strategies such as coordinating the deployment of multiple subordinates to various tasks and targets and convening regular team meetings to share information and update tactics during every investigation. Giuliani and Bratton's corporate style of managing work and getting results is thus a visible element of her professional life over the course of the series.

Dallas's relationship with Roarke, a corporate wunderkind, is also a factor in her corporate-inflected work style. While she is known to be a dogged, meticulous cop even before she meets him, her increasing adoption of COMPSTAT-style policing after they get involved is facilitated by his sophisticated off-grid computer network and data mining ability, which allows her access to protected information. In other words, she accepts Roarke's vast resources and business acumen to both crunch data for effective decision-making and apprehend suspects. She also begins mobilizing larger tactical teams with every novel, adding to her crime-solving unit in a manner that mimics COMPSTAT's (corporate-culture-based) strategy of making separate bureaus cooperate, share data, and aggressively meet goals (in this case, to identify, predict, and prevent or punish criminal activity).

Dallas also evokes the "brand" that Mayor Giuliani and Commissioner Bratton created for the NYPD in keeping with the above philosophy. Her traits and work style contain echoes of their 1994 rhetoric: that they were a new administration and police force, an ass-kicking, hardworking bunch cleaning up the mess that their predecessors and bleeding-heart liberals had made of the city (Karmen 87–92). Karmen describes that NYPD culture as follows: "A new philosophy replaced the former bureaucratic mindset: manage the NYPD like a corporation. Set crime reduction goals at headquarters. Hold local precincts responsible for meeting performance standards. Imbue commanding officers with an entrepreneurial spirit and encourage them to take initiatives and to reject the old organizational culture in which supervisors responded with caution and resisted change" (94). This "new" NYPD brand of a goal-oriented and

efficient police force is visible in how Robb portrays Dallas: incorruptible, confronting whatever and whoever comes between her and her investigation, even
if it is her chief of police (such as the one who is discovered to be corrupt by the
end of the first novel and later ousted).[13]

While these elements show the adoption of the corporate-inflected management style that was on the rise in the 1990s, the series maintains Dallas's
commitment to being suspicious of the wealthy world, both the version where
people have inherited money and power and the version where corporate capitalism has created new moguls. Dallas never overlooks the possibility of a
wealthy criminal perpetrator, even as she begins to move in the rarified circles
of upper-class New York, since she sees the working and the ruling classes as
equal in terms of criminal potential. Affluence is at the heart of NYC's persistent problems and she always keeps that in mind. In fact, before deducing the
actual killers in Naked in Death, Dallas suspects Roarke of being the murderer
because of his mysterious past, unfazed by his class position as a burgher par
excellence; in fact, as I have discussed elsewhere, her low opinion of his mon-
eyed status is pretty evident (Making Meaning 53–54). She is equally skepti-
cal of class hierarchies when the first murder victim's grandfather, a wealthy
Senator, insists that even though his granddaughter was a sex worker, she could
not have possibly associated with the other murdered sex workers; on hearing
this snobbery, she rolls her eyes inwardly, thinking "so, prostitutes had class
systems" (114). When she figures out that he's guilty and arrests him for rape
and murder, she does it on the Senate floor where his patrician privilege is on
display; later, when his aide attacks her in her home, she pummels him as if he is
the embodiment of the deadbeat father who raped her and the father who mas-
sacred his child in the incident recalled at the beginning of the novel. Both the
Senator and the aide express hostility toward her as a plebian throughout the
novel, seeing themselves as inherently superior to a salaried cop who is low on
the force's management hierarchy. She is unbothered by such characters, doing
little emotional labor to appease their expectations of deference, and holds to
her working-class tastes and attitude even after her marriage to Roarke in the
third novel in the series. She only grudgingly accepts her move into wealth and
power and continues to zip between New York's twin cities in her later cases,
quite literally swapping between her police and corporate spouse selves, with
a little help from Roarke and Summerset. It is Cinderella meets Batman, with
Dallas playing both. This is how the series finds her a revolving door out of the
double bind of wealth and working-class outsider identity.

In addition to class status, gender roles affect the practice and rewards of
labor, as noted earlier. In Dallas's case, her gender is crucial to any discussion

of how her labor situates her in relation to at least two seemingly oppositional categories (police officer and socialite wife). When one looks at the early books in the series, Dallas as a worker is written in almost pointed opposition to the so-called womanly traits and professions that reactionary gender ideology might consider "natural" to her sex.[14] Her job as a mid-twenty-first century homicide detective goes against traditional gendered occupational segregation; instead, she works in a male-dominated profession (per statistics at the turn of the twenty-first century when Robb began writing).[15] This necessitates scrutiny of the larger work culture of masculinity in which Dallas exists (and that she replicates) and how it affects the evolution of her identity.

On the face of it, the very choice of casting a romantic heroine as a cop in one of the most militarized police forces in the world associates her with "hegemonic masculinity," which researchers like Anastasia Prokos and Irene Padavic identify as "a central defining concept in the culture of police work in the United States" (442). They also cite research that argues "that the policeman's symbolic world is one of opposing qualities directly related to gender. Male officers equate women with feminine moral virtue, the domestic realm, social service, formal rules, administration, cleanliness, and emotions. In contrast, they equate men and masculinity with guns, crimefighting, a combative personality, resistance to management, fights, weapons, and a desire to work in high crime areas (Hunt, 1990)" (442). Dallas is cast in this masculine mold—a streetwise, pugnacious detective who dislikes upper management and can use weapons and weaponize her body to fight crime.

The way she is written also aligns with Prokos and Padavic's observation that cops see "policing as action-filled, exciting, adventurous, and dangerous (Brown et al., 1993) . . . [and that] male police officers . . . downplay the femininely labeled aspects of the job, such as paperwork and social service (Hunt, 1990)" (442). Dallas's behavior is marked by the above masculinist behaviors—she is one of the original kickass heroines of romance fiction. She verbally lambasts cops who make mistakes, frequently jumps in to chase or subdue unruly criminals, and rejects feminized titles, like *Mrs*. She doggedly does paperwork but is also grateful when her aide, Peabody, takes it on, and she prefers to have Peabody play the sympathetic cop during interrogations or when conveying bad news to family members of injured or dead people. The last falls into emotional labor typically expected of, and assigned to, women workers in rigidly gender-binary environments.

Dallas's macho persona seems to prove what Prokos and Padavic report of police training in the US: that the "hidden curriculum" at police academies "put[s] female recruits in a double bind: to be feminine they need to sacrifice

strength; to be a cop they need to sacrifice femininity" (450). Their observations are in line with Bradley's sociological analysis of workplaces noted above,
in which she also highlights the "double bind" forced on women who enter
male-dominated workplaces: act masculine to prove competence or be judged
as a bad worker due to your femininity (230).

Other studies outside the policing profession, like one by J. Lester, bear
out this binary that women are faced with, being "often expected to adopt
masculine traits that adhere to the masculine culture" (167). J. Lester observes
that women in masculine contexts practice a form of "passing and covering,"
downplaying their status as women and "accentuat[ing] masculinity" in order
to have authority and command respect in male-dominated contexts (169–70).
While Dallas is never shown to have such conscious motivations and is presented as just naturally being this way, her behavior exhibits masculine traits
in a manner that Lester's taxonomy would classify under "passing and covering" or Joan Acker would describe as acting as an "honorary" man—namely,
dressing plainly, asking questions abrasively, and eschewing any public display
of traditional femininity.

As noted above, she resists feminized behavior in the workplace, instead
practicing physically riskier, and grimier, behavior in the field instead (even
though as a detective she does not need to be out on the streets in physical
danger or in tactical teams during unfolding high-risk events) (133). Her actions
are more in line with Bradley's remarks on how men's work is imagined: with
associations "of the outdoors, of strength and physicality," as well as danger,
mobility, and power, not to mention creativity, intelligence, and risk-taking,
while women's work has associations of "indoor work" that is "lighter," domestic, tied to one place, and perhaps associated with beauty and glamour (9).

This sexual division of labor was birthed by Victorian domestic ideology,
referenced earlier, in which Bradley says, "women were first and foremost wives
and mothers ([Hall] 1979, p. 31). The very qualities that fitted them for this,
tenderness, nurturance, fragility, moral purity, disqualified them from the
tough and ruthless world of work and public office, for which the man's spirit
was considered to be framed" (40–41). The ideology rigidified over time with
industrial capitalism and also split the world into the outside and the private,
especially among the well-off. Sex-typing of work became far more common
and legalized.

This deep-rooted belief that a woman's primary duty is to be a wife and
mother also explains Barbara Reskin and Irene Padavic's observation that organizations still assume that the best workers are single-mindedly focused on
the job and subsequently design "responsible jobs" for men (128). As they put

it, "A man whose life centers on his job and who has a wife at home to tend to his personal needs comes closest to matching an employer's notion of an ideal worker" (128). Dallas is almost exactly this kind of model employee, and before she meets Roarke, she essentially has no personal and domestic life. Susan Halford and Pauline Leonard's observations about efficiency and the masculine orientation of Western workplaces are relevant to this characterization. In *Negotiating Gendered Identities at Work*, they cite Pringle's idea that Western work organization "should be read as a commentary on a particular form of masculinity, based on instrumental rationality which excludes the personal, sexual and feminine" and offers a "powerful discourse of how 'efficient' and 'effective' work organizations should operate" (2–3). There is a great deal of efficiency and rationality (as noted in the earlier section on Dallas's adoption of corporate work culture) and little sign of the "personal, sexual and feminine" where her work life is concerned.[16]

The series suggests the hollow and unhealthy quality of such a working world in the initial novels, though it doesn't valorize a reversal of the binary either. Instead, it dramatizes the gender bias on which such a binary rests. While Dallas enacts masculine traits and habits that she's widely respected for, she is also critiqued for the absence of some feminine ones, such as not playing as nice as required by the visibility that accompanies her rank and celebrity, a criticism that also edges into expectations of emotional labor from women employees. Her press conferences, for example, tend to be brief and matter of fact, and often end with her scolding the media for its thoughtlessness and sensationalism. The department's press liaisons either try to make her act more polite or coach her in diplomatic responses—with limited effect. From time to time, her cases involve her colleagues' personal lives and they suddenly object to her professionalism, seeing it as too rational and lacking empathy, though they eventually apologize and applaud it. In other words, Dallas routinely deals with these gendered expectations from people who admire her but occasionally want her to change her working style to one they think is more feminine and acceptable. But Robb deploys Dallas's masculine profession to thwart expectations of emotional labor and emotion work, which stifle women in a different way. Emotional labor is a nonstarter for Dallas and her identity as a cop functions to normalize that behavior.

Concurrently, the series acknowledges that women in male-dominated professions are not universally welcomed, so Dallas has to battle detractors as well; these range from people who believe a woman has no place in this fraternity, to those who are convinced that she has slept her way to the top (and crowned her corrupt behavior by marrying a rich, politically powerful white-collar

criminal). Over the course of the series, she is confronted by these expectations of who a cop should be and how she is either a lesser cop by virtue of being a woman (and later, wife) or a lesser woman and wife because she's a cop.
Apart from her divided class identity, this is her second double bind in relation
to her labor. In the first novel, when she has sex with Roarke despite his status
as a suspect in an ongoing investigation and has to reveal their relationship to
her superiors, they criticize her for abandoning her police training (rather than
trusting her evaluation of Roarke's innocence). Roarke, in turn, is furious at
her seeming objectivity when he's called in for an interrogation, accusing her
of being a distrustful lover. In other instances, disgruntled cops (newbies and
veterans) complain that her rise in the police force has been a result of affairs
with her trainer, Captain Feeney, and her commanding officer.[17] In later cases
in the series, members of the Internal Affairs Bureau and administrative higher-
ups suggest that her integrity as a cop is in doubt because she has married a man
who is suspected of criminal activity. Some even warn her that her marriage has
negatively affected her chances of promotion to captaincy.[18] While she shows
limited distress over this attitude, Roarke is angry on her behalf and upset that
he is a liability to her career advancement, in an interesting transferal of emotion work from the heroine to her partner.

On the flip side, she is found wanting (by others, but occasionally by herself)
in terms of her proficiency as a woman and a spouse, especially in doing emotion
work as a society wife, because of the very qualities that make her a good cop.
Apart from the examples of her interactions with Roarke's majordomo (and
father figure) listed earlier, people in his world occasionally wonder how she is
a fit consort for a corporate rock star with impeccable style. Summerset initially
critiques her for failing to attend business dinners and play hostess for events
Roarke must host. Early in the series, she confronts him about this disapproval,
noting that it stems from her lack of commonality with his dead daughter, who
epitomized conventional femininity and who he had hoped Roarke would
marry.[19] He concedes her point and gives up that expectation, later becoming
her snarky ally in the household. They continue to scuffle verbally, but these are
fake spats whose narrative function is to show that she can reject emotion work
without losing his approval (and by extension, the family he represents). As
the series progresses, Summerset greets her at the door when she leaves or gets
home and they trade barbs, but he shoulders some of the emotion work between
her and Roarke on that threshold, giving each a heads-up on what the other
might need that day or evening.[20] When Dallas does appear at Roarke's side,
she is often late, makes no effort to act out the gloss associated with corporate
spouses, and evokes comments and raised brows for her unrepentant demeanor.

While unapologetically wedded to her work, Dallas occasionally voices a nagging suspicion that she isn't holding up her side of what is conventionally expected of a wife, especially in a high-society marriage. She senses that there are "marriage rules" that obligate her to switch from professional work to personal (female) work/roles and minimize work spillover to home, but she is usually irritated at having to conform to these expectations (once snapping, "I've got to make dinner conversation with a bunch of snooty strangers every time I turn around, and worry about what the hell I'm wearing when I do it").[21] Taking the time to express her love and being considerate of others' feelings (like texting Roarke about her schedule, buying Christmas gifts, or planning an intimate dinner at home), are irregular practices for her. Moreover, these attempts generally befuddle Roarke, underlining the fact that it is not something he expects from her—though he appreciates the attempt. Essentially, she does domestic labor and emotion work the way men do—occasionally and often grudgingly—but Robb makes sure those clumsy efforts are recognized by others. In other words, Dallas's developing community and family rarely takes her domestic and emotion work for granted as they see her job (and its associations listed above) as her primary identity. While Robb pointedly makes a woman's labor in the domestic realm visible, other examples of highlighting emotional labor and emotion work abound in the genre.

An extension of this idea is that the domestic front is not a domain that interests Dallas, and she rarely bothers with anything traditionally considered a woman's realm, such as cooking, home decor, shopping, or socializing. (I will say more below on how she is rarely criticized directly for ignoring the domestic sphere, though Summerset needles her on occasion even as he assists her when she needs logistical rescue.) Again, while Roarke's resources play an undeniable part in her reduced labor at home, we would be remiss to overlook the fact that the fantasy is not just about upward mobility; it's about relationship strategies and technological improvements (such as automated chefs and robotic workers) that could help redistribute the mental load and domestic labor fairly in an intimate partnership in any economic class.

While Dallas's neglect of home labor is not faulted, loved ones bemoan how fearlessly and single-mindedly she throws herself into her dangerous professional life in the world outside.[22] Fueled by love or anger, her critics occasionally berate her for her soldier-like devotion to police work and the tactics she uses to solve crimes, including physical risk-taking. In *Vengeance in Death* (1997), for example, she cons a friend, reporter Nadine Furst, into doing a broadcast to lure out a suspect. The provocation results in him booby-trapping Dallas's car and injuring her. On learning how Dallas manipulated her, Furst lays into her for being a "Bitch. Goddamn *cop* bitch" (224, emphasis mine). Roarke is furious at her seeming carelessness toward her own safety (in this case, motivated by a desire to keep him safe), till she points out that he would do the same for her and that his anger betrays a double standard. Even her commander and later her mentor chide her for her professional focus, criticisms that appear linked to her unwomanly disinterest in prioritizing relationships and her own safety.[23]

In keeping with this preference for doing physically demanding tasks in her work life, Dallas is also written in a way that counters femme gender stereotypes, both in her clothing and her grooming as well as in her body type, though the former shifts away from that binary over the course of the series.[24] If viewed through the manufactured and binary understanding of gender that goes with cisnormativity, Dallas is drawn as more male than female: we are told repeatedly that she is tall, with small breasts that require no support, long legs, and lean muscles.[25] To be clear, she is never misgendered as a man but descriptions of her small-breasted, small-buttocked, rangy musculature distinguish her from other women in the series, including her sylph-like best friend, Mavis, and her curvy partner, Delia Peabody.

Though rarely in uniform, her clothes are undistinguished and fall closer to the masculine end of the wardrobe spectrum in the beginning of the series. (Her stylistic gender nonconformity is also highlighted through comparisons with the elegant dresses or feminine fashion statements of her female colleagues and pointed references to her male clotheshorse colleague, who is marked as an unusual man for his fastidious dressing.) Dallas, in contrast, is initially written as someone who barely pays attention to clothes even in their functional capacity. She frequently forgets gloves and hats while running to work for instance, and cannot color-coordinate anything she is wearing, especially at the start of the series. She also bloodies herself and her clothing in the performance of her job quite frequently. Though she has a large diamond that her husband gifted her, she wears it on a chain inside her shirts and only because she hurt him by refusing it initially; it is an act of emotion work, but it mortifies her if the pendant is seen by colleagues. Her hair is always described as short or choppily cut, sometimes by herself.

Her appearance is notable since gendered self-presentation is not a natural or even merely a social construct but has been legally encoded and enforced, especially in professional contexts, including in the US. In a 1979 judgment, for example, a court ruled against Data Von Lanigan when she sued her employer for firing her for "cross-dressing" by wearing a pantsuit (Hillman 157, Katharine T. Bartlett 2569). Such cases testify to how strongly clothing is policed and how masculinity has been firmly linked to wearing pants in Western culture. Of course, over time wearing pantsuits has become a sign of entering masculine culture rather than an offense. (See chap. 2.) While Dallas says that she doesn't care to spend more time on grooming herself, that claim itself aligns her with a masculine gender presentation, especially the specific manifestation of hegemonic masculinity in police work mentioned earlier.

Reskin and Padavic's research confirms this behavior. They argue that job sex-typing is often accompanied by an insistence that employees embody a gender role. They provide examples of employers designating a female gender to some jobs, by enforcing, for instance, wearing makeup (women US Marines), wearing uniforms that emphasize sexuality (cocktail waitress), and practicing social skills, personal services like gift shopping, and attractiveness (executive secretaries) (132). Such insistence implicitly suggests that men don't need (and probably should avoid) accoutrements or displays of such traits. Viewed in this light, Dallas's sartorial ineptitude or indifference functions as a sign of her lack of feminine frivolity or the sexualization that is associated with other women in the series, in effect making her a part of the dominant masculine group she works with.

Over the course of the series, however, her wardrobe and grooming get taken over by her friends and Roarke. While she still dresses in trousers and shirts for the most part, her clotheshorse husband slowly stocks and arranges her closet in a way that results in a more aesthetically coordinated look while also protecting her from the elements (and from bullets). Her friends, too, insist on her getting her hair cut professionally and every major injury she gets is followed by a medical as well as a spa session where she is forced to get cosmetic treatments that she otherwise abhors. While Dallas usually rages against these processes in a manner that everyone finds hilarious, essentially throwing anti–emotion work tantrums, she is getting the hang of dressing herself in a less ragtag fashion as the series has progressed. But as with the other aspects of synthesizing her professional identity as a cop and personal one as a wealthy wife and friend, there is a gradual synthesis. When she dresses for parties in dresses, for example, it's usually in something Roarke has color-coordinated and accessorized; but she throws these on after she has run home from a case with only a few minutes to spare. Thus her appearance occasionally shifts to the middle of the feminine spectrum but it requires no thought on her part, or any major adjustments to her work-life spillover into the domestic and personal. In a notable scene, she once strips off her glamorous cocktail dress but is standing in fancy heels while still having a gun strapped to her body, a sight that Roarke compliments—cop and sexy wife are integrated in one image.

Dallas's workspace and habits also challenge gender stereotypes about women being interested in home management or decoration and emphasize a masculine aesthetic, especially in the early stages of the fifty-five-book (and counting) series, but gradually undergo the same shift as her personal appearance. Unlike Reskin and Padavic's observation that women "celebrate private life at work" such as birthdays and photographs of families, partly to forge community, and Lester's observation that women college faculty enacted masculine behaviors in male-dominated departments but feminized their workspaces through cute knickknacks, Dallas barely personalizes her home, let alone her workspace. Her office at the precinct is tiny and spartan, with minimal and uncomfortable furniture; others remark on its uninviting quality—epithets range from "dump" to "dungeon"—which she admits is why she keeps it. She has a coffee maker and a stash of candy, neither of which she shares willingly or without prompting. There are no other personal touches to soften the space, such as mementos or photos of Roarke, their cat, or their friends. When exhausted during cases, she simply lies down on the hard floor and naps. A colleague looks at the space and "doubt[s] Eve realized just how completely the cramped little room suited her. No fuss, no frills, and very little comfort" (*Loyalty in Death* 134).

This is in striking contrast to Bradley's research on "gendered work culture" in her case studies of British workplaces in the 1980s, where she found that "many female work groups in factories and offices 'bring home into' the work environment, both domesticating it (making boring work more tolerable, making the office a pleasant, sociable and cosy place to be in) and also being domesticated by it (as once again the 'inbuilt' domestic orientation of women is emphasized and made visible to men). . . . Hospitals and schools mirror family relationships and in them women practice their 'inbuilt' feminine skills for the public good" (230). In other words, women shape their workplaces to appear homelike and in turn, the space reinforces their socially dictated feminine identity, visible more often in certain professions.

Dallas shows no such inclination when the series begins, an attitude more aligned with the traditional masculine stereotype of indifference to decor. Before moving in with her husband, as noted earlier, she lives in an impersonal apartment. To make her feel at home (and at work) in his house, he designs a home office that resembles that impersonal space with some minor comforts (such as a carpet, a couch, and an indoor garden by a large window) to balance out her computer and the other equipment she needs to work (*Glory in Death* 143). Here is where the hegemonic masculinity script starts to loosen a little, though Roarke is again the one to coax her into accepting something less spartan, which only applies to her home office. She is noticeably moved at his gesture of bringing some of her belongings from her old apartment, such as a battered desk, into this home office, which begins the process of synthesizing "instrumental rationality" with "the personal, sexual and feminine" (Halford and Leonard 2–3).

When Roarke proposes they redesign the space after a few years, however, she continues to defy the stereotype that women love redesigning their environment. But her anger also suggests that she has formed an attachment to the existing design. Yet instead of voicing that emotional attachment, she argues purely in terms of what is appropriate to police work, insisting, "How can I have cops come up here, work here, if you go all fancy with it? It's a work space, for solving murders, closing cases, not for showing off." He counters with "We're hardly talking about fussy window treatments and bloody divans," reassuring her that femininity is not about to take over (*Brotherhood in Death* 142–43). The final version of the new office, in *Apprentice in Death*, is in keeping with her preference for nonfussiness, and what she really approves of is the mix of efficient workspace in muted colors and functional equipment, like a concealed whiteboard, a coffee machine inside her desk, and a voice-activated computer system.[26] But the office comes with some personal touches, albeit without her own actual input: a favorite stuffed animal, a sculpture gifted by her partner's mother, a photo of her and Roarke. It's a clever synthesis of her masculine work ethic and aesthetic and the feminine one that Bradley and others noted of women workers in their research, but one that does not impose a significant burden on her mental load, since Roarke shoulders most of it.

Dallas's interactions with coworkers go against the grain as well, defying studies such as the ones Bradley reviews that demonstrate how sexual segregation of work is not just top-down but a process through which men and women act out expectations of masculine and feminine sensibilities: "Women's cultures center on their home lives, on families and domesticity: conversations, rituals and symbols are concerned with homes, romance, marriage, children, clothes, food and the feminine lifestyles. Cakes and recipes are exchanged, clothing catalogs circulated, advice on how to handle husbands and boyfriends passed on. By contrast, men's cultures are more work-centered, and also emphasize exaggerated versions of masculinity (sometimes symbolized by aggressive initiation rituals): talk features sport, heavy drinking, sexual bravado, anecdotes stress strength, audacity, resistance to authority, physical exploits of various kinds" (69). As with her appearance and her office, Dallas's behavior does not fit this gendering norm at work at the start. For one, she does not have cozy chats with coworkers, most of whom are men. She hunkers down in her office unless briefing a team in a conference room. When her female aide (and later, partner) brings up diets or boyfriends, Dallas engages only when she is given no choice and her advice is usually brutally practical. Since she does not have keepsakes, there are no objects that serve as conversation starters or bonding artifacts. She eschews traditional feminized practices such as shopping, admiring babies, and physical displays of affection in public, especially around coworkers. At work, she is happy to eat junk food someone else might have brought and is frequently seen kicking and swearing at uncooperative vending machines (that are programmed to penalize hostile behavior) but has neither ability nor interest in exchanging recipes or buying gifts. She is embarrassed or contemptuous if anyone remarks on her clothes as being unusually nice, another signaling of her distance from feminized behavior.

Dallas's prickliness is similar to Linda McDowell's observation of "microscale interactions" in organizations, including talking and joking, which often reflect and reinforce masculine values and power and "appeal to 'highly masculine values of individualism, aggression, competition, sport and drinking' (Collinson and Hearn 1994: 4)" (136). In this mold, Dallas participates in sarcastic or snarky remarks with her team when passing the bullpen and emits strength and audacity during her investigations. On more than one occasion, she tackles runaway suspects and criminals and gets clocked in the process; at other times, she joins coworkers in mocking their sharply dressed colleague. As suggested by Harriet Bradley then, as a woman in a "male" career, she outmans the men in her professional orbit, physically, verbally, and aesthetically. While she slowly starts to do more emotion work with colleagues, partly by mimicking such behavior that she observes in her husband and her aide, it is a small part of her work and domestic life. So there is a process of synthesizing gendered traits that occurs here, but Dallas maintains her dominant qualities alongside occasionally displaying new behaviors.

As noted earlier, those qualities are admired by some of the rank and file, including her aide and her team. In contrast to observations of actual "androcentric" workplaces, Dallas's behavior does not diminish her femininity in her own eyes or that of others, especially her husband. She is impatient with niceties and politics, willing to be first through the door in any arrest or search, and her lack of feminine qualities appears to find favor in the department. In many ways, this "masculine" behavior has earned the respect and affection of many of her colleagues and superiors in the chain of command. She has high status as a detective and commands a large team of junior coworkers and peers. This personal and professional network that surrounds her is in keeping with the romance dialectic and its rejection of the double bind or false binary (in this case, of working versus upper class, wife versus cop, and feminine worker versus masculine worker).

The series gives her a supportive community that appreciates who she is and what she does, irrespective of traditional notions of what kind of work women should do and what their traits should be. Apart from her professional allies, she has a husband who is indifferent to convention, including in his wife. As long as she is not endangering herself unduly, he aids her in her investigations instead of hampering them or asking for more domestic labor or emotion work, something she recognizes:

> "In my opinion, cops are mostly a bad bet in the personal arena. But some make it work. It works, I guess, when the civilian gets it. When the civilian respects and values the job, or at least understands it. I got lucky there."
> She shifted her gaze to where Roarke stood behind the range of cameras. "I got lucky." (*Innocent in Death* 181)

Unlike data that documents diminishing involvement from the male partners of women who bring work home or are dealing with work stress, Roarke routinely steps up his domestic role (including emotion work) when Dallas is on a case (Minnotte et al. 791). Additionally, instead of bringing "home into" work, a practice Bradley observes in women employees (230), Dallas often does the reverse, and then Roarke insists that any colleagues who come to her home office be fed. Again, it helps that the series is set in 2058 and she benefits from automated household appliances and a de facto housekeeper, but this fantasy is just one more way in which romance criticizes traditional gender roles and their tyranny and imagines alternatives to the false binary for its heroines. Indeed, the portrayals of many other straight couples (who are not astronomically wealthy) in the series reinforce this vision of a romantic partnership, with her female friends excelling at their jobs while also enjoying relationships with men who do emotion work and domestic tasks.[27]

In sum, this sci-fi romantic suspense series shows the operation of sex-typing and the gendered nature of professions, especially ones traditionally male or "androcentric," but also the romance heroine's move toward a work self that rejects that double bind (Bradley 231). As with her work space, Dallas gradually synthesizes the seeming opposite versions of behavior women are offered in work life, both in terms of time usage and presentation of a worker-self. Halford and Leonard mention that clock time is "tied to dominant accounts of masculinity as rational, controlled and linear," while "feminine time has been represented in terms of caring, other-oriented time, not bound by clock-watching, mechanistic time but process-driven and on-going" (13). In their hospital field study, Halford and Leonard observed male and female staff and saw that "speed and style of comportment asserted direction, authority, an unquestioned purpose" in men, while women showed "less ostentatious [behavior], both in their speed of movement and posture" (93). Dallas evinces a mix of these traits, working doggedly till a crime is solved even if she is injured or ill with exhaustion or lack of sleep because she feels an obligation to the dead and to the surviving loved ones, an extreme form of care—but she does this with authority and speed. It's a hybrid self, to modify Lester's concept of the "hybrid performance," which combines traditionally feminine and masculine gender display, and while some of the feminine is coaxed out of her by her husband and friends, it is presented as detoxifying her of the worst elements of hegemonic masculinity (Lester 169). When it comes to work pace and work space, Dallas is forging her own unique hybrid worker self.

At the start of the series, Dallas is on one side of the masculinist binary, epitomizing the findings of many studies that suggest that women in male-dominated occupations take on the traits of that culture. Her clothes, appearance, work habits, and work spaces mimic traditional masculine ethos in general and policing's hegemonic masculinity in particular. While praised in many quarters for her work ethic, she is also criticized for being too much of a hard ass and for lacking feminine qualities (i.e., being disinterested in emotional labor). After marriage, she is still deeply devoted to her job and irritated at any expectation that she act more like a traditional woman and spouse, including performing emotion work. But the series starts to imagine a less ascetic, efficient, impersonal life for her, one into which she is coaxed and aided by her romantic partner, her work partner, and assorted other people she encounters or starts to develop an intimacy with. (Many of these are also part of the small group that addresses her as "Eve.") Rather than having her replace her one-sided (work-focused) life with another (domesticity-focused society wife and mother), the series offers a new vision of how she can live out many aspects of herself (cop, friend, wife). As the series moves toward its fifty-sixth book in 2023, Dallas is a heroine whose work defines her while she also finds fulfillment in a hybrid self that exists in realms of the domestic and the social as well. While the sci-fi and mystery elements of the series allow her opportunities for traditional kinds of heroic action through her job, the romance element allows her opportunities for intimate heroism, learning how to be a long-term romantic partner and friend without giving up public (wage) heroism.

In *Dreaming of You*, people treat the heroine's creative labor as idiosyncratic or uppity, or they fail to understand how that labor is tied to her identity outside of the roles they recognize as natural. In *In Death*, the heroine's work has locked her into ignoring affective and emotional aspects of personhood, and while her professional abilities evoke respect in many people, they are also viewed as dangerous or déclassé by some and overblown by others. Despite the disapproval or incomprehension both heroines face, they hold firm to their

conviction that they have a vocation and deserve respect. While the first heroine offers one perspective on the romance novel dialectic—rejecting the false
binary of moral woman / slutty hack writer—the detective novel presents a
variation: its salaried public servant protagonist scorns conventions tied to
class, taste, and gender behavior, steamrolling over highbrow and sexist beliefs.
Both heroines allegorize the romance fiction community's snubbing of the
snobbish disapproval the genre faces for its alleged nonliterariness. Both also
have different relationships to emotion work—the former heroine having done
too much and the latter almost none—with either extreme being detrimental to
their well-being. As they build a more integrated self, they develop a healthier
balance in their mental load, partly by partnering with people and lovers who
are willing to share not just material wealth but emotion work as well. Finally,
while *Dreaming of You* is a more classic romance and its heroine's binary is similarly associated with the traditional false choice between work and domesticity,
Naked in Death extends the genre into the hybrid form of a speculative police
procedural and launches a series, testifying to the need to explore other aspects
of a woman's extended struggle to work on her own terms.

Cohn and others have regretfully pointed out that romance novels cope with
financial disparity between genders by showing the taming of the hero via love,
and then having his commitment to the heroine validate her worth and that of
the traditional domestic space and tasks patriarchy confines her to; such a resolution does not change real-world inequality where men have greater economic
power while women's work and aspirations are devalued and circumscribed.
Others, like Illouz, focus on how romance media and practices have become
infiltrated by late capitalist principles, visible in the contradictory logics of
encouraging consumerism as well as rational productivity or conformity and
individual freedom. This chapter shows that these are familiar and limited perspectives to understand romance fiction economics because they overlook the
nuances of the heroine's behaviors as an economic subject. Whether in novels
that show women trying to earn a living in a hostile society that wants to bar
them from the labor market, or novels that show them in a male-dominated
field, or novels that elevate the worth of the activities, jobs, and industries
associated with women (arts, education, human services, food, fashion, etc.),
the genre normalizes the idea that only a woman has the right to determine
how and when she does physical, mental, and creative work. Just as crucially, it
models how the heroine can choose to do or decline emotional labor.

Moreover, the genre of popular romance novels *did* change real-world economic structures for many women. As pioneering editor Vivian Stephens has
said, the women she collaborated with (in her role as an editor who bought their

manuscripts and as a founding member of the Romance Writers of America who helped them understand publishing) found their identity as writers (Julie E. Moody-Freeman "'Dance Between Raindrops'"). As she tells it, "I didn't really realize until a long time later what it did for their own psyche and for their emotional health because . . . it took them from just being someone's mother, someone's wife, to their own identity as a writer" (Moody-Freeman "'Dance Between Raindrops'"). Many of them were able to gain economic autonomy, even leaving unfulfilling or abusive relationships, because they gained confidence that they could make it as writers. The way Stephens sees it, receiving a publishing contract told a woman that "she could write something that would sell under her own name, under her own skin, that would give her the confidence that she could go on with the rest of her life. So, you never know what a simple something, like a little Candlelight Romance [novel] can do for a person" (Moody-Freeman "'Dance Between Raindrops'"). When one writer thanked Stephens for saving her by accepting her novel for publication at a time of dire financial straits, Stephens told her "You saved yourself. You had a manuscript that I liked and I was happy to buy it from you" (Moody-Freeman "'Dance Between Raindrops'"). Her modesty and deferral of praise recognize a writer's work but the anecdote reveals how the writer's life was made possible by others, mainly women like Stephens. Directly and indirectly, this leads us to the crucial matter of a heroine's rightful place and the community support that can help her become her full self, which is taken up at length in the next chapter.

NOTES

1. Barnett does note that when a woman is married to someone who mainly gets satisfaction from money and cares how his income compares to other men, he may feel less content in the marriage if his wife earns more. But this is a specific exception (162).

2. While these scholars distinguish between "emotional labor" as paid work and "emotion work" as unpaid labor, Reskin and Padavic use "emotion work" to refer to the former. They say that more jobs done by American women than men emphasize "emotion work," because "most of the emotion work is about making other people feel good—a task that society has largely given to women" (133).

3. See Jayne Anne Krentz's *Dangerous Men and Adventurous Women*, a collection of essays in which romance authors talk about their writing. Also, "Sneers and Leers" by Jen Lois and Joanna Gregson documents the disparagement and innuendo directed at romance authors.

4. I explored this phenomenon in my dissertation and in "Romance in the Media" in the *Routledge Research Companion to Popular Romance*.

5. A recent search on a library website yielded a few hundred results for Sarah Fielding and a few thousand for Henry Fielding. For more on women writers like her, see Dale Spender's *Mothers of the Novel* and *The Writing or the Sex? Or Why You Don't Have to Read Women's Writing to Know It's No Good.*

6. Regis presented the paper "The Romance Community: *A Room of One's Own* and *Écriture Feminine*" at the annual meeting of the Popular Culture Association in April 2010.

7. Pete Hamill described the city in the late eighties as one full of the criminal behaviors of panhandlers, "roaming gangs of teenagers," "armies of New York drug addicts," "regiments of the homeless," and other dangerous "derelicts" (62–65). Also see my article "From Barbarized to Disneyfied: Viewing 1990s New York City through Eve Dallas, J. D. Robb's Futuristic Homicide Detective" in the 2017 "Capitals Crimes" special issue (volume 10, pp. 72–86) of the open-access journal *Forum for Inter-American Research.*

8. In it, Joelle Attinger wrote, "Last year 1,905 people were murdered in New York, more than twice as many as in Los Angeles. In the first five months of this year, 888 homicides were committed, setting a pace that will result in a new record if it goes unchecked. . . . This summer, in one eight-day period, four children were killed by stray gunshots as they played on the sidewalks, toddled in their grandmother's kitchens or slept soundly in their own beds. Six others have been wounded since late June" (38).

9. Hamill wrote that the Queens resident (a recent immigrant from the Midwest) lost his temper with his six-day old son, "chopped up the infant and threw him to [his] German shepherd[.] When the cops arrived, there was [nothing] left of the [child] except the blood [on the] floor" (61).

10. In fact, Robb's descriptions of the shooting deaths of the prostitutes so strongly evoke the 1990 news coverage of New York by people like Attinger and Hamill that a reader familiar with that coverage could be excused for thinking that this case is actually set in that crime wave, almost always portrayed in contemporary media reports as an inexplicable pathology. Robb portrays Dallas's professional life as marked by the fallout of such madness.

11. See Kecia Ali's *Human in Death* (2017) on the ethics in the series.

12. "Zero tolerance" and "Broken Windows" philosophies advocate crackdowns on any activity that the police see as a gateway to larger offences, with the logic being that curbing petty offences prevents escalation toward worse crimes (Andrew Karmen 114). Benjamin Bowling explains COMPSTAT culture as follows:

> Regular 7am meetings at headquarters in which computer generated maps of crime and police activity are displayed on huge screens to an audience of up to 200 people including police brass, district and US attorneys, parole, schools, Port Authority police and the media (Bratton 1998: 232; Gorta 1998). In these meetings (likened by a police cartoonist to being in front of a firing squad), the Chiefs grill precinct

commanders in detail about the "hot spots"—what's going on, and what they are doing about it. At the same time resources and responsibility were decentralized to precinct level with more direct accountability to headquarters (see also Silverman 1996; Allen and Wright 1997). (543)

13. Bowling and others have noted that the NYPD was deeply mired in dysfunction in the 1980s, including corruption at various levels of the organization (538). *Naked in Death* appears to pointedly treat that as a tradition to which Dallas does not belong.

14. Bradley notes that in the gendering of work, workers themselves construct "notions of distinct sexual identities" that cast men and women as different and result in "gendered work cultures" (229). One could argue that being a police officer is a profession with the "personal care motif" associated with women's work if one takes the "Protect and Serve" motto of the police unironically. In *Festive in Death*, a holiday banner hanging in the homicide bullpen reads, "No Matter Your Race, Creed, Sexual Orientation, Or Political Affiliation, We Protect And Serve, Because You Could Get Dead."

15. Per Barbara Raffel Price, women made up 15 percent of the uniformed officers, and a far smaller percentage of higher positions in the NYPD in 1996.

16. In an early novel, a detective who is an old flame reminds us of her sexual attractiveness to other men, but by and large, coworkers call her "Lieutenant" or "LT" and treat her as one of the guys.

17. In *Conspiracy in Death*, the accusation comes from a bitter woman beat cop and in *Purity in Death*, from a young IT officer who is delirious from a virus.

18. See *Interlude in Death, Purity in Death, Survivor in Death, Vengeance in Death*. (https://indeath.fandom.com/wiki/Eve%27s_Laws)

19. In *Vengeance in Death*, Dallas's impression of Marlena from old photographs is of "Golden hair, innocent eyes, and a snowy white dress. Pure ... virginal" (196).

20. I am grateful to Courtney Wetzel for articulating this specific function of Summerset's.

21. *Vengeance in Death* (155).

22. As Bradley has noted, the inside/outside split was manufactured by sexist Victorian ideology, prompted by the knowledge that women *have* historically worked outside the home as needed by the family. She concludes that it was a deliberate measure to confine them indoors, especially to solidify gender and class hierarchies, starting in the nineteenth century.

23. See *Glory in Death* (1995) for the former and *Ceremony in Death* (1997) for the latter.

24. I have always associated her with athletic George from the *Nancy Drew* series, with her aide Peabody a stand-in for Bess, who provided a physical contrast.

25. Cisnormativity, the hegemonic attitude that naturalizes gender, trains people to see certain bodies as female and certain bodies as male; the classification is based on the presence or absence or size of certain bodily features such as breasts, shoulder width, eyelid to brow distance, and in intrusive or intimate situations, external or internal genitalia.

26. She vetoes the first design: "The colors are kind of girlie, and the stuff's sort of . . . sharp and . . . slick. So plain it's fancy"; the second is nixed because even though "It doesn't have that I'm-new-and-cutting-edge-and-really-important deal," and the "colors are strong . . . but it's a little in-your-face. Distracting." She likes the palette of the third: "the colors are good, and they're quiet but not girlie. They're not saying, Hey look at me. It's more like they've been there awhile. And the command center looks . . . commanding. No bullshit. But . . . most of the other stuff doesn't look like anybody lives with it." Even the palette that is "browns and sort of greens and whites that weren't bright and shiny" she imagines is "in some designer speak" given "bullshit names like Contented Fawn and Zen Retreat and Chocolate Drizzle" (*Apprentice in Death* 43). Roarke merges the furniture in design two with the colors of three. She approves: "The stuff doesn't look as . . . fussy in these colors like it does in the in-your-face ones. It looks more . . . real. . . . It's efficient, it's not fussy or weird" (43–44).

27. I owe this insight to Courtney Wetzel.

FOUR

CITIZENSHIP

WHETHER IT COMES TO GENDER, sexuality, or labor, elements of the false choices women face carry connotations of insider/outsider status. It is therefore apt to now turn to romance fiction's questioning of binaries via its heroine's political roots and actions, which raises the issue of women's identity in regard to community or group membership and loyalty. The operation of this dynamic can be seen in a family, a neighborhood, a town, or a workplace, and it can have national or global repercussions. While questions regarding a heroine's status are always present in some fashion in a romance novel, the stakes become more visible in ones set against the backdrop of inter- or intragroup conflict (including war) and its material and psychological aftermath. In this vein, and to varying degrees, the novels in this chapter touch on the significant realignments regarding national or group identity that individuals undergo during contentious times. Novels like these include different representations of how one may (or should) question one's political identity when one's country is involved in covert or open armed conflict. While some romance novels foreground the contingent nature of these identities, others treat them as an immutable fact. For instance, in many historical romances set in Britain (the majority of which are now written by white American authors), love for Britain (which acts as an Anglo-Saxon stand-in for the US) is usually portrayed as the only patriotic love worth defending, and Britishness (i.e., Americanness) the only honorable citizenship identity. The elision between the two nationalities betrays the historical and ideological underpinning of political identity, composed of seemingly fixed but carefully constructed labels, within and outside the genre.

In this sense, some romances engage with international conflict and national allegiance without always applying a critical lens. In other cases, when the patriotic self is found to be in opposition to the romantic one, the former may be nudged aside to allow the novel's requisite happy end. (See Kamblé *Making Meaning.*) Even Regency romance novels follow this circumscription, despite the fact that the British Regency (1811–1820) was a time of intense questioning of political identity and allegiance, coinciding as it did with one of the bloodiest eras of competing nationalisms—the Napoleonic wars and the race for colonial supremacy between Europeans. But whether directly or obliquely, romance heroines in a plot about dueling community loyalties, national or otherwise, and about a group's willingness to accept their claim of full membership in that society (which T. H. Marshall equates to citizenship) offer insight into a larger discourse about women's emotional attachments and citizenhood (Marshall 8, 28).[1]

As Marilyn Friedman notes, citizenship "can be an identity; a set of rights, privileges, and duties; an elevated and exclusionary political status; a relationship between individuals and their states; a set of practices that can unify—or divide—the members of a political community; and an ideal of political agency" (3). She also points out that citizenship is a "social practice" that has traditionally been gendered and women have often been excluded from state citizenship, with that status reserved for male people (4). Even in cases where women are granted political citizenship, there is a gender bias, and women's exercise of citizenship thus faces "practical and conceptual obstacles" (4). Melinda Chateauvert also brings up how citizenship is contingent on many factors, including gender and sexuality as well as skin color and race, in her discussion on the differences between a (neo)liberal concept of citizenship and one that centers a human rights-framework, including of sexual citizenship and the individual's right to pleasure ("Framing Sexual Citizenship"). This chapter focuses on two historical romances that grapple with these ideas.

Despite their historical setting, the novels engage with contemporary socio-legal discourse about women's loyalties and show how it affects the genre's understanding and representation of women's history as outsiders and insiders in a group. Contesting state and social rhetoric about where the heroines belong, what labels their ethnicity and lineage dictate, and what citizenship rights and responsibilities they can assume occurs through the heroine's journey (geographic and metaphorical) in these texts. The spatial connotation is especially relevant here. After all, Alison M. Jaggar reminds us that the "activities regarded as characteristic of citizens—fighting, governing, buying and selling property, and eventually working for wages—have all been viewed as masculine," and corresponding places, including the battlefield and the state, are cast as public arenas where "citizenship is performed" (92);

our heroines cross these boundaries, acting as they see fit, and refuse to let patrilineal or conjugal relationships determine their place in a community. In other words, these heroines reject the binary that women's identity based in familial or romantic relationships is incompatible with membership in the larger polity or vice versa.

Joanna Bourne's espionage novels (*Spymaster's Lady*, 2008; *Forbidden Rose*, 2010; and *Black Hawk*, 2011) are notable for engaging with the ideologies of political identity and with citizenship and its obligations in the context of war and courtship. (This preoccupation might stem from the years in which Bourne worked as a US State Department Foreign Service Officer in many countries.) In these novels, patriotic love is as central to the narrative as romantic love because the protagonists have opposing national allegiances, an opposition thrown into sharp relief by their professional and civilian ties to their respective countries. Moreover, the struggles of these intelligence-operative heroines (i.e., professional agents of the nation-state) can act as a reminder of how first-class citizen status (as worker or soldier) continues to be elusive for those who are not cis-heterosexual-males in liberal democracies even today (Jaggar 93).[2]

While historical romances have increasingly confined themselves to the British Isles or colonial America (and the few set elsewhere rarely extend their ideological landscape), these novels are set in revolutionary-era France. Bourne's French heroines and British heroes travel across a Europe in turmoil, and when they enter into a romance narrative during these intentional or coerced crossings of national boundaries, they are forced to examine their political worldview. As they clash with each other in the midst of a tense plot of espionage and double-cross, they also start to question their respective superiors and their own political identities, duties, and rights.

In his discussion of identity and identification, Stuart Hall mentions two primary approaches: the commonly understood one in which identification is "constructed on the back of a recognition of some common origin or shared characteristics with another person or group, or with an ideal, and with the natural closure of solidarity and allegiance established on this foundation" and a discursive one in which it is a "construction, a process never completed— always 'in process' . . . a process of articulation, a suturing, an over-determination or a lack, but never a proper fit, a totality" (2–3). In other words, he conceives of identification as a self-labeling based on a belief in one's likeness to others or to a paradigm, but also an ever-unfolding event of sorts, one that remains incomplete and requires effort on one's part for its continued existence. Most romances adopt the first approach, relying on stereotypes (some constructed by other romance novels), and treating group labels as natural and in no need of further examination. Bourne's novels are more in line with the second, dis-cursive, understanding of identification. In them, nothing is taken for granted by the protagonists when it comes to a macro-identity like nationality. For them, falling in love is co-terminus with realizing that one's identity is either overdetermined or lacking and often with a crisis about the moral worth of the nation with which one has identified.

In *Spymaster's Lady*, heroine Annique Villiers identifies as a French patriot but is under considerable internal and external pressure to examine what that means. A nineteen-year-old with an eidetic memory, she has worked as a cou-rier for the French spy network since she was a child during the Reign of Terror. Having been trained by her spymaster mother and her friends and colleagues to be fleet-footed and wily, she is known in the intelligence community by the *nom d'espionnage* of Fox Cub; this is one of many different identities that she assumes and juggles throughout the course of the novel. Annique meets Robert Grey, a senior British Intelligence officer, when they are both being interrogated in a French secret service prison for different reasons. They collaborate to es-cape, but she then finds herself tricked into his custody. Robert believes that Fox Cub is responsible for the death of some of his agents and wants retribution (in addition to any information he can extract from her about Napoleon's plans to invade Britain). Annique, in turn, is already in two minds about said infor-mation. She knows that revealing it to British Intelligence would be treason, but she also believes that it would save lives on both sides of the Channel and curb Napoleon, who seems to have betrayed the French revolution for his own ambition. Annique's dilemma (which intensifies upon meeting Robert), is thus a political one: how to love and be loyal to her country when the country's lead-ership might be in the wrong, particularly at a time when she is falling in love with an enemy nationalist whose political identity is inimical to hers. While tackling this dilemma, she has to constantly contend not just with her own upbringing, which inculcated unquestioning devotion to the French Republic, but also with how Robert and others define her and themselves.

Since Annique has been raised to serve her country, her core identity rests on French loyalism. Yet this identity as a good French citizen is under strain even before she enters into a romance narrative with a man who does not share her beliefs. An identity formed as a result of being "hailed" by the French state since childhood, it has started to fray in the face of the knowledge that the nation, the "object fantasy" of identification, is deeply flawed at best, tyrannical at worst.[3] Moreover, Annique's imprisonment by her French colleagues exposes the fic-tion that one's nationality can guarantee "solidarity and allegiance" (Hall 2). Her encounter with repressive state apparatuses reverses the ideological work done by the "rhetorics of nationhood," which Sonya O. Rose identifies as "strategies deployed to manage or organize the differences among people … so that individuals see themselves as national beings regardless of their loyalties and preoccupations" (9). Annique has believed such rhetoric all her life, but her arrest and mistreatment disrupt the fantasy that nationhood is about a "unitary collective identity," a fellowship of members who can trust and rely on each other (Rose 7). Her first custodian, Leblanc, is French secret police and should be her ally, yet he treats her not as a comrade in arms or even just a compatriot worthy of courtesy but as a woman he can sexually abuse and threaten. He, too, wants information about the planned invasion of Britain—not for patriotic purposes but so he might sell it for a profit. It is problematic, the narrative thus suggests, to believe that nationality is anything but a shifting sign; Frenchness clearly means different things to Annique and to Leblanc.

The disruption of Annique's straightforward relationship with France (and herself) actually predates her mistreatment at Leblanc's hands. Retroactive exposition reveals that her mentor in the secret service had become disillusioned with Napoleon after losing his two sons in Napoleon's Egyptian campaign and had confided to Annique his wish to foil Napoleon's plans of invading Britain. Annique herself is worried that the invasion will not only cause the death of innocent British civilians but also eventually bring greater retribution onto France. She is thus conflicted about her duty to her nation and to her mentor even before she is captured and imprisoned by Leblanc and meets Robert, technically her enemy. His seemingly rational arguments in favor of British lives, that is to say, against French triumph, exacerbate her crisis. Falling in love with a man who critiques her country alters the already jaundiced view she has developed of her own French identity. In the opening prison scene, for instance, she forces herself to be brave with the exhortation, "French honor demanded a Frenchwoman meet death as courageously as any English," yet the line is immediately followed and undercut by the thought that "French honor always seemed to be demanding things of her," suggesting an ironic rather than naive view of national identity, one that is not immutable, that she is always negotiating (6).

After Annique and Robert's prison break and flight across France, one marked by incidents in which they alternately fight and ally with each other, Robert eventually gets her to the headquarters of British Intelligence in London, where he holds her prisoner. Their attraction has built over the course of their journey, but they are hyperaware of the problems related to their sexual and emotional involvement. Both know that their respective patriotisms make such a relationship adjacent to treason in wartime, even if they were ordinary civilians, which they are decidedly not. Annique is especially disturbed by her unwilling attraction to an enemy combatant who is so politically different from her as to almost qualify as another species (thereby raising the specter of whether she could mutate into another nation-species herself): "He was as unsuitable for a lover as a penguin or the shadow of a large tree. A hulking, grim stranger who was an enemy and in the profession of spying, which was a type she did not admire. She could not have chosen more stupidly" (77). She views her desire for him as an infectious disease that is dangerous to her personal and professional (nationalist) self: "It disturbed her intensely to be touched by this man. She did not want to desire him. This hunger was something that had befallen her, like an illness" (77). She later worries that she has in fact become a dupe or a national traitor out of love or cowardice. Robert recognizes her fears after they have become lovers and observes that "she lay there, wanting him. Scared of it. Wondering if it made her a whore or just a fool. Halfway wondering if she was trading herself to an enemy spy, for safety" (277). Apart from these worries about patriotic integrity caused by her romantic feelings for her enemy, which run contrary to her sense of who she must be (i.e., not an Englishman's lover), she grapples with *his* definitions of who she is.

Robert formulates his definition of her as an anti-British sex worker at the beginning of the novel. As he watches her putting on a conventional gender display to scheme her way out of the prison, he ignores her professional skill and constructs her as a French seductress in his mind, thinking, "She was totally feminine in every moment, *indefinably* French" (14, emphasis mine). Yet he then proceeds to define her Frenchness in mythosexual terms: "With her coloring—black hair, pale skin, eyes of that dark indigo blue—she had to be pure Celt. She'd be from the west of France. Brittany, maybe. Annique was a Breton name. She carried the magic of the Celt in her, used it to weave that fascination the great courtesans created" (14). Apart from his absurd, yet conventional, casting of her as an exotic whore based on ethnic essentializing (which will be proved wrong soon), what makes the passage notable is the ironic light in which the context paints it. We already know from a preceding section (narrated from Annique's point of view) that she is playing a role from her arsenal as a clever spy, one she has labeled "Silly Young Harlot," to lull their jailor into a false sense of security. But Robert homes in on her actions to pigeonhole her, reading her gender display as something essential in her nature and fails to recognize her behavior as an act.

In fact, over the course of the novel, she calls up several different personas, showing us her strategic deployment of different gender displays for a professional purpose. For example, in an early attempt to distract Robert and stoke up her courage against potential torture, she thinks, "There were roles within her. . . . She would be the Worldly Courtesan" (56). Like an actor, she has invented motivation and a backstory for this character that she can call up when needed: "The Worldly Courtesan was years older than Annique, knowing and cynical. She did not give a fig whatsoever about an enemy English. The Courtesan would not worry about wearing that obscene scrap of cloth . . . or whatever else it might become necessary to do. . . . The Courtesan was not dismayed because a man desired her. It gave her power" (57). The role of a sophisticated sex worker helps her do her job without allowing sexist sexual morality to limit her actions and lets her manage the fear that being a woman amidst predatory men engenders. This display of hegemonic femininity is a tool she uses for occasional gender maneuvering. At other times, she variously assumes the personas of a pregnant and nauseous German hausfrau to escape a French patrol and of an ordinary farm woman while walking through the English countryside. In every case, she separates the roles that are necessary for her mission from herself, a woman who is alone, orphaned, afraid, and visually disabled for half of the novel—the woman she speaks of in the third person as "Annique," as seen in the above example.

Robert initially tries to reduce her identity to one of those roles—that of a prostitute. When his colleague Doyle argues that she must be respected as a fellow intelligence agent and not dressed "in some whore's castoffs," Robert retorts that "she's worn less in the service of France," implying that the service has been on her back. He thinks that by putting "Annique in this [dress], she'd look like what she was—an expensive Courtesan, a woman born to entice men" (46), exhibiting a tendency that scholars like Tammy M. Proctor observe in both popular and intelligence service rhetoric: casting women spies as sexual adventuresses (123). Annique is puzzled by Robert's prejudice and contempt, thinking, "As if he did not have his dozens of women agents working for his Service. It was illogical that he should despise her" (59). Her critique exposes a paradox in ultranationalist rhetoric: it prizes love of nation but views anyone who holds a different national identity as suspect; if that someone is a woman, she is cast not as a patriot for her nation but as its whore.[4] Again, echoes of this perspective are visible throughout the genre, even when the setting is limited to smaller communities or interpersonal conflicts (as chap. 2 demonstrates). There are innumerable novels, especially in the 1970s–1990s, that show a heroine having to battle someone's assessment of her integrity and loyalty to a hero or a group on a sexual meter.

Throughout the novel, even Annique's ostensible compatriots and enemies try to define her within the context of her work, her gender, and her sexuality.

Her fellow Frenchmen, such as the men who imprisoned her in France and are chasing her and Robert, discuss her alleged treason in sexual terms, casting her as a promiscuous turncoat, a typical disloyal woman. One of them says, "It is always a mistake to use women. You all trusted that bitch, and now she spreads herself for this Grey and squeals our secrets. It must be stopped" (242). With these multiple stakeholders attempting to exclude or include Annique when it comes to their versions of patriotic identity, the novel makes evident that such an identity is not stable but a discursive field, especially for women.

She has to skirt these definitions even as she starts to question the rightness of staying true to France in the face of the brutality of her French pursuers and the harsh retribution promised by her former colleagues for her possible treason. In particular, the character of Leblanc, her jailor and nemesis, exposes as fiction the narrative that the nation is benevolent and benign toward its citizens and therefore deserving of their loyalty. Under these pressures, she begins to question not just whether revealing French secrets is a terrible betrayal but also whether her France (i.e., the nation she believed worth defending) even exists. Any unitary, uncomplicated notion of national identity and duty is thus impossible here despite her beliefs regarding the obligations of French citizenship and of her profession. She begins to grasp that while one may choose to imagine one's nation as, in Sonya O. Rose's words, "an essentially unchanging place of like-minded people where we experience the emotional security of being perpetually at home," the nation is in fact a "reification, a conceptual abstraction" with no permanent factual reality to back up this faith (11, 7). Replace the word "nation" with ones like "family" or other communities and you can see how the phantom of Sandra J. Lindow's heroine fleeing home (as discussed in my introduction) is present in many romance novels.

Annique's fight to retain control of her identity as a French patriot becomes even more complicated when Robert's boss reveals that she is the daughter of a Welsh couple rather than a French one. On finding out about this British heritage and her birth name, Anne Katherine Jones, Annique reacts with ontological incomprehension: "It is like saying I am a giraffe or a teapot or an Algonquin Indian. I have become impossible and ridiculous" (293). Again, as in an earlier passage (77), such similes hyperbolically highlight how people are trained to believe in national identity as if it is a species category and its upending can seem to go against the laws of nature. Her parents' elaborate lie threatens her national sense of self, exposing the flimsiness of the identity one believes to be absolute but that is entirely contingent on narratives of birthplace, one's parents' alleged national origins, and one's upbringing. Worse, she is given proof that her parents were double agents loyal to the British crown, who siphoned the intelligence reports she had gathered to their London contacts. It is a crushing blow to the recently orphaned woman, bringing all her past service to *her* nation's security into question. Raised to give allegiance to France, Annique finds her identity completely torpedoed by her nonconsensual recruitment into the "enemy" camp. She says to her British custodians (and insta-compatriots), "In one hour, you have destroyed me. I have been a traitor all my life. All my life, everything I did . . . was for nothing. Nothing." She thinks to herself, "she had become insubstantial as smoke. If she was not French, she could not imagine what she might be. Maybe nothing" (295–96). The competing story they tell her of her parents' identity and national loyalty erases her citizenship and invalidates her life's work and her mission in one stroke, replacing her fixed identity with a political question mark.

Others try to tell her she is just swapping citizenship labels; but being told she is Welsh and that her parents (and unwittingly, she) have spied for the enemy nation imposes a complicated new identity that is unreal, leading her to say "I am the offspring of a mermaid and a sea cod" (296).[5] Robert is sure she will recover from her confusion, and when she responds that she won't, he tries to reassure her with, "Yes, you will, my little halibut" (297). Yet the endearment only underlines how all such labels are equally "impossible and ridiculous," merely an ideological exercise in creating the political equivalent of subspecies, yet with material repercussions and women being denied agency in categorizing themselves.

The new knowledge of her parents' loyalties in addition to her love for Robert, with his strong moral code (a direct contrast to the flaws exhibited by France's representatives), worsens Annique's quandary about her own responsibilities in the struggle between the two nations to which she is now tied. After her rage is spent, she recounts memories of a father who, despite the evidence of his British allegiance, loved France; Robert agrees, saying, "he was a man capable of loving more than one nation" (302). It is another moment in which the text acknowledges how fluid and gendered political identity can be since Robert and his fellow spies are forcing Annique to choose one side over the other: her father got to be his own decision-maker and is admired for it, but she is a woman, and they assume she must take her identity from descent or marriage. As Tamar Mayer observes, "*nation* . . . remains the property of men," and men retain the authority to determine the boundaries of a nation and label what is appropriate behavior for its citizens, women frequently occupying a very precarious position in that last group (1, 12, 14).

Robert's superior also turns out to be her Welsh grandfather by blood, and thus a symbol of the confluence of patriarchy and state authority: (Grand) Fatherland. He feels certain that she will easily select his country as her own.

He imagines her to be a "woman of strong, uncomplicated loyalties ... binding herself to him and his organization and to England," a process that he thinks will be aided by her desire for family (which now exists solely in England) and for Robert (310).[6] Despite all evidence to the contrary, he seems to think that a woman's national identity is "uncomplicated" and based on "natural" ties, such as bloodlines and marriage, and he believes that both will draw Annique to the British side (310).

The novel does not share his viewpoint, and despite Robert's personal integrity, the British side is painted in grey as well—literally his last name—making it clear that there is no blameless, perfect nation. The British secret service traffics in lies, it practices wrongful imprisonment, and its military intelligence brethren are all too willing to employ torture. Furthermore, when Annique escapes British custody and goes to fulfill one last duty to her French superior, the similarity between the two sides becomes even more pronounced. Her French handler gently but intractably declares a judgment of sexual indenture in a brothel as punishment for her affair with Robert and for revealing minor secrets to the British; he changes the order just as easily to a death sentence when he thinks she has revealed France's invasion plans. Her years of loyal service count for nothing as far as her nation's self-appointed (male) representative is concerned.

Ironically, others' definitions of her as having a derived or relational identity become the path to her survival. Her French boss retracts the death sentence when he learns of her parents' birth nationality and status as double agents; his about-face is partly to prevent that secret from being broadcast and making France and his unit a laughingstock. But an additional reason is that the revelation of Annique's Welsh blood revokes her Frenchness (and therefore invalidates a treason charge) in his eyes (as in her British grandfather's). In other words, like his British spy counterparts, he regards her identity as derived from her parent's birth and loyalties; her own lifelong beliefs and service to France are no longer relevant. This is in keeping with historical practices of gendered citizenship, with women considered chattel to be passed from one man or nation to another without agency or inalienable national identity, as Tammy M. Proctor and Deniz Kandiyoti have observed, respectively (more below). This relational way of defining Annique saves her life; she is excused for loving Robert and allegedly telling him French secrets because she is now considered British despite her involuntary draft into this identity.

But Annique herself does not relinquish her Frenchness easily, rejecting this zero-sum nationality game in favor of a kind of self-determined dual citizenship. For one, she succeeds in halting Napoleon's invasion by falsely confessing to the French that she has relayed his plans to the British, which is actually an act of French loyalty since it forestalls a deadly counterattack by Britain. She also insists on maintaining her identity as a French patriot by refusing to give information on her friends in that secret service network to the British. Even as she considers Robert's marriage proposal and his insistence that she'll have to pick one nation, she explains that her actions against Napoleon stem from her own critique of his choices when it comes to France's welfare and do not mean she is now British and willing to betray all her former colleagues: "I must fight against Napoleon, insofar as it lies within me. But marriage . . . It is a matter of loyalties, you understand. I cannot be English, even for you. I cannot tell you all I know. I have too many old friends—" (366). That ellipsis and the dash are a balancing act, a refusal to pick and choose between sides that are integral to her. She recognizes that loving a man with an adversarial profession and nationality has made her personal crisis of national identity a geopolitical matter, which will have lifelong implications for her and her birth country.

Her declaration is that of a heroine's impregnable citizenhood, rare for a genre which, as I noted earlier, acknowledges the presence of intergroup/international conflict but often sidesteps it by adopting simplistic and essentialist attitudes toward national identity and prioritizing the love narrative. Despite the novel's titular possessive that suggests that the heroine is to be identified via her spy lover/boss, *Spymaster's Lady* critiques derived female identity. Annique agrees to marry Robert and live in Britain but not to join his spy network, retaining her French identification while taking on a new self via newly discovered and forged relationships with British subjects. Robert understands and agrees to never pressure her into betraying her comrades.

The novel thus foregrounds the fragility of a complacent belief in stable political positions and hints at the true cost of hybridity, which is often offered as a solution to the multiple demands that people encounter under globalization and forced and voluntary international border crossings. This is even truer for women, who have been excluded from citizenship while also being suspected of being incapable of true national loyalties. Love, marriage, and familial ties elevate this tension for women, especially in wartime. As Proctor notes in her study of women's lives in Britain in World War I, women who married men from other nations or had family in other countries became suspect during the war. Popular and legal discourse treated their allegiances as always in question. Kandiyoti sees this in similar terms, arguing that "the regulation of gender is central to the articulation of cultural identity and difference. The identification of women as privileged bearers of corporate identities and boundary markers of their communities has had a deleterious effect on their emergence as full-fledged citizens of modern nation-states" (388). In other words, nations and communities use women to define themselves against an Other. But they do so partly by never giving female citizenship permanence and inviolable status.

Spy narratives stem from this perspective, though they swing between two sexist extremes: that women make natural spies because they are cunning and possess weak sexual morals or they make terrible spies because they tend to fall in love, forget the mission, and betray the nation. Annique, a female spy in love, thus faces the quintessential quandary of such women: how to control her citizenship and prove it to others. In an attempt to maintain a grip on shifting political identities and the demands attendant on them, she plays multiple roles. Her switches between professional role-playing and her personal identities (including that of lover) and others' attempts to construct who she is expose the gap between the essentialist idea of identity and its discursive reality. She is a hybrid subject by virtue of her gender and her profession, with love altering the political dimension of that self. It gives her new allies, both in the form of Robert as well as her powerful grandfather and his network, but she has to force them to acknowledge all the parts of her self. Love, in romance novels, is often meant to suggest a means to avoid fragmentation or unite one's splintered parts, but it can also mark the places where identities are always in crisis and under erasure. The idea that love can offer a complete, unified identity is the hegemonic narrative in romance, but the other narratives that it wrestles into submission, particularly when it comes to hybridity, are well worth examining.

Sherry Thomas's *My Beautiful Enemy* (2014), set in the overlap of the Qing and Victorian eras, hints at this as well. But it has a different approach to representing women's nationhood and citizenship in that it opens the door to discussions of the impact of Western colonization and globalization on the world. While Victorian romance is a small subset of historical romance, which is otherwise dominated by novels set in the Regency period, general fiction set in the Victorian era is a substantial part of publishing. In *Neo-Victorianism and the Memory of Empire* (2012), Elizabeth Ho argues that "the return to the Victorian in the present offers a highly visible, highly aestheticized code for confronting empire again and anew" (5). This explains the presence of so many neo-Victorian texts, all interested in "the aftermath of the empire and its reappearance in processes of globalization" (5). With these claims as my point of departure, I examine Thomas's novel, set in 1891 China and London and, via flashbacks, 1883 Chinese Turkestan (Sinkiang/Xinjiang). Through these settings, *My Beautiful Enemy* not only stages the challenges that women have faced in the recent past at the fault lines of cultural and racial identities but also acts as an allegory of what they continue to face. *My Beautiful Enemy*'s period setting looks back at colonial expansion but also serves to voice the contemporary (spatial and psychological) struggles of the female immigrant to the Anglophone Global North, with Victorian England standing for the North's continuing dominance in the global imaginary.[7]

In other words, while showing the influence of the British Empire on her Anglo-Chinese heroine in *My Beautiful Enemy*, Thomas's novel evokes today's boundaryless empire of globalization and the pressures it exerts on female immigrants from, and/or residents of, the Global South. It highlights the demands placed on women, especially immigrants, by new cultural imperatives that accompany globalization, specifically in relation to subject position, national identity, and belonging. The setting and period thus stage a conflict that is about our contemporary moment, when globalization is carrying the cultures of the Global North—particularly expectations of gender roles and display (as well as love and marriage)—across the planet. Women from the Global South experience these as normative and aspirational even while they live their lives in their home countries and doubly so if they leave those places to travel to the heart of the neo-empire of globalization.[8]

The average nonimmigrant woman from the Global North may not experience these cultural imperatives in ways identical to her immigrant counterparts, but she isn't exempt from the hegemonic cultural standards of the dominant group in her country either. This phenomenon is just more dramatically visible in *My Beautiful Enemy*. Indeed, the novel is a story of how an alien, as Sara Ahmed conceives the term, is not just one who travels to a "foreign" land but someone who is treated as an "outsider insider" in a community: "the alien is the one who does not belong in a nation space, and who is already defined as such by the Law. The alien is hence only a category within a given community of citizens or subjects: as the outsider inside, the alien takes on a spatial function, establishing relations of proximity and distance within the home(land). Aliens allow the demarcation of spaces of belonging: by coming too close to home, they establish the very necessity of policing the borders of knowable and inhabitable terrains" (3). Ahmed's framing of an alien as someone who functions to define what the homeland is, usually *inside* the border of a nation, is visible in Thomas's novels through the life of Bai Ying-Hua/Catherine Blade. She is a biracial nomad, an outsider everywhere, including in the land of her birth, someone whose familial and cultural loyalties play out across competing gender and national (British and Chinese) scripts and over geographic crossings.

In *My Beautiful Enemy*, the Sino-British heroine lives and moves across multiple cultures in nineteenth-century Qing China and Victorian England. The story of Bai Ying-Hua's parentage and youth—growing up as the illegitimate, mixed-race daughter of a woman who had been sold to a Shanghai brothel, then bought by an Englishman (who died while she was pregnant with his child), and finally ensconced as the concubine to a high-ranking Chinese noble—is narrated in the young adult prequel novel *The Hidden Blade* (set in 1870s imperial Peking/Beijing). That novel also tells of how Ying-Hua was raised to be a lady but struggled to achieve traditional feminine perfection when young. This gender struggle appears to have an underlying cultural twist, as if her biracial self lacks an essential Chineseness—her calligraphy and poetry is not sufficiently elegant, and no one thinks her comparable to her mother, the epitome of the cultured, graceful Chinese gentlewoman. In an expansion of her alienation, even that partial femininity is something Ying-Hua has to shed when she begins secretly training in martial arts (partly due to her nanny's worry about her bleak future as an Anglo-Chinese orphan) which inadvertently leads to a feud with another biracial warrior, Lin.[9]

When *My Beautiful Enemy* begins, it is 1891 and the prologue shows Ying-Hua on an England-bound ship in the midst of a brutal battle with Lin as she tries to save two British gentlewomen travelers. Soon after this incident, the first chapter shows her in London, now passing as a demure white British expat newly arrived from overseas. The contrast posed by her meek London persona to the warrior persona that readers saw in the prologue is disconcerting. Moreover, the shock experienced in this scene by Captain Leighton Atwood, who knew her in the past only in her warrior self, amplifies the reader's awareness of the artifice of Ying-Hua's politesse (mimicking Anglo upper-class femininity). We soon learn that Leighton was a former British foreign office staffer who was briefly her lover in China in 1883 and whom she tried to kill at the end of their affair.

The novel alternates between 1891 England to flashbacks of that earlier time, when Ying-Hua lived in the Chinese northwest (Turkestan/Xinjiang) and often posed as a Kazakh man. In this male disguise, she used her martial arts training to spy on local warlords for her foster father.[10] Addressed only by his noble honorific, Da-ren, he was exiled to a governorship there by the Imperial Court for his reformer zeal to modernize China, and she accompanied him to escape Lin. Her status as Da-ren's foster daughter puts her in a strange position in his household because she is neither servant nor a full gentlewoman because of her mother's concubinage. These 1883 Turkestan flashbacks are key to understanding her increasing alienation and existential solitude fueled by her mixed identity (of class and race) and the early death of her mother as well as her sense of inadequacy in comparison to her mother's traditionally feminine refinement and her seemingly hopeless quest for Da-ren's approval after her mother's death.

In other words, even before she comes to London in 1891, Ying-Hua is a misfit, an alien, in her native land, someone neither fully Anglo nor fully Chinese—especially in terms of upper-class gender expectations—due to birth, personal inclination, and a Western education (more on the last below). Furthermore, being Han Chinese in a Manchu dynasty puts her at a disadvantage even without her mixed birth.[11] Her name itself testifies to her alien status per Ahmed's definition: as Ying-Hua explains in *My Beautiful Enemy*, "Ying is the word for England, and Hua for China"—Ying-Hua is the outsider within (254). Her martial arts training separates her further from Chinese gender roles, and her decision to use that training to aid her father figure puts her at odds with the life of gentility he has raised her to assume.[12] Instead, as noted above, she dons the persona of a gruff Kazakh man and lives in the desert, a variation of Annique's roles in service of a nation, roles that keep such heroines split into multiple selves. The flashbacks tell us that this state of alienation, wandering, and unbelonging appeared to be ending when she and Leighton met and fell in love. But a subsequent misunderstanding about each other's true missions there—she thought he was a British spy, while he thought she was a Qing spy—led to their eight-year separation, during which Lin murdered the baby she had birthed a few months after Leighton left her.

When the novel's 1891 action in London begins, however, Catherine/Ying-Hua is posing as a British woman while on a mission for Da-ren, and the kind of racial/class passing she practices is a version of what spies might do as part of their jobs. But while she is on a covert op, so to speak, she is still not a government spy, since Da-ren is out of favor with the Chinese ruling family. Her passing in London is part of her quest to locate a Buddhist artifact that might help Da-ren fund China's rise against other encroaching empires. It is in service of this cause that she conceals her other self; instead, she acts the role of the British woman and uses her acquired ability to speak the Queen's English, thanks to an English tutor who worked for Da-ren.

She is also able to pass as a white British woman newly arrived from overseas because of her physical characteristics—Thomas indicates that Ying-Hua does not fit Western stereotypes of Chineseness, having dark hair but slate-blue double-lidded eyes and red lips. Her acceptance in Victorian England, where there is a rigid definition of ethnic Englishness, suggests that these markers are enough for her to be read as white. While the disguise trope is common in romance novels (such as a commoner imitating a lady or vice versa, or as chap. 2 shows, women passing for whatever version of womanhood is idealized in a particular moment), Ying-Hua's performance in England is distinctive because of the biracial narrative underneath.[13]

Despite her skilled ethnic and class passing, she feels herself to be a misfit in all cultures, an oddity who violates gender, class, and ethnic norms and has only a facade to exhibit, a simulation of the authenticity that she has been unable to acquire from the land of her birth through a natural osmosis or from the imagined one of her paternal ancestry through tutoring. In other words, she is a woman who has straddled cultures and gender roles since birth, a nomad and an alien. Time and geographic journeys have only magnified the seeming mutual exclusivity of her identities, alienating her from different communities even as she successfully passes in all. Her intent in London is to complete her search while posing as Catherine Blade and then return to China, but the encounter with Leighton brings all her conflicting selves, loves, loyalties, losses, and missions to a head. This crisis is exacerbated when she realizes that her nemesis, Lin, survived their shipboard fight and is working as a mercenary to destabilize the British. He wants to end her life by fomenting fears of a conspiracy against the British Empire, and his plan is to expose the fact that she is not a white British subject and have her arrested as a Chinese agent. Her ethnonational status and allegiance are thus at the heart of the conflict.

The novel's foregrounding of Ying-Hua/Catherine's split selves, as noted earlier, echoes one of the preoccupations of the genre, resonating as it does with the predominantly female readership and its familiarity with being forced to choose between different false binaries. Thomas goes a step further, casting Ying-Hua's selves across ethnonational lines. It is a tale not just of the kinds of socioeconomic and civic demands all women face, and that romance fiction represents, but of the specific ones that Western colonization has imposed and neo-imperial ideology now inflicts on women in the Global South, particularly those who also immigrate to the geographic centers from which those ideologies radiate. That this tale is set in 1891 England, when Queen Victoria's empire was at its peak, is deliberate. It is a moment when specific linguistic and gender norms were dispersed across the globe from the capital of the empire, just as in the present moment, when globalization, specifically Anglo-American neoliberalism, has dispersed specific ideologies of normativity to the world, especially the Global South. Just as contemporary women (particularly in the Global South) labor to fit the Anglo expectations of beauty and behavior found in Hollywood cinema, other media, and social media (see footnote 5), ideas about the ideal woman in late-Qing period China (the end of the nineteenth century) were heavily influenced by European ones.

Thomas's Ying-Hua can be read as a woman of this moment, one resulting from China's political defeats at the hands of British, American, and other European empires, which lead to internal and external pressures to rethink the existing Confucian value system, including gender roles and human worth overall. The history of Western influence on Chinese expectations of the ideal woman is summarized by Xia Xiaohong in "The Great Diversity of Women Exemplars in China of Late Qing." Xia argues that while many editions of the book *Biographies of Exemplary Women* had disseminated models of ideal women since 2 BCE, these models required reconsideration following China's increasing contact with the West, as well as its loss of power over the Qing period. Surveying the biographies of Western women (printed in books and columns in local women's newspapers), Xia notes the inclusion of women like "Harriet Beecher Stowe . . . Queen Victoria, Jean-Marie Roland (better known as Madame Roland), Johanna von Putkammer (Otto von Bismarck's wife), and Florence Nightingale" (222). Xia also mentions Queen Catherine of Russia and notes the special emphasis in these compilations on revolutionaries like French anarchist Louise Michel, Charlotte Corday, Anita Garibaldi, writer Madame de Stael, suffrage activist Dame Millicent Fawcett, and two Russian nihilists. One of these collections by Yang Qianli was meant by Yang for use as a textbook and its Western figures as models for Chinese women for the future. Such books, claims Xia, especially the ones that highlighted the independence or revolutionary spirit of these figures (rather than their status as wives of great men, as some versions did) trained girls to be New Women (227).[14] Thomas's neo-Victorian, neo-Qing novel taps into this moment of competing Chinese and Western norms of femininity.

Although she does not actually read any of the abovenamed texts and technically grows up about a decade prior to their dissemination, Ying-Hua can be read as one of the Qing-era women who encountered this historical change in female role models. Thus, apart from encountering the same expectations that all romance heroines face, Ying-Hua must address ethnoracial and linguistic expectations both from her domestic world (the old Chinese ideal of gentlewomanly grace and obedience to patriarchy) and from the world that has intruded on it (the new ideal of boldness and educated self-sufficiency). As a teenager in 1870s Peking, she is meant to walk, speak, dress, and be artistic with her mother's lauded grace, as described in the prequel novel *The Hidden Blade*. But she is also forced to become a warrior (in a Chinese martial arts tradition) so her family and she can survive personal misfortune, much of it resulting from China's political weakening. Moreover, she receives a Western education and encounters Western gender norms—the English tutor gives her Austen's *Pride and Prejudice,* starring a beloved nonconformist heroine—and marvels at the freedom these women appear to possess.

When she travels to England in 1891 then, Ying-Hua is already a complicated citizen marked by the footprints of multiple nations. London is the heart of an empire whose early forays into her birthplace have left her with competing legacies, physiological and ideological. In addition to her Anglo education, and alongside inheriting the repercussions of her mother's concubinage following the death of her British keeper (Ying-Hua's father), our heroine has to contend with other crisscrossing sociopolitical consequences: British paternity and Han maternity, her emotionally distant Manchu father figure (whose predictions of cultural and political defeat at the hands of the rising West are ignored by the Chinese throne), a heart broken by an Englishman, and a lonely pregnancy followed by solitude after her Anglo-Chinese nemesis murders her baby. Despite the weight of this complex history, she has to conceal her genealogy and Chinese upbringing when in England and display the manners and mannerisms prized by the British upper class if she is to move in those circles till she completes her mission.

She knows she may have to pay a price, socially and legally, if her heritage, athleticism, or lethal skills come to light, hence her charade as Catherine Blade.[15] When asked to describe how she saved the British ladies on the ship, for instance, Ying-Hua is relieved that no one witnessed "the details of [her] strength and dexterity," and she downplays the incident with, "I had the advantage of surprise on my side, a great deal of luck, and the experience of taking a pot to a miscreant's head once in a while" (17). Leighton, who knew her as a deadly Central Asian warrior woman disguised as a coarse horseman, observes her well-mannered female display in disbelief. He cannot fathom her being a lady, in this or in any culture: "To experience her speaking the Queen's English almost without accent and in general conducting herself with ladylike modesty—his disorientation, fierce to begin with, turned dizzying.... He could not place her in [China], a place that hid its women behind walled courtyards and covered litters. Could not imagine her without a fast horse and a gleaming sword. It would be like locking a wolf in a broom cupboard.... He could not get used to her demureness: The most decorous of spinster aunts would barely rival her in propriety" (38–39).

Ying-Hua has become an alien to Leighton, both in terms of gender presentation, class position, and ethnicity; she is unnerving to him because her mannerisms resemble those of British ladies and the lethal woman he knew seems to be restrained (or has restrained herself) in normative femininity. But she herself doesn't see the role-playing as a contradiction. She believes that if they had married, she could have fit easily into his British world despite having lived as a "nomad girl" because of "the long years [in China] confined behind high walls, the sea of etiquette through which she swam daily, the elaborate pretense she was capable of putting on, to appear the most docile and ladylike of creatures. She would not have had a bit of trouble negotiating the relatively uncomplicated English rules of politesse" (76). In other words, Ying-Hua has been passing *all* her life in terms of gender role conformity, which in fact contributes to her greater skill in racial passing. Forced to present as a genteel Chinese lady at home before and even after she becomes a warrior, the text suggests, has given her the faculty to don different gender, class, and ethnic identities in China and in Britain.

It is not hard to see the story as representing the author's trajectory—her grandparents went to English-language colleges and had adopted a Western sensibility, making them something of an oddity in northwest China in the early twentieth century (Bette-Lee Fox). Many of Thomas's family members immigrated to the US, and her mother moved there to study while Thomas stayed behind and arrived in the US later. She has talked about being a teenager at the time and feeling like a misfit (linguistically and culturally), struggling with the immature stories in children's primers in ESL classes when her literary sensibilities were far more developed due to linguistic fluency in Chinese and a wider acquaintance with Chinese literature.[16] She gained proficiency in English partly by reading romance novels with the help of a Chinese-English dictionary. So the specific allegory within *My Beautiful Enemy* can be traced to the fact that Thomas is a Chinese immigrant to the United States.

But even without this possible autobiographical component, Ying-Hua's journey reflects elements of contemporary women's self-restructuring when faced with multiple cultures and differing expectations, especially the well-documented journeys of recent immigrant women. Caroline Plüss discusses this phenomenon in her study of Chinese-Singaporean repeat migrant women.[17] She argues that migrants are deemed different by locals, and this difference is used to block their ability to "access new and desired resources" (126). Per her survey of women migrants, some of them change their characteristics to resemble the local majority community in order to fit in and to gain the resources needed to build their cultural capital, and "forge hybrid or cosmopolitan cultural identities" in the process: "To overcome such exclusion and devaluation, migrants can try to construct new cultural capital by changing some of their cultural characteristics and, therewith, their identifications (Plüss 2005, 2011). Such changes often involve adopting characteristics of those who control access to desired resources" (126).

Ying-Hua experiences similar demands and displays such adaptive behavior (as Thomas has done: beginning her career in a publishing industry that traditionally centers the white Anglo-American experience by writing English-language romance novels with Victorian characters and from a white subject position). Interestingly, Plüss adds that in some cases hybrid identity might include "asserting cultural characteristics" that the migrant possesses and the resource-holders consider important, thus turning a potential liability on the migrant's part to an asset. Both Thomas and our heroine construct such a hybrid, transcultural identity in the sense of performing one cultural self over another when needed to achieve personal, familial, and national goals—for Ying-Hua, this includes fighting off physical dangers and unencrypting Pali verses on ancient tablets to locate a historical treasure, and doing so while presenting as British when necessary and Chinese at other times.

In effect, the novel performs two actions: it uses its Victorian setting to tell a historically faithful tale of a woman with a mixed-race identity forged by the impact of British influence in China in the late Qing period; second, when read through Plüss's analysis, and in light of Thomas's own trajectory, it tells a story of how contemporary women in the Global South may cope with living in a cultural neocolony, this one created by globalization (particularly via mass media that is manufactured in the North). It also hints at how these new visions of womanhood and personhood in both eras can force the formation of a hybrid identity, with one face masking many. Such masking becomes even more pronounced for those who migrate to neocolonial metropoles. This hybridity, a dialectical resolution for an ongoing contemporary dualism, is one that Thomas accomplishes for Ying-Hua by having her selectively adopt the "characteristics of those who control access to desired resources" without giving up existing characteristics (Plüss 126). In other words, Ying-Hua/Catherine is a hybrid character, putting on or taking off one of her many selves depending on the nation-space in which she finds herself, and the novel foregrounds this cultural negotiation and its costs via her interactions with others in these settings.

Thomas also achieves hybridity for Ying-Hua through a deft fusion of the traits of Anglo-American romance with a genre that is Chinese in origin. Moreover, after a decade of only publishing white Regency/Victorian romance, the emphasis Thomas places in this novel on Chinese history and culture suggests the kind of "asserting [of] cultural characteristics" that Plüss observes of immigrants. To elaborate, My Beautiful Enemy possesses a sophisticated multiculturalism that goes beyond the inclusion of the names and descriptions of multiracial and multiethnic characters' skin, hair, cuisine, clothing, and ethnocultural festivals.[18] Both novels in the duology draw on a genre called wuxia, a literary and cinematic form that has a centuries-long history in mainland China, as well as Hong Kong and Taiwan. While I argue elsewhere that Thomas's use of wuxia is a transculturation of the romance genre, what is relevant here is her adaptation of wuxia and how it can tackle the binary of citizenship and ethnonationality that Ying-Hua faces.[19] As I note there, in explaining the wuxia genre, William Leung says that the phrase wuxia stands for an instantly recognizable form of "narrative where traditional ideas about good and evil are played out in the stylish adventures of skillful, spiritually attuned warriors" (43). Typical structural features of wuxia fictions are "larger-than-life heroes, inventive rewriting of historical events, celebrations of heroic comradeship and dazzling fighting sequences" (43). Additionally, scholar Raechel Dumas observes that wuxia's key features were "the construction of a world of martial arts characterized by fantastic depictions of local spaces of the past, superhuman feats, and, often, dramatic and even dangerous romantic liaisons."[20] Thomas, who grew up in China, mentions wuxia as an inspiration for these novels on her site. Without explicit mention of the term in the novels themselves, she fuses the hallmarks of wuxia and wuxia pian (wuxia cinema) with a second-chance-at-love plot and the historical subgenre, both staples in mass-market Western romance.[21] In drawing on wuxia, Thomas brings to romance new possibilities of female motivation and action as well as plot lines based on notions of duty and happiness from another literary and cinematic culture. This also stretches the romance genre beyond its current circumference, especially in imagining a nonderivative, nonbinary version of women's national identification and citizenship.[22]

Wuxia encounters occur in what is termed *jianghu* (or *jiang hu*, literally "lakes and rivers," loosely meaning an underworld distinct from the quotidian political state, itself called *jia guo*) (Ken-Fang Lee 284). Thomas highlights Ying-Hua's position between these two worlds throughout the novels, in addition to juxtaposing Peking (Beijing) against Xinjiang (Chinese Turkestan), and China against England. The martial training Ying-Hua started as a teenager, and her later decision to use that training to aid Da-ren, leads her into *jianghu*, a feud-filled, realism-defying space. The flashbacks to 1883 that narrate her initial acquaintance with Leighton tell us that she might have exited *jianghu* when she fell in love, but their misunderstanding resulted in her resigning herself to this underworld, outside of romantic and national belonging and political citizenship, and in conflict with various state powers.

It is a classic wuxia story since ethnic and national identity and its struggles are integral to the genre—scholars argue that wuxia has been about Chinese nationalism and establishing authentic Chineseness since its start. Stephen Teo says that "Within wuxia literature itself, it has long been the practice to regard xia as a concept often equivalent to a declaration of the national" (10). He points out that wuxia cinema was an expression of China's "industrial nationalism" alongside a desire to articulate Chinese nationalism through "traditional, native

genres" (10, 41–42).[23] In other words, wuxia cinema's "historicist" quality—
it's typically a period costume drama—was a way to create Chinese identity based on the past but it contained a modern, transnational layer as well.
Thomas brings this Janus quality into Ying-Hua's young adult and adult
romance novels through a heroine who straddles multiple age-old and modern
sensibilities and expands romance fiction's political field of vision.

In keeping with the wuxia genre's dual interest in the old and new, past and
present ethnic and national identity is a key theme in *My Beautiful Enemy*. The
motif is visible in Ying-Hua's hybrid identity of British and Chinese heritage
and her entanglement with nineteenth-century Chinese national politics and
British meddling in Asia (with its subtext of contemporary national identity
conflicts). Ying-Hua, like Annique, is embroiled in a personal and national
struggle in parallel with the romance plot. The latter leads her on the larger quest
for her community as represented by her reformist Chinese foster father (versus
the short-sighted Manchu rulers who fail to see that Britain's growing power
is tied to its evolving modernity). In this, she fulfills the wuxia feature of "the
xia or knight-errant [acting] as an agent of history, conscious of his or her role
in shaping events and the destiny of the nation" (Stephen Teo 7). Ying-Hua is
key to imagining a China (and by extension Chineseness) that can be modern
and yet true to its past identity, steeped in mainland traditions and yet able to
instrumentalize other cultural traits.

This is in line with Rong Cai's observation that "the knights' interactions
with orthodoxy ... are as exciting as their private acts of vengeance," suggesting
that the stories are not only about personal feuds for wrongs done but also about
a fight for a larger just cause in the face of state or institutional ossification. This
is visible in Ying-Hua's service towards her foster father's goals (more on this
below), but her mission gets muddied by non-Chinese political actors in the
form of Leighton and those he represents. In 1883 Turkestan, he is posing as a
surveyor but secretly spying for Britain while Ying-Hua is seeking information
for her foster father by spying on local warlords and their factions.[24] The deserts
of Chinese Turkestan function as *jianghu*, where Ying-Hua in her Kazakh male
persona first encounters Leighton in a tavern and then grudgingly allows him to
accompany her on her journey. He sees past her facade but understands that her
warrior skills are not fake even if her male presentation is. His easy acceptance
of her multiple mysterious selves leads to their eventual romantic involvement.
But their national differences mean that the couple's relationship in *jianghu*
goes from love to heartbreak. In other words, in keeping with the romance
genre's imperative for some obstacle to be resolved and also demonstrating the
abovementioned claim that wuxia can feature "dangerous romantic liaisons,"

Thomas complicates Ying-Hua's relationship with Leighton using cultural as well as political factors that put multiple national loyalties at cross-purposes.

As noted earlier, it is understandable that Thomas, a Chinese immigrant to the US, centralizes the issue of nationality (making it responsible for the novel's point of ritual death, in fact). Ken-fang Lee argues that the wuxia genre, especially the wandering knight, is key for Chinese in the diaspora to imagine a China they cannot otherwise access (because they or their parents emigrated from the mainland to Taiwan or elsewhere). As he puts it, "This wandering spirit can be seen [as] a specter of the modern Chinese diaspora. Those Chinese émigrés leave native homeland and inhabit another world (Ng 1999: 601–602), but still feel affiliated with Chinese culture" (286). This tension is dramatized in two ways in *My Beautiful Enemy*: one, Ying-Hua has to deal with the fallout of disagreements among her Chinese compatriots over national vision and the strategies to build a stronger China, a struggle in which she chooses tactics not authorized by the existing Chinese government (a wuxia trait); two, her own national self is divided, with the Chinese half warring with the British one, as projected onto Leighton, the British Empire's representative.

Apart from grounding the novels in wuxia themes, Thomas deploys other wuxia elements throughout the duology that are helpful in understanding Ying-Hua's journey as a heroine constructing herself across many worlds. In distinguishing wuxia cinema from kung fu film, for example, Stephen Teo notes that wuxia is associated in Chinese film mythology with developing one's qi, which allows for flight with swordplay (as well as the use of other weapons) (5). Ying-Hua is this kind of *qi*-warrior, specifically a *nuxia*, or female righteous knight-errant who employs martial means that are almost supernatural. To be sure, William Leung has noted that female xia (*nuxia*) were secondary to the Confucian prioritization of the male hero's adventures, despite having appeared in the literature since the tenth century. But Thomas's novel rejects the stereotype of the woman as lesser or less central to the story even as it maintains some *nuxia* conventions, such as in the origin story of the heroine: similar to the story of *nuxia* Nie Yinniang recounted by Rong Cai, *The Hidden Blade* shows that Ying-Hua's life in *jianghu* began during childhood and it also draws on other motifs from wuxia tales of women warriors.[25]

The female knight is an old, staple character type in Chinese literature and in wuxia film, as scholars Li Wai-Yee and Catherine Gomes have shown, respectively.[26] Thomas begins her story with this type and a world whose gender conventions are those of wuxia tales, but she alters them as the plot unfolds. Initially, the novel establishes a gulf between living an independent warrior life and the traditional feminine one, a theme many have noted is common in *nuxia* stories. The theme appears in mass-market romance as well, with many heroines chafing against gender prescriptions, physical and economic. (See chap. 2.) As with Western gender norms, there is a binary at play in wuxia that *My Beautiful Enemy* first stages—a warrior woman cannot be sexual or a mother. Instead, she must be a wanderer without a home, living for honor and conflict alone, a nomad whose relationship to the official nation and community is nebulous. As Cai observes, women warriors in wuxia are frequently divested of the feminine because they fall outside gender expectations; subsequently, they are often divorced from domesticity and family (446–48). Furthermore, "To maintain gender coherence, the woman has to renounce the essence of femininity, motherhood, thus avoiding a dangerous confusion and impasse. Although female knights-errant in *wuxia* fiction take part in fighting and may consequently cause death, they are rarely mothers" (448). He also says that the traditional "martial arts imagination" de-eroticizes the woman warrior: "A defeminized being vacated from the conventional pattern of domesticity, feminine charm, and sexuality, the woman warrior is neither enchanted nor disenchanted by love" (448). Stephen Teo notes that female knights-errant often don masculine garb and indeed that "a woman, in order to be seen to have the attributes of *wen* and *wu* applied to her self, must first be transformed into a man [in the genre]" (118). (*Wen* is the civilian-scholar quality and *wu* is the martial quality.)

Thomas starts our heroine's journey in *The Hidden Blade* from this convention that warrior and womanliness do not go together and the flashbacks in *My Beautiful Enemy* show it in her life as a young woman. I've already touched on how her own personality does not lend itself to the ideal of upper-class Chinese womanhood and that her later training in martial arts, and then espionage practices in Turkestan, exacerbates her alienation from that model. When Leighton meets her there for the first time, she presents as rough and disheveled and continues so in public throughout their acquaintance. After the split from Leighton, she is pregnant but emotionally isolated and then becomes unmothered following her child's murder. Losing her lover and her baby underlines her separation from traditional heterosexual womanhood, and she wanders for almost a decade in the *nuxia* persona. As mentioned above, the issue of the incompatibility of femininity and "masculine" action recurs in exactly the opposite way when she is in England—while living as a *jianghu* warrior in China seems incompatible with having a traditional woman's life, posing as a gentlewoman in Britain necessitates concealing any martial or androgynous qualities.

When love, marriage, and motherhood—the core drivers of a mainstream romance novel narrative—prove elusive for Ying-Hua in Xinjiang/Turkestan,

My Beautiful Enemy reveals other impulses that propel her, which are tied to her community obligations. Cai mentions "loyalty to one's master and friends" and "chivalric justice" in a discussion of wuxia (445) and Karl Kao explains that xia tales feature two kinds of reciprocity (termed *bao* and *baoying*) that are key to Chinese sociocultural life; the former suggests repayment for good and bad deeds and the latter, some version of divine reflexive retribution visited on a person (120, 125). Thomas infuses the Anglospheric romance with *bao*, which plays a role in the heroine eventually conquering the contradictions of her outsider-insider status. In effect, Ying-Hua's dialectical identity rests on the wuxia narrative drive of *bao* reciprocity; she acts from both kinds of *bao* (paying back good and bad actions), a path that finally unites her selves. Her loyalty to her foster father *and* personal vendetta power the plot, with the former leading her on a larger quest for her kinship community and the latter leading to the private pursuit of justice against an evildoer—the man who killed her baby. The two kinds of *bao* also converge in her interactions with Leighton, her eponymous beautiful enemy in both a national and personal sense.

Ying-Hua feels like she owes Da-ren her loyalty because he supported her even after her mother's death and pays him back through her spying in Turkestan, her dangerous mission to Britain and, in the end, to Ningxia/Ning-hsia province in northern China to locate the treasure he seeks. *Bao* as grateful recompense is thus the key motive for her actions in this sphere, and while there are examples of a similar sense of obligation felt by romance heroines in mass-market romance, the wuxia tradition frames this first obligation in her life as the most important one, placing family (filial piety) above the romance in the wider arc of the duology. Thus, an element of Ying-Hua's Confucian Chineseness is prioritized over the affective individualism that is integral to romance fiction as well as foundational to the post-Enlightenment Anglo-European self and Western nationhood.[27]

Bao related to personal vengeance is the driving force of Ying-Hua's actions toward Lin after he murders her daughter, and she kills him at the end with Leighton's assistance. She and Lin are mirrored Anglo-Chinese orphans (as mentioned in note 6), but Lin refuses to value his mixed ancestry, rejecting it and instead selling his deadly skills to the highest bidding state against the countries of his parents. Ying-Hua's triumph over him suggests the long-term sustainable nature of her evolving hybridity over his self-hating one. Additionally, Thomas includes vengeful *bao* or righteous action separate from personal interest as well; the flashbacks in *My Beautiful Enemy* tell us about a second manifestation of *bao* that is unusual to the romance tradition: Ying-Hua's attempt to kill Leighton via poison in 1883.[28] Her action is brought on by her sense of justice when she believes he toyed with her while he was following his own national agenda that ran counter to hers. It is an error stemming from an extreme application of wuxia principles: punishing someone who not only betrays the knight herself but also appears to threaten a larger just cause—in her case, her father's vision of a strong China.

She later comes to regret her action and believes that her childless state is a form of punishment for her unjust act (*baoying*). She wanders for eight years, devoting herself to her father's goal of bettering China while believing that she is the murderess of her baby's father. Having done Leighton harm, when she meets him years later, she attempts to practice beneficent *bao*: offering *qi* therapy to lessen the pain of the long-term disability she has caused, protecting his fiancée despite her malice, and even withholding from him the crushing revelation of their baby's short life and murder. *My Beautiful Enemy* thus allows three kinds of narrative paths or agency for Ying-Hua: acting per grateful *bao* in a plot about filial piety, expressing vengeful *bao* in confrontations with her old nemesis, and a mix of both kinds toward her lover. Her filial piety, romantic love, and martial power stem from her Chinese upbringing *and* her willingness to step outside its limits. The positive effects of this choice benefit more than one nation—killing Lin prevents a further clash between imperial powers, including France—and demonstrates the worth of her many selves working in concert.

This dialectical impulse is also what overrides the split between a pair-bonded female self and warrior self (which is tied to celibacy and solitude). Thomas overcomes the problem by creating a blended narrative, which involves altering the conventions of both parent genres (romance fiction and wuxia). She remaps both the trajectory of lonely vengeance and righteousness that is dictated by wuxia for the female knight as well as the traditional markers of settled coupledom dictated by mass-market romance while also allowing Ying-Hua an ethnonational flexibility. Ying-Hua gets her revenge against Lin but also a stable relationship with Leighton without being reintegrated into a prescribed gender role or exclusionary statehood. Where the gender role is concerned, she is depicted as the less voluble and less overtly nurturing or emotional partner throughout *My Beautiful Enemy*. It is Leighton who has the traditionally feminine role and does emotion work; he takes joy in cooking and caring for her, both during their initial relationship in 1883 and after they reunite in 1891. Her gender display of androgyny or presenting as male, which is a commonplace of *nuxia* stories, is a prominent feature throughout the novel, as is a strategic display of traditional feminine traits and nationalities.[29] She dresses as a man when she and Leighton meet and have an affair in China, and she sustains that act at length. The novel also challenges other heterosexist gender commonplaces in that we never learn if the couple have another child after they marry, skirting one of the seminal expectations of heterosexual romance—the heteronormative family centered around romanticized motherhood (Kamblé, *Making Meaning* 141).

The novel ends with the suggestion that Ying-Hua will not be confined to one national self. Indeed, she leaves England after she and Leighton pledge themselves to one another and travels to Ningxia/Ning-hsia province in China with Da-ren to complete her quest for the artifact; in this way, the novel indicates that the love plot may not always conform to the idea of joint adventure promised by the genre's HEA for its more peripatetic protagonists, nor will Ying-Hua have to prioritize her husband's allegiances or obligations.[30] In other words, her mission in support of Da-ren and his reformist hopes for China both preserves her Chinese *nuxia* and familial self alongside her British heritage and romantic relationship. After her search for treasure is complete, Leighton travels to China to ask Da-ren's permission to marry her and it is hinted that they will travel across Asia and perhaps re-enter *jianghu* in the future without settling into a traditional life. The episode symbolically preserves her natal national ties and the warrior-self she built in her time as *nuxia* even post their betrothal.

—∭—

The theme of conflicting national identities or some form of community membership comes up often in romance, women's citizenship and political identity having always been contingent and precarious and therefore of concern to the genre, which traditionally centers women. Moreover, as noted earlier, marriage can destabilize women's nationalities at various points in history, with states giving or withdrawing rights and protections from them based on their relationships with men or the state project du jour. While analyzing women's shifting status in anti- and post-colonial nationalist discourse that is based in patriarchal tradition, Kandiyoti says:

> Wherever women continue to serve as boundary markers between different
> national, ethnic, and religious collectivities, their emergence as full-fledged
> citizens will be jeopardised, and whatever rights they may have achieved
> during one stage of nation-building may be sacrificed on the altar of identity
> politics during another.
>   Women may be controlled in different ways in the interests of demarcating
> and preserving the identities of national/ethnic collectivities. As Anthias and
> Yuval-Davis point out, regulations concerning who a woman can marry and the
> legal status of her offspring aim at reproducing the boundaries of the symbolic
> identity of their group. (382)

Women are political pawns, traded, labeled, and exchanged (along with their children) in an ideological chess game of a community's self-assertion through difference. *My Beautiful Enemy*'s take on this niggling problem (of women being denied multiple citizenships and identities) is refracted through wuxia conventions and permits another route to imagining its resolution. In eventually reuniting Ying-Hua with Leighton in England after years of an ethnonational misunderstanding and having her return to China and succeed in her mission to regain a lost piece of Chinese religious history, the novel proposes a dialectically chosen identity for the biracial, once-alienated heroine.

With its warrior heroine and setting (neither solely Western or white), Thomas's duology is part of a strain of the genre that is broadening the possibilities of cultural representation to foreground not just women of previously elided races and ethnicities but other genres with their own cultural and literary traditions, possessed of their specific limitations and strengths. Late Qing China and the politics of imperial Europe shape Bai Ying-Hua into a multifaceted protagonist; she is neither the subservient Oriental figure that is still the dominant stereotype of Asian women, nor the frivolous or genteel Anglo-European associated with the Victorian "Angel in the House," nor the anachronistic Caucasian kickass or bluestocking more commonly found in historical romance. As a *nuxia*, she brings the authority of another genre from a different culture to the romance heroine and thus a capacity to expand the romance's character and narrative boundaries. In writing a wuxia romance, Thomas thus writes both eastward, toward the Chinese genre, as writers in the Chinese diaspora have done since the 1930s, and westward to romance, expanding its narrative landscape and the possibilities for national identity and heroic action by the heroine.

Ying-Hua gets a happy ending in both romance and wuxia terms but without glossing over the real heartbreak and long struggles around bicultural and biracial identity in a world that continues to be marked by the intersecting legacies of colonialism, racism, and sexism. As noted earlier, the novel confronts the reality of gender prescriptions in different cultures. Moreover, Ying-Hua's biracial birth and facades provide a reminder not just of colonial histories but also of the continuing political and cultural impact that the British Empire and the Global North have on populations across the globe, especially women consumers of Anglospheric media (from all classes).

My Beautiful Enemy also confronts the truth of the Othering of the self for the woman from the Global South living in the Global North by foregrounding Ying-Hua's status as an outsider in the British Isles. When innocently asked by Leighton's brother why an Englishwoman like her waited so many years to come to England from the Far East, she speaks tellingly of the very alienation that Sarah Ahmed conceptualizes: "Sometimes, I, too, wonder why I didn't venture out of China sooner—I'd always wished to see England, and in China I will always remain a foreigner. But the familiar does have a powerful hold. And part of me was afraid that perhaps in England, too, I would always be a foreigner" (14). She is not wrong to fear that she would be an alien there. Her physical traits, as listed earlier, mean she can evade European racist discourse, but she occupies a precarious state as a mixed-race person passing as fully white and upper class in England. Her Othering in China, for both racial and gender reasons, is done by her intimates, while in the British Isles, the care that she and Leighton take to not reveal her Chinese and *nuxia* identities highlights colonial structural inequality and throws Britain's class hierarchies and racialized political machinations into stark relief.

It is an unavoidable fact at the end of *My Beautiful Enemy* that Ying-Hua's true self, Anglo and Chinese, may never be fully expressed outside of her marriage if she and Leighton are in England or China. But the novel does not sacrifice one for the other—she was and continues to be a *nuxia* with a Chinese mother, a white British father, a Chinese foster father, and a white British husband. She may have to continue wearing many faces, masking all but one at any given time, yet at least with the hero, she can be all of them. As with many romances that foreground or allude to issues of a woman's right to be accepted in her full self, this is the personal resolution the genre offers to a larger political problem, articulating the local relationship as the first step in a heroine's march to a more global self-assertion and coherence.

NOTES

1. Marshall sees modern citizenship (i.e., full membership in a society) as endowing a "uniform collection of rights and duties," leading to equality among members (12, 28). He also sees citizenship as comprising of a civil, political, and social element, with the first relating to rights that ensure individual freedoms, the second to the right to participate in political power, and the third to the "right to a modicum of economic welfare and security," "to share to the full in the social heritage and to live the life of a civilized being according to the standards prevailing in the society" (10–11).

2. Jaggar highlights the work of feminists who contest citizenship conceived on exclusionary "masculine norms," and advocate for one based on other characteristics and activities usually associated with women, for instance, "the social, the domestic, and the personal rather than on the state and the market" (95). While the heroines in my chosen texts are closer to the traditional

citizenship model—the women act in the public sphere and are spy-warriors—these gender-corrected conceptions of citizenship can be applied to other romance novels where a heroine's citizenship does not concern international conflict or competition (93).

3. See Louis Althusser's *Lenin and Philosophy* where he discusses "interpellation" or "hailing" as a way through which powerful ideological structures make people into a subject within that ideology.

4. See Julie Mostov's "Sexing the Nation, Desexing the Body" in *Gender Ironies of Nationalism*.

5. For a Welsh person to be hailed as a British subject is arguably equivalent to such an odd union, if not an act of denying Welsh nationality.

6. His use of "England" rather than "Britain" or the "United Kingdom" is a fracture in the text—to conflate Britain with England is to call up the history of the takeover of Wales by a different nation. Despite Annique/Anne's Welsh or Celtic ethnicity, she is supposed to be loyal to England and her Welshness is then just as subsumed as her Frenchness. In other words, her citizenship and national identity are always under erasure.

7. As Nour Dados and Raewyn Connell note, the use of the term "Global South" (and by extension, Global North) instead of "Third World" or "Periphery" highlights "geopolitical relations of power" rather than development or cultural difference (12). The "Global South" covers parts of Asia, Africa, Oceania, and Latin America. The term was brought into use when economically and politically marginalized countries saw their interests as being in conflict with both First and Second World industrial countries. It became even more common in academic circles as the Cold War ended and there was growing resistance to the economic might of the "old imperial centers" (13). Dados and Connell note that the term "references an entire history of colonialism, neo-imperialism, and differential economic and social change through which large inequalities in living standards, life expectancy and access to resources are maintained" (13).

8. Numerous studies have examined this phenomenon, often in terms of the effect of the hegemonic status of Anglo beauty standards on Hispanic, African, African American, and Asian women and of the spread of Western values in general. In her dissertation on the influence of global media on South Korean women, Jong Mi Kim provides numerous examples of how women can potentially feel themselves to be Other and perhaps inferior to Western women (128, 135, 138).

9. Lin and she are both outsiders in Chinese society because of their biracial status. While this could have been grounds for solidarity, their training by different masters and factions pits them against each other, a common trope in the Chinese wuxia genre. (See also note 14.) In the novel, his status as

her nemesis could also be read as an allegory for an internal struggle about "Eurasianness" experienced by biracial Chinese in China. As Vicky Lee notes, biracial Chinese inhabited a fluctuating social position in port cities like Shanghai versus foreign settlements in places like Chengdu in the late nineteenth century, some enjoying privileges when the British Empire was powerful. But in other cases, biracial persons found themselves ostracized and/or in danger when anti-foreign sentiment was high and forced to change their names and/or choose one ethnicity at the cost of the other (23–24).

10. The Hua Mulan legend is an allusion, but there is no explicit mention of Mulan as an ideal Ying-Hua aspires to during her own upbringing. Her martial qualities, and the Chinese genre and heroines that inspire them, have more immediate historical sources.

11. Ying-Hua's Han heritage in a Manchu empire alludes to China's ethnic diversity (as opposed to the current rhetoric of Han purity) and its long history of power changing hands from one group to another.

12. Like Annique, Ying-Hua has many names, some chosen, others given. The latter function to show how social and political identities act on her. Her identity as a well-brought-up lady is seen in the title "Bai gu-niang," or "Young Lady Bai," that servants use when addressing her. Catherine Blade, the name she uses in England, is one her father wished for his unborn child to have. Additionally, she is occasionally called "Ying-ying," a diminutive for intimates that she uses for herself in her own mind. She is also "the Kazakh" in Turkestan, including to Leighton, who addresses her as "My beloved" in his letters since he does not know her name.

13. The novel itself tells us that many ethnic groups, with vast physical variations, populate Chinese territory and that diversity means that she can pass as fully Chinese in China despite her British paternity (if there is such a thing as "fully" any ethnicity).

14. Also see Joan Judge's review of how Chinese women who were starting to get radicalized in the early twentieth century looked for models in the West and often turned away from their own compatriots as "abhorrent" (798–99).

15. Ying-Hua's concealment of her mixed ethnicity and her relationship with Leighton is not technically illegal under Victorian British law. But as Roxann Wheeler notes in her study of the representations of racial mixing in the English mid-eighteenth-century novel, social acceptance of interracial sex (between an English and an unenslaved, non-English person, termed "amalgamation") and any resulting children declined in the nineteenth century. Public opinion became more racist and there was a reactionary opposition to "miscegenation" (particularly when it came to relationships between white English and Africans), even though it was not illegal in Britain, and the Marriage Act of 1753 forbade marriages between people mainly on the basis of *religious* difference (143, 145).

Wheeler also finds that marriages between British working-class men or army officers and Asian women in late-eighteenth-century British India were viewed positively and "Eurasian" male children had more privileges than native males, but this situation changed in the nineteenth century (166). In late-nineteenth-century China, argues Emma Jinhua Teng, mixed-blood (*hunxue*) was lauded as a desirable state in the writing of many late-Qing eugenics philosophers, who saw white and yellow as superior (and proximal) races and the creation of a hybrid Eurasian race as the way for China to get to the top of a racial hierarchy.

16. Thomas has mentioned this in many interviews (such as "Guest Author Day: Learning English the Passionate Way by Sherry Thomas").

17. The "repeat" indicates a demographic of migrant workers who cross borders frequently.

18. A multicultural strain has developed in the genre in recent decades, with novels starring one or more protagonists of Black/Asian/Latinx/multiracial descent and including the cultural traits listed above (some integrated more adeptly than others). See Renee Bennett-Kapusniak and Adriana McCleer's "Love in the Digital Library: A Search for Racial Heterogeneity in E-Books." *My Beautiful Enemy* develops this trend beyond the above listed elements by modifying the genre's very components.

19. See "When Wuxia Met Romance: The Pleasures and Politics of Transculturalism in Sherry Thomas's *My Beautiful Enemy*."

20. As mentioned earlier, wuxia is a form with at least a century of history and an even older pedigree. Dumas traces the presence of Chinese martial arts in popular culture texts to the second century BCE and situates the rise of wuxia martial arts fiction in the early twentieth century. Stephen Teo explains that "xia is a noun to denote a breed of male and female . . . warrior figures in the Warring States Period (403 BC–221 BC) whom we may loosely call 'knights-errant'" (3). Ken-fang Lee says that wu xia fiction reaches its zenith in the 1920s and 1930s after starting to take a specific shape in the late Qing period. (There is variation in how the genre is named, with scholars like Lee using "wu xia" especially in the adjectival form, while Leung and others use "wuxia.")

21. Wuxia stories are known to worldwide audiences through their manifestation in martial arts movies. (The hits *Crouching Tiger, Hidden Dragon* and *House of Flying Daggers* as well as *Mulan* and *Kung Fu Hustle* are the *wuxia pian* most widely recognized by non-Chinese viewers.)

22. In *A Nationality of Her Own*, Candice Lewis Bredbenner explains how women's citizenships have often been derived from their status as wives, rather than their own birth or desire.

23. Though it borrowed techniques from Hollywood and was always already transnational as well.

24. In placing her wuxia story in this time and place, Thomas is using the somewhat apocryphal theory of the Great Game, allegedly an espionage struggle between Britain and Russia over Central Asian land and power in the nineteenth century. The conflict serves to highlight the clash of nations that gets in the way of Ying-Hua's happiness with Leighton and also fills in the background for the politics of colonization, Cold War, and globalization in the century that is to follow. In terms of historical events in late-nineteenth-century Xinjiang, Russia and local Muslim factions did create allegiances that challenged Chinese sovereignty, but the latter crushed any separatist impulses (James Ciment 199).

25. After our heroine discovers her maid's role in a gang, the maid forces her to join the martial sorority and Ying-Hua is forced to become a part of the maid's feud with another group. By the end of this YA novel, she kills a rival leader by mistake and makes a mortal enemy of Lin, his star pupil, a conflict that spills into *My Beautiful Enemy*, as mentioned earlier.

26. It must be noted that even in the historical periods favored in wuxia, Chinese Confucian patriarchy restricted women's lives, limiting their sociopolitical freedoms; that is the equivalent of the *jia guo* society in the tales. In other words, the female knight is a familiar and respected character, but she is not necessarily evidence of women's freedom. Even by the start of the twentieth century, as Joan Judge clarifies, though the gendered dichotomy between talent (*cai*, for men) and virtue (*de*, women's only option) was no longer treated as a given, there were arguments about how publicly a woman might display her talent. Radical Chinese nationalists insisted on public virtue as essential to nation-building, while the conservatives felt that women's actions toward helping the nation should be confined to teaching good morals at home (768–69). Judge also lists many women educated in this first wave of Chinese nationalism who became radicalized and joined in revolutionary actions.

27. For discussions on the prioritizing of family or kinship love over all others, see Y. An's "Family Love in Confucius and Mencius." Confucianism also dictated that a woman prioritize her husband's family over her natal one after marriage (Daniel K. Gardner), which the novel does not require.

28. Loretta Chase's novel *Lord of Scoundrels* is a well-known and aberrant example of a heroine doing a deliberate physical injury to a hero.

29. This differs from romance, which does not typically permit crossdressing or masculinized gender behavior other than as a temporary episode, usually in the first half of a story.

30. I can only think of one other example of a heroine going on a mission without the hero after their betrothal/marriage—Alyssa Locke in the short story "Waiting" in Suzanne Brockman's *Troubleshooters* series.

FIVE

—ɯ—

INTERSECTIONS

THERE IS NO BETTER WAY to understand the romance heroine and her resistance to binaries than by looking at heroines who balance their lives across multiple axes of marginalization. As Kimberlé Crenshaw stated in 1989, she focused on Black women and sex *and* racial discrimination to "contrast the multidimensionality of Black women's experience with the single-axis analysis that distorts these experiences" (139). Crenshaw insisted that a feminist and antiracist theoretical framework must include the many spaces of bias experienced by Black women "because the intersectional experience is greater than the sum of racism and sexism" (140). Arguably, romance novels with Black women heroines lend themselves to, and demonstrate the need for, such intersectional analysis. To grasp the full extent of the romance heroine's heroism then, one must look to the Black romance heroine and her fight to resist, simultaneously, the bigotry of racism and the pigeonholing of sexism, gender roles, exploitative labor, and exclusionary citizenship.

In 1996, Beverly Jenkins published *Indigo*, a romance set in 1858 in the US between a formerly enslaved woman who is part of the Underground Railroad and a wealthy free Black man who helps enslaved people free themselves. Frequently mentioned as a landmark in the genre, the novel gives us a pioneering heroine in the character of Hester Wyatt, a young woman in Michigan whose hands and feet are permanently colored indigo from a childhood of forced labor on an indigo plantation in the Carolinas. While Jenkins took her inspiration from Julie Dash's *Daughters of the Dust* (Julie E. Moody-Freeman "Beverly Jenkins") and Rita Dandridge notes parallels to Harriet Tubman, the heroine's name and hands also evoke Hawthorne's Hester Prynne for me, who also stood up to a world that branded her an outcast with a visible marker.

Hester's story of enslavement is historicized by the prologue, in which a letter from her father documents that though he was a well-to-do free Black man, he sold himself into slavery in order to form a family with an enslaved woman he had fallen in love with. Numerous scholars, including Wilma King and Tera W. Hunter, have documented that such an arrangement would not have been unusual, thanks to the convoluted nature of slavery laws and statutes in the antebellum US. The outcome was dismal for Hester's parents. Despite the original slave owner's assurance that their family would be kept together, Hester's mother and she were sold and the father died alone soon after, but he wrote to his sister to find and protect the child. A few years later, a slave broker/ speculator located her and facilitated her freedom/manumission and eventual journey to her aunt, an activist on the Underground Railroad. The adult Hester is thus a free woman who was born into slavery and sold into freedom, but her citizenship as a full human is constantly under threat. While her nemesis is a slave catcher named Shoe, he is a symbol of the larger culture of enslavement that pollutes the country and treats African Americans as subhuman and Black women as the lowest in the country's racialized and gendered hierarchy.

The binary Hester consistently battles is of Black womanhood posed against human status and American citizenship, since, as Melinda Chateauvert has pointed out, "citizenship, as a status and as an identity determined by the state, is contingent upon race as well as sexuality; gender, nativity, and family status are also factors" (198). Hester's assertion of full humanity and citizenship is represented by the documents that attest to her freedom but even with the papers, the novel reminds us that the passing of the Fugitive Slave Act of 1850 menaced every Black person with dehumanization and enslavement, whether they were technically marked as a white person's chattel or not. Tera Hunter quotes from the 1853 opinion of a slaveholding chief justice of the Supreme Court of Georgia on the limits of manumission: "The free black resides among us, and yet is a stranger. A *native* even, and yet not a citizen" (86). Moreover, the Dred Scott v. Sandford Supreme Court decision of 1857 denied citizenship status to all African Americans (and I use the compound nomenclature here deliberately), free or enslaved.[1] From the beginning of the novel, however, Hester counters attempts to make her choose between full citizenship on the one hand and her racial heritage and sovereign Black subjectivity on the other, aided partly by a community engaged in fighting chattel slavery. Throughout the novel, she insists that she is both Black *and* a free citizen. As Wilma King reminds us, "many free women fought to maintain their liberty and make it more than an illusive spirit or fleeting ephemeral sense of liberty. . . . Free persons, many of whom had been enslaved, were also resourceful and resilient. Pernicious legislation could have reduced them to slaves without owners, but their agility in developing survival techniques while protecting themselves from the furies of racism points to their will to make their freedom meaningful" (1–2).

This is Hester incarnate. At the onset of the novel, she is a young woman without any known living family who lives in Michigan in the house she inherited from her aunt, surrounded by an apple orchard. She is immersed in the rescue efforts of the Railroad, using her house as a waystation to shelter new fugitives escaping the South and moving them safely to the next stop. She is engaged to a free Canadian Black man who is a teacher and a philosopher she respects but for whom she has no romantic feelings. In a way, she sees their engagement and future marriage as a part of the collective project of African American racial uplift. Hester's life takes a turn with the arrival of a fleeing family and the Black Daniel, a legendary figure who conducts enslaved people to freedom but was temporarily caught and severely beaten by a slave catcher patrol. Her initially prickly interactions with Daniel (a.k.a. Galen) as she nurses him to health soon become sexually and emotionally complicated. Though resigned to their connection being short-lived, Hester starts considering whether her anti-racist activism could coexist with romantic love in a world where Black people are constantly degraded and if those parts of her (activist and lover) might strengthen each other in the fight to assert Black humanity.

It is not an easy path, thanks to her own emotional self-protectiveness and a society that wants to deny her rights, including to legal recognition of intimate relationships, i.e., her sexual citizenship (Chateauvert 199). While Shoe is in the vicinity to track and apprehend the Black Daniel, he fixates on Hester and is determined to reduce her to a state of undignified enslavement. He even breaks into her home and steals the freedom papers she has hidden in a wardrobe, confident that without them, Hester's own word or even that of others in authority will not save her from being kidnapped and taken to the South to be sold into slavery. Anticipating just such a possibility, however, she has had the papers copied and certified at a sheriff's office. But Shoe's violation and desecration of her home and the fragility of such documentation in the face of the inhumanity of legalized slavery is a concrete representation of the romance heroine's usually more abstract and conceptual fight for a place in society. Laws about enslavement varied across the country at this time, with slaveholding states doing their utmost to treat all Black people in their territories as enslaved while kidnappers abducted citizens of nonslaveholding states and dragged them into chattel slavery, thus divesting them of citizenhood by rebranding them as property (King 152). In the final episode of Hester's *agon* with Shoe, he bribes another Black woman to trick Hester into leaving her home and captures her with this intent, but she stays unbowed, confident that her personhood is inviolate.[2] Many states had indeed passed "Personal Liberty" laws to thwart chattel slavery's long reach, but it is her sense of self and Galen's quick actions and money that foil the kidnapping attempt and maintain her free citizenship; this is in keeping with historical evidence that private actors fought for individuals' liberty and that direct action became a primary means of doing so after 1850 (King 153–55).

The climax of Hester's fight for her racial identity alongside full membership in humanity and American polity is foreshadowed by her work in sheltering and conducting fugitives to other safe houses en route to Canada. She is willing to go without food and even sell off her land for the money required in these endeavors. As noted earlier, the novel begins with such an incident, while another one involves her spiriting away a Black woman that Shoe has labeled a fugitive and imprisoned in the local jail. The latter episode is based on several such direct actions that free Black women executed in the mid-nineteenth century. In a different episode, she helps a fleeing enslaved woman leave her white enslaver, who claims to love her and their two daughters and promises to free them all soon; when the woman falters in the face of his pleas, Hester boosts her courage and helps her make the break.

It is thus established early on that Hester's HEA is bound up with her fellow Black women being free and in possession of their full selves. Hester admits her love for Galen after she is convinced that the freedom to be fully herself lies within the emotional bonds of marriage, but even then, her personal happiness is only one part of a longer arc to the HEA. She represents the free Black women abolitionists for whom there was no liberty if another was in chains or, as King puts it, "The final linkages in making the *true* essence of liberty a reality for free women emerged when their enslaved people were also free" (4). Fittingly, while the novel follows a classic Cinderella plot arc, with Hester gaining financial and emotional security through a loving husband, Jenkins makes a crucial innovation: the novel's actual end is Hester's reunion with her lost mother, a move that departs from most other novels' conclusions with a romantic declaration/betrothal/childbirth. Her dialectical journey of bringing together her racial identity and the human status that others wish to deny her extends beyond her romance arc (though Galen acts as the catalyst or facilitator of her self-unification when he finds and brings her mother, Frances Wyatt Donaldson, to her). In reuniting with her mother, whose freedom Galen has secured, and establishing a family home with her, Hester is able to repair her splintered self—indeed, the metaphor is literal, as her mother amputated baby Hester's little finger so she could always recognize her child even if slavery separated them and tried to erase her daughter's individuality and family roots.

Another element of the attempts of the racist world to divest Hester of her freedom and human dignity because of her color is the bigotry of racialized sexism. When Shoe first meets Hester, he insultingly asks her to sexually service him and his team and addresses her as a sexual commodity more than once (20). Hester is well aware of the hateful myths that Black women are "voracious in pursuit of the vices of the flesh and willing to accommodate anyone to satisfy their carnal cravings" (203). While she knows the narrative is racially motivated, she has lived a chaste life almost as a riposte to it, thereby becoming an example of King's observation that many Black women adopted a Christian morality as they "sought to free themselves of negative sexual referents," and aimed to be seen as "respectable" (37, 39).[3] At the start of the novel, Hester is engaged to schoolteacher Foster Quint but sees their future marriage as one based on mutual interests and political compatibility rather than a sexual companionate one. When her fiancé breaks off their engagement, he doesn't really apologize as he considers her interest in him largely platonic and perceives her as "practical" rather than passionate (117).

As is true for all women under patriarchy though, any respect this seeming celibacy invites is easily overturned. When Foster's new wife tries to cover up her own infidelity by spreading false rumors that Hester is having a sexual affair with Galen, Foster immediately believes Hester to have become sexually corrupt and maligns her as such in the community. The distance between being a "good" woman and a "whore" appears very narrow, especially for a Black woman, even if she is free and not legally designated as a sexual commodity (239). On the flip side, Galen repeatedly reminds himself of Hester's sexual innocence, putting her in a different category from the more sexually adventurous women he has known (93, 233). Though it seemingly endows her with higher status, this assignment of moral worth to a woman in inverse proportion to some carnality scale means she is being pushed into the virgin/whore binary.

Even when they start to become intimate, Galen holds himself back from penetrative sex, seeing it as a form of preserving her chastity. Having internalized these beliefs, initially Hester thinks, "Proper women aren't supposed to enjoy [sexual acts] are they?" (93) and worries that Galen's friend Raymond might consider her a "loose woman" (151). After she experiences oral sex with Galen for the first time and orgasms, she reacts with "Glory . . ." and later muses that "being a woman of the 1850's she did know properly raised women weren't supposed to enjoy this, yet she had" (191). But she starts to take charge of her sexual desires, asking Galen about sex and the intimacies they've already initiated. Eventually, she elects to fully consummate their relationship, stating that she is capable of making the decision. Notably, she sees it as a temporary joyful departure from being "Saint Hester" (225). Since she has no interest or hope that she and Galen will be married, her overture is entirely an act of carnal courage, where she sets aside a lifetime of white racist sexism and gender essentialism, accepted as morality and respectability politics among some people of color, and chooses to experience sexual satisfaction with a Black man.[4] It is a bold claim to sexual citizenship.

As the relationship develops, both she and Galen start to depart from the hegemonic patriarchal racist binary notions of correct sexuality. While Galen originally only sees her as a potential mistress, he realizes he wants more and corners her into a wedding after her former fiancé declares her alleged promiscuity to their neighbors. Notably, while Foster is calling her sexually dissolute, her community is excited to think she is in a marriage courtship with Galen—the twin sides of the mistress/wife dichotomy. After the wedding, she asks him if he will stray to other women once she gets pregnant; he responds that he will take no other mistress because she will be his wife and mistress (249, 317). Galen's vision of her as a "wife-mistress" enables her to fuse the two parts she has been taught to think of as mutually exclusive: a self that is regarded as worthy of respect through legal and religious sanction and one that exists beyond social approbation for its alleged tie to sexual pleasure and luxury (284–94).

This distinction between a woman who is allowed to have sex within the bonds of matrimony and one condemned for doing so outside them is part of a white Christian binary, which also extended to African Americans. But wife-status, and the respect that theoretically comes with it, was contingent for Black women, especially ones bound by chattel slavery. To be an enslaved Black woman in the antebellum US was often to be forced into the sexual labor associated with mistresses/sex workers (and be blamed for it [King 34]) and denied access to the inviolable position of wife, even to a Black man—the slave owner was the "third flesh" whose power superseded the bond of husband and wife (Hunter 54). In Bound in Wedlock, historian Tera Hunter notes that various US legislatures withheld the right to marry from enslaved Black Americans till 1866 and also notes that among the many assaults faced even by free Blacks, a critical one was that Black marriage was legally polysemic and unsettled up to the first half of the nineteenth century. Consequently, "Free blacks were increasingly forced to take extreme measures that were incongruent with their presumed status in order to protect their most viable assets—marriages and families. . . . Black couples were the least privileged and most fragile among the free married couples in their communities" (87). But Black couples also desired this right and privilege, and the playful bantering between Hester and Galen about her becoming a "mistress-wife" in pre-1866 Michigan not only nullifies the virgin/whore binary, it also reminds us that many African Americans aspired to monogamous marriage and contested legal and social barriers to this institution. Jenkins's move narratively writes back to the history of African-descended women denied an unassailable wife status just by virtue of being Black and also undercuts the sting of being labeled a sexually "voracious" Jezebel.

Over the course of the novel, Hester learns to accept her sexual self and slowly divests herself of any shame or recrimination. Early in their marriage, she thinks, "On the one hand she found the idea of playing the role of his wife-mistress terribly intriguing, but on the other she remained staid, conventional Hester Wyatt who was a bit embarrassed to be caught nude in a tub by a man— even if the man was her husband" (284). But she soon conquers this seeming dichotomy. The above passage is followed by one in which she accepts Galen's invitation to bathe together, since that "is what a mistress would say" (286), and then a long sex scene in which she participates fully and which ends with them joking about how they are thankful she is both his mistress and wife (290).

Further, not only does Jenkins write Hester as sexually desirable to Galen, Hester herself expresses her pleasure in their sexual relations; she is both sexually active and morally principled, with or without the benefit of clergy and marital law in pre–Emancipation US. After having sex with him for the first time, she has a frank conversation with a local healer to understand sexuality and its potential consequences even though she assures the healer that she is not weaving daydreams of marriage to a man whose higher class status makes such a union unlikely. Though later coerced into a wedding, in marrying Galen and enjoying their sexual and emotional intimacies, Hester claims her right to humanity, including the legal codification of her intimate relationship, and to other rights that follow.[5] Jenkins thus gives her a combination of the (neo) liberal and human-rights definitions of citizenship status that Chateuvert outlines as usually being two opposite sides of the debate about sexual citizenship (203–4).

Moreover, Hester interprets the "mistress" part of her mistress-wife status as entitling her to fewer constraints and more intimate freedoms with Galen than a wife might claim. Instead of shrinking herself into the prescribed gender role of a discreet helpmate who doesn't speak or act in certain ways with her husband, she considers herself freer to be open with him: "He wanted her to be his mistress as well as his wife, and although Hester had never met a mistress in the flesh, she had the distinct impression that they were far less constricted than traditional wives. A mistress would probably discuss matters such as [her period] with her lover" (267).

Additionally, even after Hester becomes sexually active, Jenkins does not immediately have her conceive a child, which is a departure from the genre's predisposition to celebrate this biological fate for heroines; while she does get pregnant after her wedding, Hester is initially of the same mind as many Black people: that "bringing children into a society such as this is nearly as great a sin as slavery itself" (82). Though romance novels often romanticize and even eroticize childbearing and motherhood, these are physically and legally fraught choices for most women and even more so for Black women; attentive to this reality, Jenkins reframes this gender-essentialized feature of romance heroines for the Black heroine within the perils of a nineteenth-century US that sanctioned chattel slavery (perils present in a different form even today).[6] Though Hester is no longer enslaved, her free status is a precarious technicality as I noted earlier, and what shadows her prospective motherhood is the specter of potential slavery and its implications for any future children, since it was "an article of faith . . . that masters held the rights to the increase of slave women. . . . The mother served as the vessel for the replication of capitalism's most valuable commodity, capable of transferring only her own ceaseless subjugation" (Hunter 65). Slavery and racial discrimination also justified splitting up Black families under the claim that Black people were incapable of real feelings for each other—that women would be indifferent to being ripped from their children (Hunter 17, King 58). Thus, we cannot forget that not only could Hester easily lose her own selfhood through false claims that overturn her free status, any children she might subsequently birth would inherit the condition of enslavement.[7] So while Hester is poised for motherhood by the end of the novel, it is her reunification with her mother—a scene that attests to their loving bond across decades of separation—plus the protection of love, wealth, and status that her Creole husband brings to their family, which allow her to embrace this element of her gender role.

Galen also plays a role in convincing Hester to reject a different kind of gendered dichotomy she had internalized—of female beauty being incompatible with dark skin.[8] Part of Hester and Galen's sexual compatibility rests on the fact that he sees her as a beautiful woman, with her dark skin being fundamental to his attraction to her. There are references to his desire being focused on her "dark sable breasts" (90) and "dark nipples" (287) and he compares both her nipples and dark eyes to precious stones (61, 93, 287). He thinks her "as beautiful as a black velvet sky; beautiful as sunrise," applying the phrases of romantic poetry to her body (134). Jenkins has discussed how unusual this portrayal of Hester was when the novel first came out since not only racism but colorism often excludes darker-skinned Black women from being considered beautiful (Moody-Freeman "Beverly Jenkins"). So while Hester is not beautiful to many, including Foster (134), or classy enough for some (including other Black and mixed-race freeborn people), Galen certainly sees her as stunning. We know of his bedazzlement with her physical appearance through phrases written from his point of view, such as "She had skin like silk, he noted, dark indigo silk" (188), which leads to her accepting that she is Black and beautiful (188). She likes that the way he touches her reveals that he thinks she is "made of silk, as if her arms were the rarest black porcelain and her back unburnished gold" (231) and her darkened hands (evidence of her birth into slavery and plantation work) are praiseworthy because they can heal (35). He even nicknames her "petite Indigo" because of her hands, turning a feature she felt compelled to cover up into one that inspires a loving endearment, and he terms those hands "exotic indigo orchids" (47). When she voices her chagrin over them (and her darkened feet), he reminds her that she is the one who defines her selfhood, so the world's attempt to "brand" her is irrelevant:

> "I was once told my hands would brand me a slave for the remainder of my years."
> "They were correct, but as long as it doesn't brand who you are in your heart, the color of your hands, like the color of your skin, is of no consequence." (28)

In other ways, too, Jenkin's portrayal of Hester flexes against the boundaries of the conventional feminine gender role. She is written as inhabiting modes of dress and behavior that don't adhere to typical limitations. Galen gifts her delicate negligees early on, and later, an ivory silk gown and accoutrements for a party; the silk is a fabric she had admired in a Detroit Free Produce store but had regretfully not bought because she was "practical Hester" who only did and wore sensible things (159).[9] Despite her initial misgivings that his gift of the gown is inappropriate, she finally dons it with pleasure because it helps her show the world that she is "indeed a desirable woman" (171). After the party, she even feels daring enough to try on one of the nightgowns after "imagining how it would feel to wear something so provocative" (183), and when she looks at a mirror, she glimpses "a woman she didn't recognize as herself" (183), as if discovering a heretofore unknown sexy female self. When Galen makes a surprise appearance in her room, their attraction is palpable, but intriguingly, Jenkins has her cover herself with a coarse robe at his request so they can discuss who might be betraying the Underground Railroad. In this moment, Hester's twin aspects (sensual woman and abolitionist) come together as she takes pleasure in the feel of the silken garments against her skin while walking to a writing desk to think through the problem of the traitor and make a list of suspects. Even as she executes that task, her sensible side is an internal argument with the corporal one that is aroused by the silk and Galen's presence: "The no-nonsense Hester scolded her mightily for being so brazen, even as the other Hester wanted to kiss [Galen] until dawn" (187). After their wedding, however, she keeps her daily wear limited to plain attire of cotton skirts and blouses (Egyptian cotton, since she shuns American cotton manufactured using en-slaved labor). The thought of changing into expensive and elaborate dresses several times a day is anathema to her, and she has no interest in joining the ranks of women from his elite circles who do so. It is evident then that despite enjoying the Cinderella element of being clothed in finery, Hester's pleasure in luxuries is personal and sensual rather than socially constructed or inhibited.

She has of course stepped outside the limitations of gender roles when it comes to labor—as have many Black women for hundreds of years, either forced by slavery or other financial necessity (King 25, 62). She supports her-self through occasional tutoring and laboring on her land, and the work she has been doing on the Road for much of her life has no room for a "cult of woman-hood" or "Angel in the House"–style modesty. When she is assisting an injured Galen at the beginning of the novel and wants him to move from the cellar into her house with her, he asks if her reputation will suffer. Her response is "on the Road here, we women don't always have the luxury of worrying about our reputations when there's work to be done" (55). Born and indentured into slave labor as a child on the indigo plantation, she now tends to her orchards, knows how to use a cart and mule in performing her Road-related tasks, and feeds and heals her refugees even at the cost of her own comfort.[10] When Galen enters her life, that's who he sees—a cash-strapped activist who has some inherited property and who does not shrink from the work that needs to be done.

Moreover, while she is capable of physical labor, she is also mentally resolute, including in dismissing male chauvinism. In commenting on the sexism Hester faces early on, Dandridge draws parallels between an injured Galen's initial pig-headedness and subsequent dismissal of Hester's methods or instructions and the way enslaved men first rejected Harriet Tubman's aid (910–11). Dandridge sees Galen as hierarchizing "the work that black men and black women perform as abolitionists" and as a symbol of "the strong black man who regards his public role as more important than Hester's" (910). Hester is not one to accept this un-equal valuation. We know she is a good cook and traditional healer, but this trait is clearly not hitched to others traditionally coded as feminine, such as subservi-ence to men. Not only does she not bend to Galen's bullying but she stays calm in the face of Shoe's threats and insinuations. She even arranges to smuggle out a jailed woman by impersonating her, and after she is arrested for helping the fugitive escape, she holds Shoe off with a gun when he tries to rape her in her cell.

Later, when Galen and Foster arrive to post her bond, Foster scolds her. He and Galen don't want her to take risks on the Road, their response echoing a prevailing line of thought about women's activism, as King points out: "The *Colored American* looked askance at the women who 'so degraded themselves' in an 1837 attempt to stave off kidnappers. In fact, the *Colored American* cast aspersions and begged their husbands 'to keep them at home and find some better occupation for them.' However, to fulfill their duty to themselves and others against the loss of liberty was more important to these women than perceptions of what constituted proper behavior for women and negative remarks" (156). Hester is just as brave and selfless as her real-life contemporaries and refuses to be reprimanded or to blame her fellow women abolitionists for her situation. She avers that the decision to play her part in the smuggling operation, though dangerous, was hers to make. Aware of the danger posed by Shoe, she flatly states, "I'm not going to stop my work just because he wants to see me on the block" (207), and even as she appreciates Galen's help and concern for her, she declares, "I've been on the Road most of my life, I can take care of myself" (208). In this portrait, Jenkins evokes the free Black women who, though surrounded by exhortations to bend men, did not think this fair, necessary, or desirable (King 54, 167). Galen learns to respect this principled assertiveness and self-worth.

When Galen tries to convince Hester to marry him, however, she brushes him off partly because of their class difference. She knows that some free Black people (including those whose enslaved ancestry is far back in the family tree), view enslaved or recently free Black people as lower class, and as noted above, she is self-conscious of her own childhood enslavement being visible through her hands. Galen's wealth makes this divide more vast. After they marry, she learns that people in his estranged family circle do have contempt for working-class and darker-skinned Black people, with his rich grandmother having disowned his mother for marrying such a man.[11] But there are other women in his circle who accept her marriage with alacrity, welcoming her into the fold, and coaching her on what to expect in that community. As a result, Hester is unfazed by the hostility with which some treat her when she visits Galen's family home for the grandmother's funeral; she thinks to herself, "They'd be nothing more than nodding acquaintances; her world encompassed more than gowns, hemlines, and hair dressing" (309). While her self-worth lies in her work and principles, not upper-class finery, she also comes to see her new fancy clothes as an external representation of her innately equal status with Galen, economics and birth notwithstanding. At the funeral ball, when she dresses in a new gown he has had made for her, she notes that his gift changed her "from simple Hester

Wyatt into La Petite Indigo Vachon. In the beautiful dress she looked as if she truly did belong at his side" (310). Her fine couture performs a vital function beyond a simplistic interpretation of it as gender-conforming—it asserts a class and social position that has historically been denied to Black people, certainly to formerly enslaved, dark-skinned Black women.[12] While some people still snub her and two spiteful Black socialites ask her to uncover her hands as if she's a circus freak, she maintains her cool till Galen swoops in and affirms her primacy in his life. She is proud of both her heritage and her present state and also confident of the rightness of her union with Gale.

Admittedly, marriage to him does change her everyday domestic labor. While this reduction in the heroine's labor is not uncommon in the Cinderella trope, it has a different resonance in an African-American romance. Black women were racialized as fundamentally different from white ones from the colonial period on, and their labor was exploited both in everyday work and under the tax code (Hunter 9). Within this context, the life of financial security and luxury that comes with Hester's marriage to a wealthy free Black man who loves to heap comforts on her showcases the romance heroine's journey of labor more starkly; while the non-Black heroine's journey may include a fight for the right to earn a living, or nurture individualistic career aspirations, or have her domestic burdens eased, for a Black heroine, freedom from domestic drudgery or financial precarity is freedom from an inhumane racist culture that adds to the inequalities of a sexist one.

But wealth does not preclude Hester from engaging in abolition and activism. When her new married status comes with a cook who refuses to let her work in the kitchen, she directs her energy to other labor on behalf of the abolitionist cause, including driving a cart to deliver an important newspaper even in bad weather. When scolded by the cook for risking her health and advised to use her new wealth in ways that align with her politics, she considers the many options she now has to help the cause such as "benevolent societies," "fugitive relief," and "aiding parentless children" (272).[13] To Dandridge, she belongs to a Black tradition of female abolitionists like Harriet Tubman "that allows them greater vision into the human condition and an identification with a cause greater than themselves" (909). Hester adds to her long resume of aiding the cause by organizing a fundraising fair, which was "a tradition amongst Black women of the North" to support abolitionist publications, fugitives, and institutions like orphanages (294). Hester arranges the fair to raise funds for fugitives resettled in Canada and for a local church's efforts to aid poor community members. She teams up with other women in this endeavor, as she has in her other work for the Road (including Bea the healer, other safe house volunteers, and the group that helps her plan a jailbreak). She herself is an abolitionist not just because of her former enslavement but also because her aunt was one—hers is a family lineage of female abolitionists, as was true of many free Black women of her time (King 163–64). Just as Hester's own HEA is tied to that of other Black women's freedom, so is her labor part of a cooperative effort by Black women. Her husband's wealth doesn't lessen her work—it supports and affirms her abolitionist and communal identity and labor.

As part of this group, she has no allegiance to the elements of the female gender role that involve women being meek, staying home, and limiting themselves to chores, but there is another element that she resists that is often associated with women—the desire for love and marriage. The knowledge that her father chose to enter slavery for the love of her mother haunts her, and she thinks that love must be a "terrible thing" (30). The incident mentioned earlier where she helps a Black woman break away from the white slave owner who claims to love the woman and children that he treats as chattel disturbs Hester. These cases suggest to her that love without freedom is just dehumanization. Hester also finds it sad that her aunt and the man who loved her never got together because that man felt loyal to the wife he left behind when he fled enslavement three decades ago, a complication caused by slavery that Hunter discusses in her study of African-American intimacy. But while Hunter documents how Black men and women found alternatives to the restrictions placed on their intimate lives, Hester is initially resistant to any form of romantic intimacy because it seems a liability in the context of the "peculiar institution" of slavery and racial discrimination in the US (Hunter 11). Examples proving her right abound— such as the unhappy love story between the local white sheriff's son and a Black burgher's daughter—and reinforce her conviction that the continuing presence of racial inequality can only lead to heartbreak. Early on, she defends her choice to marry for cerebral companionship by telling Galen, "I don't wish to marry for love. I don't need misery in my life" (82). But as her desire for Galen and her admiration for his work grow alongside the realization of his commitment to her, she conquers her own fears about the vulnerability and danger inherent in love and embraces its strength. For Hester to admit that she has feelings for Galen is an act of courage—one she engages in after reminding herself that "during her years on the Road she'd faced numerous real dangers: slave catchers, dogs; being afraid of her feelings was silly" (172). A key element of this trust is the fact that not only does Galen love and protect her, he learns to respect her Road mission, giving it the same importance as his own continuing mission as the Black Daniel. This love resembles the practice of freedom that bell hooks has called for in *Outlaw Culture* (248), including working in community against a "culture of domination" that is anti-love (247).

Striving for her race is intertwined with Hester's bond with her husband, and the novel's end, with her being pregnant and anticipating a life with her own free mother, holds the promise of a community in which women join hands with men in traditional and untraditional ways to work toward communal freedom. In portraying her and her relationship with Galen, Jenkins provides us a love story that epitomizes what Tera Hunter notes of the ties between enslaved Black people: "Although African Americans struggled to nurture and uphold vibrant, genuine, intimate relationships that buffered their degradation as human beings, they did so with eyes wide open, with vigilance and trepidation given what infringements lurked around them" (31). Hester Wyatt, the daughter of a free man who gave himself into bondage and a mother whose freedom was stolen, creates an integrated self in antebellum America while continuing a collective movement for human status and full citizenship for others like her, joining a "black helping tradition" (Dandridge 918). Love becomes part of the practice of freedom for her, one that helps her also piece together disparate elements of a female gender role. As such, her journey epitomizes Linell Cady's claim that "the self is no substantial entity, complete and defined, but a reality always in the process of being created through the dynamic of love, which continually alters its boundaries and identity" (qtd. in Dandridge 145).

While Jenkins applies the Cinderella tale to an 1858 abolitionist's journey to embracing her many facets, in *A Princess in Theory* (2018), Alyssa Cole cleverly updates the trope to the present moment by fusing it with a well-known scam of the internet age—spam emails promising you a windfall through the largesse of an African (usually Nigerian) prince. Only, Cole's protagonist is an overworked epidemiology grad student in New York who has no patience for fairy tales (which she equates to cons). She is immersed in her doctoral research, multiple jobs, and coping with the slights that come her way as a Black woman scientist. The novel—published at a time when the White House appeared to have turned away from science and from funding public health research and toward nakedly racialized politics—resonates even more in the age of the COVID-19 pandemic, the Black Lives Matter protests, and the heightened awareness of various forms of misogyny and sexual harassment.

Naledi "Ledi" Smith (née, unknown to her, Ajoua) is already living on the fault lines of this society when she starts to get blitzed by what she thinks is a targeted scam. She is annoyed but does not think for a moment that the email claims about her royal descent and family history in the African kingdom of Thesolo are authentic. Orphaned as a young child, she is struggling to finish her doctorate, and her work is her life, except for a rare outing with a rich socialite friend. Meeting a handsome stranger named Jamal at her second job as a server in a dining hall, followed by bumping into him again in her apartment building, tempts her into a semblance of a personal life. When his secret identity as Prince Thabiso Moshoeshoe (who also happens to be her childhood fiancé) is revealed, Ledi feels betrayed but is persuaded into the professional opportunity of a lifetime in his (and her) home kingdom. Cole thus brings to the genre the intersecting axes of Blackness, working-class life, female gender, and STEM academia, and imagines how these can impact the romance genre's core narrative of finding a partner and creating a family.

A Princess in Theory is the first in a series titled "Reluctant Royals," and in it Ledi faces this binary: is she a poor orphan and a scientist-in-training in a country that deems her a lesser minority while it appears to be drifting away from scientific rationalism, or is she a scientist with living blood relatives as well as being a princess from an African nation that resisted white colonization and racial degradation and that blends folk traditions with science? In other words, it's not so much that she has to choose between one ethnic identity and another, or between a traditionally feminine and nonnormative female self, or between a working-class identity and aristocracy, or between singlehood with casual sex and coupled intimacy; instead, the choice she faces is between a version of herself that has limited clout, due to the intersection of her class, gender, and race in the US, and a potential past and future via an African nation that can give her access to a powerful (albeit not quite democratic) version of all her identities. The potential Cinderella life via a rich prince is again not a fantasy of escaping economic precarity as much as it is about the power to continue the work that the heroine wants to do while being valued for it.

Cole has her bridge those selves through Thesolo, a fantasy space akin to Wakanda in *Black Panther*, and the romance plot. The spatial reset through the love story permits Ledi to splice together a self that is both thoughtful and empathetic (because she has known what economic hardship, sexism, and racism feel like), and one that has an unbroken, proud African lineage as well as the capacity to improve the lives of others through her training and her new wealth. As an epidemiologist, she has the research skills and perspective to contribute to public health, and as a Black woman with political power (if she accepts her fairy tale prince and their childhood engagement), she can combat inequality to enact large-scale policies. Equally important, the trip to Thesolo can symbolically reverse her family's forced exile from Africa to the US, and the subsequent loss of a loving community, and help her retrieve and integrate the parts of herself she blocked off after orphanhood. In other words, the most deep-rooted binary the American foster care system locked her into—intimacy versus emotional safety—is assailable if only she can embrace her heritage and the stranger who is her fiancé.

The challenges in Ledi's life as a Black woman scientist are dramatized through specific interactions she has with a white male post-doctoral researcher in the lab where she works and with other key individuals in her field. While Ledi admits that she entered the discipline knowing that racism made it tough for Black people to pursue a career in STEM, her frustration is compounded by intersecting structural issues: "She hadn't foreseen all the other variables that went into life as a woman in STEM: politicians who treated her profession with contempt and threatened her future—and the world's. Fellow scientists like Brian, who thought that women in the lab were their personal assistants instead of their equals" (5). While Ledi opted for this field because she was inspired by a magazine article featuring a Black woman scientist, it is an uphill battle (5).

Not only does Brian subject her to the sexism that women in STEM often document, but his behavior is also tinged with racism. In their first interaction, he assumed she was a cleaner, and he has subsequently mansplained basic scientific concepts to her in public while pointedly asking a junior white male student for advice (4). Yet he routinely asks her to do his tasks and assigns her extra grunt work instead of the junior scientist. When she points out the imbalance of work assignments between her and that student at the beginning of the novel, Brian accuses her of shirking work; rather than fight back, she just draws in a breath at the unfairness of his accusation and scolds herself for voicing any dissent, thinking, "Why did I even say anything?" (6). Such self-silencing is a traumatic aspect of emotion work and labor, one that minoritized genders like women undertake at home as well as in professional spaces, as do ethnic minorities, to keep the peace as Ledi initially attempts to do. More poignantly, she remembers how "challenging the people who held power over you made you undesirable, and undesirability meant gathering all of your things into a black plastic bag and being sent back to the group home," drawing a through line between her personal experience of being disenfranchised and this professional mistreatment she tolerates, both of which split her into a polite facade and an unhappy interiority (6).

Despite the fact that she shows Brian conciliatory behavior, including a "tone she'd heard secretaries on old syndicated TV shows use to placate their sexist bosses," he has reported to the lab head that she is "giving him attitude" (5). It is clear that he wants to invoke the "angry Black woman" stereotype often weaponized against Black women and that she prefers not to complain than have that stereotype associated with her. The irritation that Ledi's Indian female colleague, Trishna, expresses about Brian validates Ledi's perception of his behavior as unfair. Moreover, Trishna's reaction suggests that even other women of color in STEM don't get as much racist sexism directed at them—or feel as pressured to tolerate it—as Ledi does. Handling the microaggressions of people like Brian requires a significant amount of emotional labor from Ledi, and it is visible in the contrast between her calm, polite attempts to resist his bullying and her internal state, which swings between angry thoughts like "This motherfucker" (5), self-soothing reminders like "Asshole postdocs are temporary, but scientific discoveries are forever" (7), and reactions like nausea and a mounting sense of fatigue over maintaining her poise while hoping "her expression wasn't as murdery as she felt" (7).[14]

Additionally, the zeitgeist in which science funding, particularly for the unglamorous field of public health, is on the wane is a constant source of anxiety to Ledi, as is the lack of mentorship and information about a future fieldwork opportunity that could bolster her résumé. At the start of the novel, her adviser, who heads the Disease Task Force she was to join, has not communicated with her for a while, and she soon learns that the task force's funding has been cut, leaving her without that opportunity. Ledi recognizes this denial of funds for a crucial cog in the public health field as evidence of the larger failures of the US in maintaining social services and infrastructure. Once, when Thabiso expresses incredulity at the ways in which the grimy reality of New York doesn't befit its fame, she responds, "One fun thing you learn when you study Public Health, especially infectious diseases, is that most societies are one step away from dystopia, really" (153); her remark not only highlights Thesolo's superior public health policy later but is an eerie (though predictable) foretelling of the COVID-19 pandemic and its mishandling in the US by people who dismissed science and pushed policies that supported a racist political agenda. As an epidemiologist whose work is being undermined by short-sighted politics, she is thus being devalued and endangered professionally and as a citizen.

Collectively, Ledi struggles with a precarity brought on by the intersectional disadvantages of her identities and her (foster) country's political failures. Her home life bears the marks of it: she lives alone, and a foster childhood full of rejection means she never confides in anyone about how she lost her parents early in life; her apartment is small, rent-controlled, and in a walk-up (elevator-less apartment building) in Inwood (an ethnically diverse, relatively affordable neighborhood in northern Manhattan); she has second-hand furniture; her roommates are two mice that were once part of a science experiment (a nod to her profession but also to the Cinderella story).

This initial setup is a contrast to the life she is offered in Thesolo when her fiancé, Prince Thabiso, comes into her life in search of his missing promised bride. While he initially hides the truth from her in order to ease her into that reality, the revelation occurs halfway through. Subsequently, Ledi has to grapple not only with Thabiso's dissembling and her own growing feelings for him but also with facing a new self that she finds scary. As a result, while the romance plot is about their reconciliation after she forgives him, there is a parallel narrative about unifying her own splintered self that is in line with the ones explored in previous chapters and in the section on *Indigo*.

Cole thus configures a multidimensional arc in the heroine's journey—two versions of a Black woman scientist and what she can accomplish, one within a system where racism, classism, and workplace sexism dominate and one where that system can be reimagined and improved. This fits Crenshaw's argument that the societal position of Black women cannot be understood, nor the problems they face alleviated, without considering a universe of material and discursive spaces.

—⁂—

When Ledi mentions Brian's unfair exploitation of her labor to Thabiso/ Jamal, he wonders why she puts up with it, leading her to explain how society punishes women, especially Black women, who complain: "Men make life harder for women who say no, especially women who look like me. . . . STEM is already hard to navigate—being marked as someone who doesn't work well in teams or contribute enough could tank my career" (81). She is surprised but pleased when Thabiso thinks it over and says that he has read research that "a woman who speaks once or twice in a professional or academic setting is seen as monopolizing the conversation," which corroborates her experience (82). Unlike Thabiso, Ledi's former boyfriend just dismissed her complaints, having never experienced sexism himself. Intrigued by the possibility that this man— a Black man, but unmistakably a wealthy Black man—can understand sexism, Ledi teaches him about gaslighting: "It's when you point out something that upsets you, or you try to set boundaries, and the other person tries to make you feel like you're overreacting or it's all in your head. Like when I tell Brian it's not fair that he's offloading his work on me, and then he acts like I'm the one being difficult" (82). Thabiso goes one step further and frames that behavior as Brian "being an asshole," but even more importantly, he realizes that he himself had exhibited arrogance toward her when they first met, which Ledi confirms. Verbalizing her lingering disapproval and anger at his past behavior is her first step in calling people out rather than quashing all emotional reactions (i.e., doing emotional labor and emotion work), which racism, sexism, and the foster system had trained her to do. Their exchange also links structural sexism in the workplace to sexism in an intimate partnership but models how it can be unlearnt as well. This is of course the promise of heterosexual romance—that the love story is not just about romance but about a woman getting treated equitably by a male lover and feeling free to express herself with him (as well as outside their relationship).

When she later discovers that Jamal/Thabiso lied to her, it becomes the impetus for her larger revolt against being quiet. Subsequently, she begins speaking up to claim her space and her rights as a scientist and a woman. The next time Brian tries to assign her more of his grunt work, Ledi says no, standing her ground despite his accusation that she isn't being a team player. The confrontation finally reveals how she has been suppressing a part of herself in a vain attempt to not cause a fuss and cannot do so anymore: "Apparently, oh-sure-I'll-do-that Ledi had been incinerated by the flames of her frustration and I-wish-a-motherfucker-would Ledi had risen from the ashes" (213). Riding on this phoenix-like militant reincarnation, she calls him out for being a bad supervisor, and when he tries to railroad her into being quiet in the presence of their lab head, she exposes his unfair past treatment to the head with "I was actually about to do my own work. I'm pretty tired of doing yours, too" (213).

As mentioned earlier, she has suppressed such negative affect and self-assertion due to childhood trauma and systemic racism and sexism, but this has also meant divorcing herself from true attachment to anyone. Having grown up a Black girl in foster care in the US, Ledi has trained herself to armor her heart or, to use her scientific metaphor, maintain a "social phospholipid bilayer: flexible, dynamic, and designed to keep the important parts of herself separate from a possibly dangerous outside environment" (8). Yet, despite a conviction that no one wants her or would care about her needs, she has an attachment to the Disney movie version of romance and once dreamt about living in a castle amongst royalty. Learning that she is in fact a long-lost princess is thus a shock because it pits those two instincts (attraction and avoidance) against each other while shaking up the identity she has created for herself. A second shock is that she learns that some of her family is still alive in the country of her birth but stricken by a mysterious illness that has spread there. Nevertheless, she downplays the importance of familial ties at the beginning, declaring, "My friend got me one of those DNA tests and I still haven't looked at the results. I'm Naledi Smith. I eat biostats for breakfast and produce the cleanest gel images on the East Coast. I don't need a past" (167). In her insistence that her identity comes from her work in the present and not in lineage or genetics, she denies any possibility of a self outside one that is self-made and that rests only on her scientific labor and acumen, not family history.

In keeping with that identity, when Thabiso dangles the carrot of a fieldwork opportunity in Thesolo that would also give her extraordinary data for her doctoral thesis, she succumbs to visiting her birth country. But her determination to separate professional motivation from personal attachment is compromised from the start as Thabiso asks her to pretend they're still engaged to counter the growing belief among his compatriots that their unfulfilled betrothal caused the epidemic. As a result, Ledi confronts the possibility of research success, gaining family, moving up in the socioeconomic hierarchy—and ridding herself of racist pigeonholing by becoming African royalty, all in one fell swoop. The problem is that this powerful potential unfractured self and future terrifies her, promising cohesion but also the specter of loss: "Living in the dark had allowed her to go through life in her self-contained way. Now he was offering to bring her into the light, and that would change everything. Fear gripped her tight with this one simple truth: if she knew who her parents were, she would know what she'd lost, what she'd been denied" (218). It is not difficult to hear echoes of the stolen past of an entire people in her apprehension or in her longing for a country she has no memory of but whose presence has haunted her. Thabiso himself is troubled by her losses, thinking, "The reverence of the ancestors was ingrained into every Thesoloian, whether they were a beggar or a king. The remembrance of those who came before you and the passing on of familial knowledge was something sacred. To not even know one's parents or one's roots . . ." (105). The trailing off of that thought captures the unspeakable trauma such a sundering must inflict. For Ledi, grief over a severed familial tie and wider African lineage and a reluctance to risk new intimacies squares off against the promise of a complete self—along personal, professional, and societal dimensions. She thinks as she leaves New York for Thesolo, "She had lived her entire life—what she could remember of it—rootless, being passed around like brussels sprouts at dinner before they became trendy. Now she was about to take a trip to the motherland, her actual motherland, and she had no idea what she should be feeling" (225).

In other words, Ledi's journey to Thesolo is spatial as well as psychological, not to mention a kind of time travel to a prosperous parallel-universe African kingdom never colonized by Europeans, thanks to Thabiso's grandfather "[fighting] off colonizers with his bare hands" (29). Thesolo has mineral deposits that give it leverage in international trade, strong kinship traditions, and a robust social services network: "In Thesolo, when a child was orphaned, they were placed with relatives, or with a family who could not conceive, or in one of the communal orphanages that tried very hard to reproduce the feeling of a family and usually succeeded" (104). And "Thesolo was consistently listed as one of the most progressive countries in the world, with more technological and environmental advancements being put in place" (254).

Ledi is thus transported to a place that is separate from the history of the white conquest of Africa and the triangle trade, of American slavery, Jim Crow, and present day anti-Black systemic racism, as well as of stereotypes about postcolonial African countries. And by virtue of discovering her birth, she has the chance at an identity that puts her in the most powerful tier of this society. It is a complete reversal from the life of an orphaned, indigent grad student scientist who has always faced structural inequality in terms of race, class, and gender. The new identity of Naledi Ajoua over the generic one of "Ledi Smith" also forces her to be more visible, to participate more fully, to not fade into the background: "Smith had given her anonymity, ensured she was always at the back of the class and at the bottom of lists. Ajoua was a front of the class, top of alphabetically ordered lists kind of name. It was a name that didn't allow for shrinking" (224).

In her new (old) country, her family, the royal family, and other Thesoloians offer her a mixed reception that mirrors her own internal divide about her community citizenship. While her uncle appears affectionate, he has a political agenda, and Thabiso's parents see her as the child of traitors and unworthy of him and the throne. His mother critiques her jeans and t-shirt combo on arrival as "unbecoming of a supposed future queen," speculates if she's trapped him with a pregnancy, and makes snarky comments about her public health career, suggesting she wasn't good enough to be a doctor (or the next queen) (243). The populace is assessing her to decide if she is one of their own or an outsider, and a makeup artist assigned to her tells her she must look like a princess or risk the catty retaliations of competitors: "You may have been born here, but right now you're a greedy American coming to take what's ours" (249). So the irony is that she has never known full citizenship in the US, but is now faced with natal compatriots who think of her as an American outsider.

The cosmetician is one of several women who assist her fractured self's repair. When she is coiffed and dressed in the Thesoloian fashion before her welcome party, she stares at her new look, thinking that the primping "had transformed her into someone else entirely. Perhaps the woman she would have been if her parents had never taken her to New York" (251); the mirror reflects a self and a life that she feels disconnected from even as she is trying it on. Her other allies, in addition to Thabiso, are two Thesoloian women—Thabiso's assistant Likotsi and her own cousin, Nya. While opposites in personality, they each provide her with a support system and access to the country's culture and history as she gets the lay of the new (mother) land. She attempts to speak the language, though regretful that her parents have made her a stranger to her own native tongue, and her attempts solicit kindly laughter (266). Her constant push and pull toward this new national identity are thus a result of her own past experiences of being an undesirable misfit as well as the structural fault lines of legal national identities and the complications caused by forced displacement and the severing of kinship networks for such populations.

Though drawn to the idea of roots and a family, Ledi continues to skirt the emotional dangers posed by the potential deaths of her sick grandparents even as she works to discover what might be causing the mysterious epidemic in Thesolo. During a ritual ceremony, however, the region's priestesses (another form of a female community) give her their blessing, and even as a part of her warns her to stay aloof, their words overcome her fear that she's never good enough to belong: "Ledi's heart felt like it would burst as the women graced her with their joyous smiles. They were happy she was there. Ecstatic. *These women don't know you. This is an act.* It might have been a performance for the royal court, but Ledi couldn't fight the warmth that flowed through her, the sense of belonging. She couldn't fight the fact that she felt like a princess" (294).

Following the ritual, Thabiso and the court bow to her in a moment of welcome because she has accepted the betrothal, but she is still unwilling to fully accept the situation, convinced as she is that she's like bad Velcro that nothing sticks to. On a visit to her ancestral village with Thabiso, she wonders "what it would be like to be his future queen. To have such responsibility would be nerve-racking, but the trade-off would be getting to help people. Being royalty might have its upside, but thinking about it in relation to herself was asking for trouble" (310). As is evident, her internal battles are constantly about this attraction she feels toward the parts of herself she lost but that she cannot quite commit to in this new world, with its motley attitudes toward her. Her epidemiology task partly serves to reconstitute her scattered history and identity.

While working to understand the outbreak, she combines ancestral and cutting-edge knowledge in the exercise of her public health skills. She listens to the local narratives about the outbreak's cause, and though listening can be emotional and gendered labor, here it stems from her disciplinary training (rather than from a pressure to perform affect), which advises students that superstition or religious explanations can lead one to the scientific cause of a problem. She receives confirmation that some blame Thabiso's unmarried state for the epidemic, and there is discontent with the powerful class her grandparents belong to, though it is at odds with the actual useful policies put in place. Moreover, public discussion about the illness, spawning a kind of hysteria, has convinced people that they have been infected by the "Prince's plague" (317).

Following this listening tour of sorts, which provides her with political and cultural insight, Ledi jumps into doing patient intake, thanks to the high-tech setup at the hospital where she is to intern, earning Thabiso's gratitude and praise. This is the turning point in their relationship, where she starts to see him and the country as inalienable parts of herself and her future.

Before Thabiso, her fear of being hurt has meant that she denied all intimate connections (and separated sex from sentiment) other than a dysfunctional relationship with her friend Portia. When it comes to romantic ties, she had labeled most men as pointless outside of sexual activity, having filed her most recent unfaithful boyfriend "in the Annals of the Journal of New York City Fuckboys" (21). Rather than being hurt by his cheating, she was relieved because she didn't love him, and though she wondered what it would be like to have a real partner who stuck with her, her instinctive reaction to that thought was "That would be terrifying" (24). Like Hester Wyatt, romantic intimacy and trust do not come easy to this orphaned woman in a racist and sexist world. This avoidance behavior is in full force when she meets Jamal/Thabiso but she also feels an immediate attraction; so when he finagles his way into her life in New York, she gives him non-verbal consent to initiate their sexual connection, and then responds to his wish to kiss her with brief verbal cues like "okay" and lets him pull her closer (125–26). Over the course of their rollercoaster relationship, however, her skittishness eventually changes to assertion as she notices how he looks at her as they have sex, a look that reveals his focus on her as a person he really values (131). When they reconcile in Thesolo, he still initiates their first kiss but she participates fully, even pushing him onto his back and straddling him as they have make-up sex.

The scene occurs when they are forced to seek shelter in a shepherd's cave due to a storm on the way home from a remote village. The forced proximity and the knowledge that Thabiso held out hope they'd be reunited ever since their childhood separation, lowers her guard, making her wonder if the goddess had indeed decided they were a correct match (329). Her acceptance of a female divine principle shows her growing connection to the matriarchal religious tradition of her lineage alongside coming to terms with her own suppressed or seemingly incompatible selves. These warring sides finally start to come together at this time as she sees that Thabiso also has two sides but both love her. As they lie in each other's arms, she understands that she is "being held by a man who had presented her with two separate identities and seemed to care for her regardless of which he inhabited" (331). Like her, Thabiso had two sides, and in accepting his, she moves toward accepting her own duality that mirrors his in a way. Having shared her sexual self with him, she finally initiates emotional intimacy as well, dropping her stoic mask.

She confesses her inexperience with being part of a couple and her puzzlement over why her parents chose to sever her from her people, and he assures her she won't be alone again.

Just as they reconcile with each other (and she is reconciling with her own atomized parts), she briefly falls ill but recovers thanks to Nya's timely intervention with a local tea; subsequently, she and her doctor try to triangulate what factors, environmental or genetic, might have caused that sequence of events. The investigation brings her uncle's machinations to light, solving not just the current mystery but the motivation behind her parents' flight from the country years ago. While the discovery of this family member's duplicity absolves them, and thus Ledi, of the charge of treason, it is her newly established trust of Thabiso and his sincere desire to protect his people and her that contributes to her acceptance of her new role and past. Moreover, she is able to compile the entire experience in Thesolo for her thesis, "combining the fields of infectious disease, sociological epidemiology, and the degree in law she'd unofficially received after watching too many marathons of *Law and Order*" (353). Thabiso's mother apologizes, admitting she was wrong to blame Ledi for her parents' flight but also confessing that her anger stemmed from her love for Ledi's mother and a sense of betrayal at her seeming abandonment of her friends and family. Following the settlement of these past griefs—possibly a metaphor for the complicity of some Africans in the violent expulsion of others across the Atlantic—as well as a reconciliation with Portia, who engineered the reveal of Thabiso's true identity because she was jealous, Ledi is free to pave the path to her HEA with Thabiso in the twin worlds of New York and Thesolo. Undoubtedly, this is a jet-setting HEA, with the hero-helpmate's wealth facilitating the heroine's success in a financial, national, professional, and emotional realm—an arc that is unusual even in a genre that fantasizes resolutions to real-life dilemmas for the average woman. It's a turbo-charged fairy tale and one can rightly ask if it has any significance outside this specific plot.

While Ledi tells herself she no longer believes in fairy tales, whether that be *Cinderella* (or *Beauty and the Beast* [259], or *Sleeping Beauty* [261]), they are ubiquitous in mass-market romance and *A Princess in Theory* shows how these tales need to be reconceived for a Black heroine. She is not appreciated—not in her home, as is true for many heroines, and not outside the home (in the US). Her beauty, intelligence, and dignity are in question in a world that discounts Black women on multiple fronts. Indeed, her name, Naledi, is a play on No-Lady, alluding to the denial of "lady" status to Black women. For abolitionists, acquiring this marker of bourgeois virtue was crucial in the fight against the racist ideology that supported slavery and is a category that continues to be contested even today. Black women in a racist culture are treated as incompatible with being lady-like, in terms of both class status and sexual morals.[15] Thanks to a history of racist sexism and classism then, Ledi's identity as a Black woman is more overwritten than other women's and places her full citizenship in doubt. Moreover, the contemporary rhetoric among her peer group that sexual expression is (or should be) separate from emotional intimacy leaves her even more isolated.

While these challenges are hypervisible in Black romance, they appear in muted or partial form for many romance heroines. A prince can give this heroine access to power and wealth, but she needs to draw on her own past to make her way forward, building networks not just with a fairy godmother but also other women, like the Black women in this chapter. The Black romance heroine is inextricably linked with the solidarity offered by a Black female community and a secure romantic partnership, for without these, her HEA would be precarious and incomplete. Finally, as every chapter in this study has tried to show, each romance heroine can be all things—professionally accomplished, emotionally fulfilled, sexually open, and socially secure so long as her journey breaks out of celibate and cerebral solitude in a tower.

NOTES

1. Some of the relevant elements of the Scott v. Sandford decision:

   4. A free negro of the African race, whose ancestors were brought to this country and sold as slaves, is not a "citizen" within the meaning of the Constitution of the United States.

   5. When the Constitution was adopted, they were not regarded in any of the States as members of the community which constituted the State, and were not numbered among its "people or citizen." Consequently, the special rights and immunities guarantied to citizens do not apply to them. And not being "citizens" within the meaning of the Constitution, they are not entitled to sue in that character in a court of the United States, and the Circuit Court has not jurisdiction in such a suit.

   6. The only two clauses in the Constitution which point to this race, treat them as persons whom it was morally lawful to deal in as articles of property and to hold as slaves.

   7. Since the adoption of the Constitution of the United States, no state can by any subsequent law make a foreigner or any other description of persons citizens of the United States, nor entitle them to the rights and privileges secured to citizens by that instrument. ("Dred Scott v. Sandford (1857)")

2. Among the many ways that free Blacks were menaced by legalized slavery was "manstealing," which King describes as "the physical abduction of

persons with the intent to enslave," a practice in which "free blacks . . . could be 'mistaken' for slaves. In slaveholding states, it was commonly believed that all blacks were enslaved; consequently, free blacks were subjected to kidnapping and enslavement" (152).

3. In the chapter "This Modest Bending of the Head," King examines how white society constructed and deployed these stereotypes and how Black women reacted to them (34). Alongside the "Jezebel" stereotype, she also shows how its polar opposite—the asexual "mammy"—was also a caricature that fit a racialized virgin/whore binary (35).

4. For more on how gender conventions, ideas about the "cult of true womanhood," and values such as "modesty in actions, words, and dress" were spread through the Black press and via Black women's societies in the antebellum US, see King (39–42). On the mixed reactions among Black communities in the nineteenth century to white Christian sexual morality, see Hunter's *Bound in Wedlock*.

5. The right to be married presumes one's human identity. As Hunter says,

> African Americans understood the importance of contesting the standing of their relationships as integral to any prospects that freedom might hold for them on the most basic level. Marriage was by no means synonymous with freedom, but slaves and free blacks knew that their future as liberated people was less certain without the guarantee of marriage—or the right to choose whether to wed or not. How far could they go in the world without beloved kin, the foundation of which was secured on the bedrock of publicly protected marriage? . . . Marriage in U.S. history has always been intertwined with a person's gender, race, and identity and place in the social order. How men and women relate to the public world has been tied to their status as married or potentially married people. As such, marriage has been linked to citizenship and civil rights. (7)

6. See Kamblé *Making Meaning* for more on the association of an HEA in romance with pregnancy, childbirth, and the nuclear family. King notes that children under five made up nearly 40% of deaths in the nineteenth century, irrespective of the mother's demographics (58). Today, Black infant mortality is still the highest of all ethnic groups in the US ("Infant Mortality"). Moreover, pregnancy-related deaths in the US show significant racial disparities, with Black women experiencing the highest mortality ratio per 100,000 live births according to the Centers for Disease Control ("Pregnancy Mortality Surveillance System"). Motherhood versus life is a disturbing binary that continues to menace Black women far more than other groups, indicating racism within health systems and socioeconomic structures overall.

7. Hunter notes that "Black women gave birth to the capital that helped forge the nation's wealth, typically under the duress of coerced sex with the very men who sired biracial progeny and turned them into commodities. They also give birth to children by enslaved black men whom neither mother nor father

possessed according to law and white society, and whom their enslavers literally capitalized" (4). To bear a child as a Black woman prior to emancipation was not the final seal of the romantic HEA that the American romance genre has enshrined for its white couples (true even in novels that acknowledged maternal and infant mortality as high); especially for the enslaved, though even for a free woman like Hester, it was an element of Black intimacy always experienced with the full knowledge of its fragility within an inhumane racist system.

8. King cites an 1859 essay by Martin H. Freeman that references Black veneration of Anglo-Saxon ideas of beauty and the cause of this tendency, as well as suggestions to reject such "colorphobia" and build Black self-esteem (46–47).

9. For more on Free Produce, see King (164–65).

10. Dandridge terms her one of the "formidable heroines in the battle against race prejudice" and also notes that Hester aids people by using black folk culture: "She heals with spirituals, home-made unguent, and handpicked herbs" (909). She is also a reminder of the many free Black women who transgressed gender role conventions to labor as needs required. See King on New Englander Addie Brown's various jobs, including being a teamster: "Driving teams of draft animals required crossing gender boundaries but Brown's economic welfare was more important than social constraints" (62).

11. The grandmother's death also reveals her extraordinary methods of maintaining power and building wealth through blackmail and other unsavory practices. There is some data on the small proportion of slave-owning or other wealthy free Black people who watched out for their own economic interests and created insular networks (Margo Jefferson 24, King 79, Lawrence Otis Graham 37–38).

12. King discusses specific functions of clothing for nineteenth-century African Americans and the racist criticism and moralizing directed at them (70–71).

13. For more on Black women's societies in the antebellum North, see King (86 and note 82 on 217).

14. While King reminds us of the "humble pose" and "mask" that Black people in the antebellum period often adopted around whites so as to conceal negative affect and avoid retaliation, Ledi shows us how contemporary racism still makes it necessary, especially of Black women (69).

15. See Wahneema Lubiano and Lisa B. Thompson for a history of the "Black lady" idea, in which Black women are supposed to perform the gender, sexuality, and class display that middle-class white morality anointed as "good." Though a tool meant to combat racist ideology about people with African heritage, the "Black lady" trope is pernicious for the intersectional burdens it forces on Black women and because a society that holds racist biases often pivots to viewing such women with suspicion. One can be Black or a lady in this system, not both.

CONCLUSION

BOTH ACADEMIC CRITICS AND THE popular press have centered the idea that romance fiction is about avoiding reality or about not being familiar with reality through ignorance, willful or otherwise. Janice Radway documents her subjects' use of romance reading as "escapism" or temporarily stepping away from the responsibilities of physical and emotional caretaking.[1] As she notes, the readers' "conception of romance reading as an escape that is both literal and figurative implies flight from some situation in the real world which is either stifling or overwhelming, as well as a metaphoric transfer to another, more desirable universe where events are happily resolved" ("Women Read the Romance" 60). If Radway speaks of escapism by paraphrasing what her subjects say about their reading, other critics have used the concept to find fault with the genre. Laura Vivanco has written a roundup of this tendency of romance critics to label romance reading analogous to Marx's description of religion as an "opiate" (i.e., an escapist addiction) for the wretched. My own essay on critiques of romance in the popular press and media hints at their reliance on the negative connotation of the term escapism. (See "Romance in the Media.")

Of course "escapism" crops up in the discourse on mass media at large in this vein as well, but some scholars offer more nuance. In discussing British TV shows in *The Popular Arts*, Stuart Hall and Paddy Whannel make a distinction between escapism that is "the wish-fulfillment of becoming absorbed in something which is wholly alien from popular experience" (263) and the escapism of stories that narrate lives similar to that of the viewer/reader but without "the intensity and the complications of experience" found in our quotidian world (264). They also identify different class-based escapist experiences: one, escapism that is about a fantasy of wealth and is "normally associated with the portrayal of desired freedom offered to the characters by the possession of riches and high social position" (264) (which is partly what billionaire/ aristocrat romances offer); and two, escapism that is about "compensation and consolation" offered in stories about an ordinary, simpler, "cosier" (263) life, but with all its "unpleasant features glossed over" (264). As such, Hall and Whannel stress that escapism is not the portrayal of just one kind of world or experience but can be found via a variety of tales, including naturalistic ones that lay false claims to realism; to them, what actually makes some stories "escapist" is the "eye which observes those lives" and whether it avoids complexity in the way it sees them (264).

I hope that this book has revealed some examples of romance that show an eye for distilling and representing the complexity and the often discomfiting nature of women's lives. Romance can offer a momentary escape into fantasies of wealth or coziness or exotic spaces, or of supernatural or sci-fi worlds, yet it often does so alongside what Hall and Whannel call a "commitment" to portraying challenges. In doing this, it can fulfill what they see as a key role of art and entertainment: "to encourage us by showing us new qualities and new possibilities in life" (264). While I make no claims that every reader seeks or notices such complexity, though even a casual look at the genre's community online can surface such discernment, the texts themselves are not devoid of it.

As conceived by romance authors and romance publishing, romance heroines find their HEA/HFN in the process of reaching for new qualities and new possibilities, in a reflection of contemporary women's contestations of their situations at home, in the workplace, at school, and in overtly political spaces. The heroines both notice and imaginatively confront or circumvent the limits that heteropatriarchy, racial capitalism, and normalized in-group/out-group ideology place on women. When representatives of patriarchal policing chastise them for being sexual gourmands or not sexual enough, romance heroines explore their sexuality with a partner who either has no allegiance to that policing or who unlearns it. When gender role regulators invoke shame or punishment or refuse to accept deviations from traditional gender display/presentation, romance heroines only redesign their appearance based on their own needs and aim at maximizing their goals. When family or coworkers give romance heroines a choice between wage work that gives them professional fulfillment and unpaid traditional domestic labor and emotion work, they dialectically synthesize their own worker identities out of discrete traits and habits rather than only selecting mates rich in money and emotional support (who might make that choice unnecessary). When polities draw exclusionary lines and marshal immigration paranoia or nationalist/ethnic/other purity discourse, romance heroines embrace the strengths of their diverse heritages and create new societies with a partner and others who already are, or gradually become, iconoclasts. In a reflection of all the spheres that women inhabit in the world and the boxes that that world keeps trying to shove them into—as workers, gendered and sexual beings, citizens of different groups—romance heroines stare down false choices and weave together past selves and new ones.

Romance authors scaffold these dialectical journeys with supporting characters, including intimate partners, who affirm the heroines' desires for wide-ranging intellectual, emotional, and physical growth, for sexual and gender expression, and for belonging and identity. All along, they imagine structural alternatives to the limitations of our existing world, where ideologically-motivated hegemonic groups gaslight women that "having it all" is a fantasy just to conceal the fact that they are actively ensuring an unequal world stays immutable; witness all the recent legislation in the US against reproductive and voting rights as well as climate justice, BIPOC reparations, affirmative action, and unions, not to mention the policing of women's gender presentation in schools as well as in international sports. It is unsurprising that a genre that poses alternatives to this structural inequality faces flack for dwelling on sentiment, which has been gendered female and alternately uninteresting or dangerous (as opposed to the masculine preoccupations of honor, power, violence, and death); yet romance fiction continues to dialectically develop its own identity with every year.

Before I end, I want to acknowledge again that this book has left out a range of stories that are increasingly ascendant in the genre. I began conceptualizing this book in 2014, when these were not a part of my own reading or of the romance discourse I followed in scholarly or social media spaces. As the endings of academic books are always an HFN, not an HEA, however, I conclude with brief remarks on these journeys yet unexplored and hope that others will join me in writing about them in the coming years.

First, despite the time I spent on gender presentation and display, none of my selected works examine two other elements of the body—fatness and disability. Romance novels have, until recently, made the slim body type the unmarked or default state. While heroines may express anxieties about possessing an unattractive body, its nonfatness is only now starting to be denaturalized and questioned. Even so-called "curvy" heroines were rarely portrayed as fat-positive and certainly never represented by a fat model on the covers. A careful reading of the descriptions of those curvy heroines often revealed that, like Bridget Jones, they were actually not large or plus-sized. Heroine status versus fatness is a crucial binary that reflects another ubiquitous real-world dichotomy imposed on women: be thin at all costs or resign yourself to labels like sinful, lacking discipline, lazy, and undeserving of love, desire, money, career success, or food. Only as recently as the last three to five years have authors who challenge this fat-phobia-driven centering of the slim body started entering mainstream romance consciousness and reflecting wider conversations around body- and fat-positivity. There will soon be a significant enough corpus to study how romance has changed its representation of heroines' body types and some scholars are already putting it under a critical lens.

Disability finds varying representation in the genre, and heroines with physical challenges or differently abled bodies are still uncommon. There have occasionally been visually-disabled or hearing-and-speech-impaired heroines and a few who use accessibility aids. Neurodiverse characters are equally rare, and while Kresley Cole's Holly is signaled as being on the behavioral spectrum, she is an outlier from that decade when it comes to traditionally published romance. We have to look to more recent romance novels to see the first harbingers of a pushback against the binary of the lovable abled body and neurotypical mind versus the desexualized sidekick or villain that is associated with an atypical physical or cognitive self. But changes are afoot and the genre is rising to the challenge, as will its academic readers.

Furthermore, my book does not include same-sex romance because I wanted to unpack the female heroine's journey within the heterosexual romance narrative. But it is an aspect of the genre that deserves its own comprehensive analysis. Starting from the terminology itself, questions abound: is gay/lesbian romance the same as MLM (Men Loving Men) or WLW (Women Loving Women)? Is MLM or WLW using gender essentialist terms? What of male/male or slash? Is the dialectical building of identity in queer romance similar or different from the patterns I observe in straight/heterosexual romance? Should queer romance characters written by straight-identifying or cis authors be read with a different analytical framework than ones by #OwnVoices authors?

In addition to these shifts, there is more visibility in indie/nontraditional romance novels for intimate bonds and family structures beyond coupledom or pair bonds. Plots based on ménage à trois, polyamory, or open relationships, while still a niche subgenre, may extend the configurations that mass-market romance has enshrined for much of the last century. I am eager to see how someone could apply my analysis of romance heroines to these reconceived relationship formations and explore how they are resolving or dissolving other binaries. It would be fruitful to track the growth of these patterns against legal decisions on marital and conjugal rights, questions about parenting decisions and responsibilities, and issues such as the recalibration of domestic labor, equal pay, universal basic income, senior living support, taxes on the ultra-rich, etc.—in effect, a reconceived Happy Ever After in the "real world."

Finally, the big one: this analysis rests on the gender binary of man and woman, which is central to the genre's history, but leaves out the ways other minoritized genders understand the self and intimacy. Mass-market romance has for decades been a genre written by and marketed to cis women and has foregrounded the journeys of cis women. Yet it is increasingly clear (and of course has always been true) that "woman" is a category that falls into a gender binary, and its place in upholding heteropatriarchal norms, especially in Anglo-European culture, is rightfully under scrutiny. To speak of a "romance heroine" is itself, therefore, to be complicit in this history of binaries in some way. Even so, I hope that readers see this work as useful, within limits, in understanding a structural problem in this gender-restrictive world, with its masculine/feminine, male/female, man/woman dichotomies, particularly as represented in mainstream romance fiction.

For much of its existence, mass-market romance has remained tied to these divisions, largely as a reflection, but also as an enabler, of these ideologies. In the last decade and a half, however, the novel half of its DNA has been reworking itself and more romance novels featuring protagonists who may identify differently are showing up on readers' radars.[2] This change is driven by indie and self-published romance novels that have been featuring other main characters for much longer as well as absorbing real-world conversations about trans, nonbinary, and gender fluid subjectivity and building a more inclusive society. Thanks in part to the growing digital reach of self-published authors and smaller, less traditional, publishing houses that can bypass mainstream publishing and distribution gatekeepers, romance protagonists are further challenging many commonplaces in the genre, including the centrality of gender binaries. A significant offshoot of this trajectory is trans romance, which raises other intriguing possibilities beyond the ones in this study: can a character who identifies as a trans woman be read as a romance heroine, or does (or should) the term entirely loose valence and critical usefulness? What does such a confrontation or dissolution help us make of our world and its arguments over boundaries that people wish to call "natural" or "normal"?

Whether the romance heroine as a construct continues to exist or not, I hope this analysis provides food for thought to my fellow romance enthusiasts, whether they be academic scholars, independent researchers, romance readers, or the romance-curious. The romance heroine as a reflection of our gender-essentialized world has siblings in other literary and nonliterary forms as well;

I believe those of you studying the female-identifying protagonists in music, cinema, TV, poetry, and nonfiction essays can use this analysis to provide insight into what sociopolitical dichotomies they represent. Finally, it is my hope that the journey of the heroine will lead you on paths to our collective freedom from false choices and toward a whole self.

NOTES

1. See also Heike Mißler's (careful) reading of Radway in the second chapter of *The Cultural Politics of Chick Lit: Popular Fiction, Postfeminism and Representation.*

2. See the Introduction of *Making Meaning in Popular Romance Fiction* for my DNA analogy of the two strands of a romance novel's genetics.

AFTERWORD

AS I WAS REVISING THIS manuscript during the peer review process, the pandemic upended many lives and women shouldered its challenges on multiple fronts, sometimes in isolation and sometimes with supportive communities. Simultaneously, protests for the rights of ordinary people—the right to life, to dignity, to assembly, to protest, to just and fair due process—erupted across the world, including in the country of my birth, India. I am in awe of the courage of citizen activists, especially generationally oppressed minorities. Women, cis and trans, have put their bodies on the line in an extraordinary display of heroism. They are truly an inspiration.

This book recognizes that heroines exist in many spaces, domestic and public, in times of hardship and of plenitude, and romance novels distill their struggles within an arc of hopeful resolution. I started writing about heroines as I was finishing my previous book, which had profiled romance heroes. While I wrote that monograph to provide an analytical framework for the undertheorized half of heterosexual romance, I had always intended to develop a similar framework for romance heroines.

In the years I worked on this book and refined my ideas about romance heroism, ranging from asserting one's gender presentation and sexual identity to occupying and demanding recognition for labor and citizenhood, world events continued to show the grief and resilience of women in the face of sexual assault, political trolling, legislative inequity, and climate injustice. I have tried to study equivalents to these qualities in novels that I have found compelling, whether when I first read them or in retrospect.

A final thought, one that I hope to develop in the future (since endings always call forth expectation of new beginnings for romance readers!): The use of the term "formula" as a dismissive remark against romance novels has always intrigued me. For one thing, formulas are not simplistic and inherently deserving of contempt, are they? Second, there isn't one romance formula to rule them all, as it were. Moreover, does the existence of such a formula make everyone capable of creating something intriguing or entertaining? I think not. With every year that passed as I worked on this manuscript, I kept encountering new subgenres, new series, new character types, and new versions of an HEA or HFN. This is why I respect those who can synthesize a meaningful romance from an alleged formula and why I consider romance-writing a profound act of creativity.

I have also wondered whether those who dismiss genre fiction do so because they see it as unoriginal or because it reminds us that all writing borrows from others. In this light, "original" "creative" writing is coy about its citational history, with palimpsests of predecessors that are cherry-picked, covertly incorporated, and only meant to hail select readers, while romance fiction is an example of literary honesty, wearing all its formulaic hearts on its sleeve for anyone who chooses to see them. I hope this book has modeled inquiry into these romance fiction formulas and how practitioners aren't merely repeating them but re-configuring elements they learned from their forebears into new formulations.

APPENDIX

One or more of the false binaries I have discussed appear in all heterosexual romance novels to some degree, with varying emphases. Here are some examples in each domain in addition to the ones I have examined:

SEXUALITY (VIRGIN / WHORE, BUT COULD ALSO BE MOTHER / COUGAR, SEXUALLY ACTIVE / ICE QUEEN, ETC.)

The Flame and the Flower (Kathleen Woodiwiss, 1972)
Entwined Destinies (Rosalind Welles, 1980)
Winter Bride (Iris Johansen, 1992)
The Shameless Hour (Sarina Bowen, 2015)

GENDER (MAINLY GENDER PRESENTATION / DISPLAY AND GENDER ROLES, SUCH AS PRETTY AND STUPID / SMART AND FASHION-CHALLENGED, EMOTIONAL AND FEMME / GRUMPY AND BUTCH, YOUNG AND SEXY / OLDER AND FRUMPY, ETC.)

House of Mirrors (Yvonne Whittal, 1983)
Gentle Rogue (Johanna Lindsey, 1990)
Plain Jane MacAllister (Joan Elliot Pickart, 2002)
The Dare (Elle Kennedy, 2020)

WORK (MAINLY LABOR, PHYSICAL AND EMOTIONAL, WITH OR WITHOUT A WAGE, AND CLASS IDENTITY, SUCH AS WORKING CLASS / SOCIALITE, GENTLEWOMAN / PROFESSIONAL, CRUDE PHYSICAL LABORER / WELL-MANNERED, ETC.)

Breakfast in Bed (Sandra Brown, 1983)
Dawn of Valor (Lindsay McKenna, 1991)
Halfway to the Grave (Jeaniene Frost, 2009)
Office Hours (Katrina Jackson, 2020)

CITIZENSHIP (COMMUNITY MEMBERSHIP, SUCH AS CITIZEN OF ONE NATION / TRAITOR, SPY / PATRIOT, AFFILIATION TO ONE RACE OR TRIBE VERSUS MIXED RACE OR LOYAL TO MANY, ETC.)

A Kingdom of Dreams (Judith McNaught, 1989)
The China Bride (Mary Jo Putney, 2000)
Magic Bites (Kate Daniels series book 1) (Ilona Andrews, 2007)
The Devil Comes Courting (Courtney Milan, 2021)

INTERSECTIONS (TWO OR MORE OF THE ABOVE)

The Kadin (Bertrice Small, 1978)
The Color of Love (Sandra Kitt, 1995)
Ayesha at Last (Uzma Jalaluddin, 2019)
Like Lovers Do (Tracey Livesay, 2020)

BIBLIOGRAPHY

Ahmed, Sara. *Strange Encounters: Embodied Others in Post-Coloniality*. Routledge, 2000.

Ali, Kecia. *Human in Death*. Baylor UP, 2017.

Allan, Kenneth, and Scott Coltrane. "Gender Displaying Television Commercials: A Comparative Study of Television Commercials in the 1950s and 1980s." *Sex Roles*, vol. 35, no. 3–4, 1996, pp. 185–203. *EBSCOhost*, https://doi.org/10.1007 /BF01433106.

Althusser, Louis. *Lenin and Philosophy and Other Essays*. Translated by Ben Brewster, Monthly Review Press, 2001.

An, Y. "Family Love in Confucius and Mencius." *Dao*, vol. 7, no. 1, 2008, pp. 51–55. *Springer*, https://doi.org/10.1007/s11712-008-9041-5.

Andrews, Ilona. *Magic Bites*. Ace, 2007.

Attinger, Joelle. "Decline of New York." *Time*, 17 Sept. 1990, pp. 36–41.

Avey, Tori. "Who Was Betty Crocker?" *The History Kitchen*, Public Broadcasting Service, 15 Feb. 2013. http://www.pbs.org/food/the-history-kitchen/who-was -betty-crocker/. Accessed 28 Aug. 2019.

Barnett, Rosalind Chait. "Women and Multiple Roles: Myths and Reality." *Harvard Review of Psychiatry*, vol. 12, no. 3, 2004, pp. 158–64.

Bartlett, Katharine T. "Only Girls Wear Barrettes: Dress and Appearance Standards, Community Norms, and Workplace Equality." *Michigan Law Review*, vol. 92, no. 8, pp. 2541–82.

Bennett-Kapusniak, Renee, and Adriana McCleer. "Love in the Digital Library: A Search for Racial Heterogeneity in E-Books." *Journal of Popular Romance Studies*, vol. 5, no. 1, 2015. jprstudies.org/2015/08/love-in-the-digital-library-a -search-for-racial-heterogeneity-in-e-booksby-renee-bennett-kapusniak-and -adriana-mccleer/.

Bourne, Joanna. *Spymaster's Lady*. 2008. Berkley, 2010.

Bowen, Sarina. *The Shameless Hour*. Createspace, 2015.

Bowling, Benjamin. "The Rise and Fall of New York Murder." *British Journal of Criminology*, vol. 39, no. 4, 1999, pp. 531–54.

Bradley, Harriet. *Men's Work, Women's Work: A Sociological History of the Sexual Division of Labour in Employment*. U of Minnesota P, 1989.

Bredbenner, Candice Lewis. *A Nationality of Her Own: Women, Marriage, and the Law of Citizenship*. U of California P, 1998.

Brockmann, Suzanne. "Waiting." *Headed for Trouble*. Ballantine, 2013, pp. 34–51.

Brown, Sandra. *Breakfast in Bed*. Loveswept, 1983.

Cai, Rong. "Gender Imaginations in *Crouching Tiger, Hidden Dragon* and the *Wuxia* World." *Positions: East Asia Cultures Critique*, vol. 13, no. 2, 2005, pp. 441–71.

Carriger, Gail. *The Heroine's Journey: For Writers, Readers, and Fans of Popular Culture*. Self-published, 2020.

Chase, Loretta. *Lord of Scoundrels*. Avon, 1995.

Chateauvert, Melinda. "Framing Sexual Citizenship: Reconsidering the Discourse on African American Families." *The Journal of African American History*, vol. 93, no. 2, Spring 2008, pp. 198–222.

Christine. "Little Progress, Lots of Repetition." *Amazon*, 26 Aug. 2009. www .amazon.com/Dreamfever-Series-Karen-Marie-Moning/dp/0440244404 /ref=pd_sim_b_3. Accessed 21 Mar. 2013.

Ciment, James. *World Terrorism: An Encyclopedia of Political Violence from Ancient Times to the Post-9/11 Era*. Routledge, 2011.

Cohn, Jan. *Romance and the Erotics of Property: Mass-Market Fiction for Women*. Duke UP, 1988.

Cole, Alyssa. *A Princess in Theory*. Avon, 2018.

Cole, Kresley. *Dark Desires after Dusk*. Pocket, 2008.

Connell, Raewyn. *Gender and Power: Society, the Person, and Sexual Politics*. Stanford UP, 1987.

Crenshaw, Kimberlé. "Demarginalizing the Intersection of Race and Sex: A Black Feminist Critique of Antidiscrimination Doctrine, Feminist Theory and Antiracist Politics." *University of Chicago Legal Forum*, vol. 1989, no. 1, 1989, pp. 139–67. http://chicagounbound.uchicago.edu/uclf/vol1989/iss1/8.

Cyranowski, Jill M., and Barbara L. Andersen. "Schemas, Sexuality, and Romantic Attachment." *Journal of Personality and Social Psychology*, vol. 74, no. 5, 1998, pp. 1364–79.

Dados, Nour, and Raewyn Connell. "The Global South." *Contexts*, vol. 11, no. 1, 2012, pp. 12–13. *JSTOR*, www.jstor.org/stable/41960738.

Dandridge, Rita. *The Black Helping Tradition in Frances Harper's* Iola Leroy *and Beverly Jenkins'* Indigo *and* Through the Storm. National Association of African

American Studies, 2001. *ProQuest*, rpa.laguardia.edu/login?url=https://www
.proquest.com/conference-papers-proceedings/black-helping-tradition
-frances-harpers-iola/docview/192408967/se-2.

Devor, Holly. "Gender Blending Females: Women and Sometimes Men." *The American Behavioral Scientist*, vol. 31, no. 1, Sept.–Oct. 1987, pp. 12–40.

Dixon, jay. *The Romance Fiction of Mills & Boon, 1909–1990s*. Routledge, 1999.

"Dred Scott v. Sandford (1857)." National Archives, https://www.archives.gov
/milestone-documents/dred-scott-v-sandford. Accessed 12 Aug, 2022.

Dumas, Raechel. "Kung Fu Production for Global Consumption: The Depoliticization of Kung Fu in Stephen Chow's *Kung Fu Hustle*." *Style*, vol. 43, no. 1, 2009, pp. 65–85.

Erickson, Rebecca J. "Reconceptualizing Family Work: The Effect of Emotion Work on Perceptions of Marital Quality." *Journal of Marriage and Family*, vol. 55, no. 4, 1993, pp. 888–900. *JSTOR*, www.jstor.org/stable/352770.

———. "Why Emotion Work Matters: Sex, Gender, and the Division of Household Labor." *Journal of Marriage and Family*, vol. 67, no. 2, 2005, pp. 337–51. *JSTOR*, www.jstor.org/stable/3600273.

Factora, James. "Katie Hill's Resignation from Congress Over a Sex Scandal Played Out Unfairly." *Teen Vogue*, Oct. 2019. www.teenvogue.com/story
/katie-hill-congress-scandal.

Flesch, Juliet. *From Australia with Love: A History of Modern Australian Popular Romance Novels*. Fremantle, 2004.

Foucault, Michel. "What Is an Author?" *Twentieth-Century Literary Theory*, edited by Vassilis Lambropoulos and David Neal Miller, State U of New York P, 1987, pp. 124–42.

Fox, Bette-Lee. "Q & A: Sherry Thomas." *Library Journal*, vol. 133, no. 3, 2008, p. 88.

Frantz, Sarah S. G., and Eric Murphy Selinger, editors. *New Approaches to Popular Romance Fiction: Critical Essays*. McFarland, 2012.

Friedman, Marilyn, editor. *Women and Citizenship*. Oxford UP, 2005.

Friedman, Vanessa. "It's 2018: You Can Run for Office and Not Wear a Pantsuit." *New York Times*, 21 Jun. 2018, www.nytimes.com/2018/06/21/style/female
-politicians-dress-to-win.html.

Frost, Jeaniene. *Halfway to the Grave*. Avon, 2007.

Garber, Marjorie. *Vested Interests: Cross-Dressing and Cultural Anxiety*. Routledge, 1992.

Garcia, Luis. "Sex-Role Orientation and Stereotypes about Male-Female Sexuality." *Sex Roles*, vol. 8, no. 8, 1982, pp. 863–76.

Gardner, Daniel K. "Confucianism in Practice." *Confucianism: A Very Short Introduction*. Oxford UP, 2014; online ed, *Very Short Introductions* online, Aug. 2014. https://doi.org/10.1093/actrade/9780195398915.003.0006.

Gilbert, Sandra M., and Susan Gubar. *The Madwoman in the Attic: The Woman Writer and the Nineteenth-Century Literary Imagination*. Yale UP, 1979.

Gleason, William A., and Eric Murphy Selinger, editors. *Romance Fiction and American Culture: Love as the Practice of Freedom?* Ashgate, 2016.

Goffman, E. "Gender Display." *Gender Advertisements*, Palgrave, 1976, pp. 1–9.

Gomes, Catherine. "Wu Xia Pian and the Asian Woman Warrior." *Traffic*, no. 7, July 2005, pp. 95–112.

Goris, An. "Happily Ever After . . . and After: Serialization and the Popular Romance Novel." *Americana: The Journal of American Popular Culture (1900–present)*, vol. 12, no. 1, Spring 2013. www.americanpopularculture.com/journal /articles/spring_2013/goris.htm.

Graham, Lawrence Otis. *Our Kind of People: Inside America's Black Upper Class.* HarperCollins, 1999.

Grescoe, Paul. *The Merchants of Venus: Inside Harlequin and the Empire of Romance.* Raincoast Books, 1996.

Halford, Susan, and Pauline Leonard. *Negotiating Gendered Identities at Work: Place, Space and Time.* Palgrave, 2006.

Hall, Stuart. "Introduction: Who Needs 'Identity'?" *Questions of Cultural Identity*, edited by Stuart Hall and Paul Du Gay. 1996. Sage, 2011, pp. 1–17.

Hall, Stuart, and Paddy Whannel. *The Popular Arts.* 1964. Duke UP, 2018.

Hamill, Pete. "City of the Damned: A Baby Fed to a Dog? So What? Welcome to New York." *Esquire*, vol. 114, no. 6, 1990, pp. 61–65.

Hecht, Laura M. "Role Conflict and Role Overload: Different Concepts, Different Consequences." *Sociological Inquiry*, vol. 71, no. 1, Winter 2001, pp. 111–21.

Heller, Dana. *The Feminization of Quest-Romance: Radical Departures.* U of Texas P, 1990.

Hillman, Betty Luther. *Dressing for the Culture Wars: Style and the Politics of Self-Presentation in the 1960s and 1970s.* U of Nebraska P, 2015.

Hird, Myra J., and Sue Jackson. "Where 'Angels' and 'Wusses' Fear to Tread: Sexual Coercion in Adolescent Dating Relationships." *Journal of Sociology*, vol. 37, no. 1, 2001, pp. 27–44.

Ho, Elizabeth. *Neo-Victorianism and the Memory of Empire.* Bloomsbury, 2012.

hooks, bell. *Outlaw Culture.* Routledge, 1994.

Hourihan, Margery. *Deconstructing the Hero.* Routledge, 1997.

Howard, Linda. *To Die For.* Ballantine, 2005.

Hunter, Tera W. *Bound in Wedlock: Slave and Free Black Marriage in the Nineteenth Century.* Harvard UP, 2017.

Illouz, Eva. *Consuming the Romantic Utopia: Love and the Cultural Contradictions of Capitalism.* U of California P, 1997.

"Infant Mortality." *Centers for Disease Control and Prevention.* 10 Sep. 2020. www .cdc.gov/reproductivehealth/maternalinfanthealth/infantmortality.htm.

Jackson, Katrina. *Office Hours.* Self-published, 2020.

Jaggar, Allison M. "Civil Society, the State, and the Global Order." Friedman, pp. 91–110.

Jalaluddin, Uzma. *Ayesha at Last*. Berkley, 2018.

Jefferson, Margo. *Negroland*. Penguin Random House, 2015.

Jenkins, Beverly. *Indigo*. Avon, 1996.

Jensen, Margaret Anne. *Love's Sweet Return: The Harlequin Story*. Canadian Scholars, 1984.

Johansen, Iris. *Winter Bride*. Loveswept, 1992.

Judge, Joan. "Talent, Virtue, and the Nation: Chinese Nationalisms and Female Subjectivities in the Early Twentieth Century." *American Historical Review*, vol. 106, no. 3, 2001, pp. 765–803. *JSTOR*, www.jstor.org/stable/2692323.

Kamblé, Jayashree. "From Barbarized to Disneyfied: Viewing 1990s New York City through Eve Dallas, J. D. Robb's Futuristic Homicide Detective." *Forum for Inter-American Research*, vol. 10, no. 1, 2017, pp. 72–86.

———. *Making Meaning in Popular Romance Fiction: An Epistemology*. Palgrave, 2014.

———. "Romance in the Media." Kamblé, Selinger, and Teo, pp. 269–93.

———. "When Wuxia Met Romance: The Pleasures and Politics of Transculturalism in Sherry Thomas's *My Beautiful Enemy*." *Journal of Popular Romance Studies*, vol. 9, 2020.

Kamblé, Jayashree, Eric Murphy Selinger, and Hsu-Ming Teo, editors. *The Routledge Research Companion to Popular Romance Fiction*. Routledge, 2020.

Kandiyoti, Deniz. "Identity and Its Discontents: Women and the Nation." *Colonial Discourse and Post-Colonial Theory: A Reader*, edited by Patrick Williams and Laura Chrisman, 1994, pp. 376–91.

Kang, Mee-Eun. "The Portrayal of Women's Images in Magazine Advertisements: Goffman's Gender Analysis Revisited." *Sex Roles: A Journal of Research*, vol. 37, no. 11/12, 1997, pp. 979–96. https://doi.org/10.1007/BF02936350.

Kao, Karl S. Y. "Bao and Baoying: Narrative Causality and External Motivations in Chinese Fiction." *Chinese Literature: Essays, Articles, Reviews*, vol. 11, 1989, pp. 115–38. *JSTOR*, www.jstor.org/stable/495528.

Karmen, Andrew. *New York Murder Mystery: The True Story Behind the Crime Crash of the 1990s*. New York UP, 2000.

Kennedy, Elle. *The Dare*. Self-published, 2020.

Kim, Jong Mi. *Global Media, Audiences and Transformative Identities: Femininities and Consumption in South Korea*. 2008. London School of Economics and Political Science, PhD dissertation.

King, Wilma. *The Essence of Liberty: Free Black Women During the Slave Era*. U of Missouri P, 2006.

Kitt, Sandra. *The Color of Love*. Signet, 1995.

Kleypas, Lisa. *Dreaming of You*. 1994. Avon, 2003.

Krentz, Jayne Anne, editor. *Dangerous Men, Adventurous Women: Romance Writers on the Appeal of the Romance*. U of Pennsylvania P, 1992.

Lee, Ken-Fang. "Far Away, So Close: Cultural Translation in Ang Lee's *Crouching Tiger, Hidden Dragon*." *Inter-Asia Cultural Studies*, vol. 4, no. 2, 2004, pp. 282–95.

Lee, Vicky. "Erasure, Solidarity, Duplicity: Interracial Experience across Colonial Hong Kong and Foreign Enclaves in China from the Late 1800s to the 1980s." *Asia Pacific Perspectives*, vol. 14, no. 2, 2017, pp. 20–40.

Lester, J. "Acting on the Collegiate Stage: Managing Impressions in the Workplace." *Feminist Formations*, vol. 23. no. 1, 2011, pp. 155–81.

Leung, William. "Crouching Sensibility, Hidden Sense." *Film Criticism*, vol. 26, no. 1, 2001, pp. 42–55.

Lindow, Sandra J. "To Heck with the Village." *Heroines of Comic Books and Literature: Portrayals in Popular Culture*, edited by Maja Bajac-Carter et al., Rowman and Littlefield, 2014, pp. 3–15.

Lindsey, Johanna. *Gentle Rogue*. Avon, 1990.

Livesay, Tracey. *Like Lovers Do*. Avon, 2020.

Lois, Jennifer, and Joanna Gregson. "Sneers and Leers: Romance Writers and Gendered Sexual Stigma." *Gender & Society*, vol. 29, no. 4, Aug. 2015, pp. 459–83. https://doi.org/10.1177/0891243215584603.

Lorber, Judith. *Paradoxes of Gender*. Yale UP, 1994.

Lubiano, Wahneema. "Black Ladies, Welfare Queens, and State Minstrels: Ideological War by Narrative Means" in *Race-ing Justice, En-gendering Power: Essays on Anita Hill, Clarence Thomas, and Construction of Social Reality*, 1992, pp. 323–63.

Lynch, Katherine E., Ruth E. Sternglantz, and Len Barot. "Queering the Romantic Heroine: Where Her Power Lies." *Journal of Popular Romance Studies*, vol. 3, no. 1, 2012.

Mains, Christine. "Having It All: The Female Hero's Quest for Love and Power in Patricia McKillip's Riddle-Master Trilogy." *Extrapolation*, vol. 46, no. 1, 2005, pp. 23–35. https://doi.org/10.3828/extr.2005.46.1.5.

Mäkelä, Veera. "Reading Response in Mary Balogh: A Critical Engagement." *Journal of Popular Romance Studies*, vol. 10, 2021.

Malacrida, Claudia, and Tiffany Boulton. "Women's Perceptions of Childbirth 'Choices': Competing Discourses of Motherhood, Sexuality, and Selflessness." *Gender & Society*, vol. 26, no. 5, 2012, pp. 748–72.

Markert, John. *Publishing Romance: The History of an Industry, 1940s to the Present*. McFarland, 2016.

Marks, Michael J., and R. Chris Fraley. "The Impact of Social Interaction on the Sexual Double Standard." *Social Influence*, vol. 2, no. 1, 2007, pp. 29–54.

Marshall, T. H. *Citizenship and Social Class and Other Essays*. Cambridge UP, 1950.

Mayer, Tamar. "Gender Ironies of Nationalism: Setting the Stage." *Gender Ironies of Nationalism*, edited by Tamar Mayer, Routledge, 2012, pp. 1–22.

McAleer, Joseph. *Passion's Fortune: The Story of Mills & Boon*. Oxford UP, 1999.

McAlister, Jodi. *The Consummate Virgin: Female Virginity Loss and Love in Anglophone Popular Literatures*. Palgrave, 2020.

McBride, Angela Barron. "Mental Health Effects of Women's Multiple Roles." *The American Psychologist*, vol. 45, no. 3, 1990, pp. 381–84. https://doi.org/10.1037/0003-066X.45.3.381.

McClean, Jedidiah. "Gender Maneuvering over Coffee: Doing Gender through Displays of Hegemonic Masculinity and Alternative Femininity." *The Journal for Undergraduate Ethnography*, vol. 4, no. 2, 2014, pp. 19–31.

McDowell, Linda. *Gender, Identity and Place: Understanding Feminist Geographies.* Polity Press, 2018.

McKenna, Lindsay. *Dawn of Valor.* Silhouette, 1991.

McNaught, Judith. *A Kingdom of Dreams.* Pocket, 1989.

Milan, Courtney. *The Devil Comes Courting.* Self-published, 2021.

Minnotte, Krista Lynn, et al. "Emotion-Work Performance among Dual-Earner Couples: Testing Four Theoretical Perspectives." *Journal of Family Issues*, vol. 28, no. 6, June 2007, pp. 773–93. https://doi.org/10.1177/0192513X07299676.

Mißler, Heike. *The Cultural Politics of Chick Lit: Popular Fiction, Postfeminism, and Representation.* Routledge, 2016.

Modleski, Tania. "The Disappearing Act: A Study of Harlequin Romances." *Signs*, vol. 5, no. 3, U of Chicago P, 1980, pp. 435–48. *JSTOR*, www.jstor.org/stable/3173584.

———. *Loving with a Vengeance: Mass-Produced Fantasies for Women.* Shoe String Press, 1982.

Moning, Karen Marie. *Bloodfever.* Kindle ed., Bantam, 2007.

———. *Darkfever.* Kindle ed., Bantam, 2006.

———. *Dreamfever.* Kindle ed., Bantam, 2010.

———. *Faefever.* Kindle ed., Bantam, 2009.

———. *Shadowfever.* Kindle ed., Bantam, 2011.

Moody-Freeman, Julie E. "Beverly Jenkins." *The Black Romance Podcast* from The Center for Black Diaspora at DePaul University, Sep. 2020, blackromancepodcast.libsyn.com/.

———. "'Dance Between Raindrops': A Conversation with Vivian Stephens," *Journal of Popular Romance Studies*, no. 11, May 16, 2022. https://www.jprstudies.org/2022/05/dance-between-raindrops-a-conversation-with-vivian-stephens/.

Moore, Kate, and Eric Murphy Selinger. "The Heroine as Reader, the Reader as Heroine: Jennifer Crusie's *Welcome to Temptation*." *Journal of Popular Romance Studies*, vol. 2, no. 2, 2012.

Moore, Mignon R. "Two Sides of the Same Coin: Revising Analyses of Lesbian Sexuality and Family Formation through the Study of Black Women." *Journal of Lesbian Studies*, vol. 15, no. 1, 2011, pp. 58–68.

Mostov, Julie. "Sexing the Nation, Desexing the Body: Politics of National Identity in the Former Yugoslavia." *Gender Ironies of Nationalism*, edited by Tamar Mayer, Routledge, 2012, pp. 89–110.

Murdock, Maureen. *The Heroine's Journey: Woman's Quest for Wholeness.* 1990. Shambhala, 2020.

Mussell, Kay. *Fantasy and Reconciliation: Contemporary Formulas of Women's Romance Fiction.* Praeger, 1984.

———. *Women's Gothic and Romantic Fiction: A Reference Guide.* Greenwood, 1981.

Napier, Susan. *Love in the Valley.* Mills & Boon, 1985.

Pearson, Carol, and Katherine Pope. *Who Am I This Time?: Female Portraits in British and American Literature.* McGraw-Hill, 1976.

Pearson, Quinn M. "Role Overload, Job Satisfaction, Leisure Satisfaction, and Psychological Health among Employed Women." *Journal of Counseling & Development,* vol. 86, no. 1, 2008, pp. 57–63.

Pickart, Joan Elliot. *Plain Jane MacAllister.* Silhouette, 2002.

Plüss, Caroline. "Chinese-Singaporean Repeat Migrant Women: Transnational Positions and Social Inequalities." *Living Intersections: Transnational Migrant Identifications in Asia,* edited by Caroline Plüss and Chan Kwon-bun, Springer, 2012, pp. 125–47.

Poovey, Mary. *Uneven Developments: The Ideological Work of Gender in Mid-Victorian England.* U of Chicago P, 1988.

"Pregnancy Mortality Surveillance System." *Centers for Disease Control and Prevention,* 25 Nov. 2020, www.cdc.gov/reproductivehealth/maternal-mortality/pregnancy-mortality-surveillance-system.htm?CDC_AA_refVal=https%3A%2F%2Fwww.cdc.gov%2Freproductivehealth%2Fmaternalinfanthealth%2Fpregnancy-mortality-surveillance-system.htm.

Price, Barbara Raffel. "Female Police Officers in the United States." *Policing in Central and Eastern Europe,* edited by Milan Pagon, College of Police and Security Studies, 1996. https://www.ncjrs.gov/policing/fem635.htm.

Proctor, Tammy M. *Female Intelligence: Women and Espionage in the First World War.* New York UP, 2006.

Prokos, Anastasia, and Irene Padavic. "'There Outta Be a Law against Bitches': Masculinity Lessons in Police Academy Training." *Gender, Work and Organization,* vol. 9, no. 4, August 2002, 439–59.

Putney, Mary Jo. *The China Bride.* Ballantine, 2000.

"Q & A." *Lisa Kleypas,* www.lisakleypas.com/readers-ask/.

Radway, Janice. *Reading the Romance: Women, Patriarchy, and Popular Literature.* 1984. U of North Carolina P, 1991.

———. "Women Read the Romance: The Interaction of Text and Context." *Feminist Studies,* vol. 9, no. 1, 1983, pp. 53–78. *JSTOR,* www.jstor.org/stable/3177683.

Regis, Pamela. *A Natural History of the Romance Novel.* U of Pennsylvania P, 2003.

———. "The Romance Community: *A Room of One's Own* and *Écriture Femina.*" Popular Culture Association conference, 2 Apr. 2010, St. Louis MO. Conference Presentation.

Reskin, Barbara, and Irene Padavic. *Women and Men at Work*. Pine Forge Press, 1994.

Riederer, Rachel. "Is Dolly Parton the Voice of America?" *The New Republic*, 18 Dec. 2020, newrepublic.com/article/160596/dolly-parton-appeal-divided -america.

Roach, Catherine M. *Happy Ever After: The Romance Story in Popular Culture*. Indiana UP, 2016.

Robb, J. D. *Apprentice in Death*. Berkley, 2016.

———. *Brotherhood in Death*. Berkley, 2016.

———. *Innocent in Death*. Kindle ed., Berkley 2007.

———. *Loyalty in Death*. Berkley, 1999.

———. *Naked in Death*. Berkley, 1995.

Rose, Sonya O. *Which People's War?: National Identity and Citizenship in Wartime Britain 1939–1945*. Oxford UP, 2003.

Russ, Joanna. *To Write Like a Woman: Essays in Feminism and Science Fiction*. 1972. Indiana UP, 1995.

Schippers, Mimi. "Recovering the Feminine Other: Masculinity, Femininity, and Gender Hegemony." *Theory and Society*, vol. 36, no. 1, 2007, pp. 85–102.

———. *Rockin' Out of the Box: Gender Maneuvering in Alternative Hard Rock*. Rutgers UP, 2002.

Serfaty, Sunlen, et al. "Katie Hill Admits to Relationship with Campaign Staffer." *CNN*, 2019. www.cnn.com/2019/10/23/politics/house-opens-investigation-into -katie-hill/index.html.

Shapiro, Lila. "'I Really Thought He Was Going to Kill Me and Bury My Body': A Romance Author Accused Her Husband of Poisoning Her. Was It Her Wildest Fiction Yet?" *Vulture*, 19 June 2019, vulture.com/2019/06/romance-author -sherrilyn-kenyon-said-her-husband-poisoned-her.html.

Small, Bertrice. *The Kadin*. Avon, 1978.

Snitow, Ann Barr. "Mass Market Romance: Pornography for Women is Different." *Radical History Review*, no. 20, 1979, pp. 121–41. https://doi.org/10.1215/01636545 -1979-20-141.

Sommer, Will. "Blundering pro-Trump smear artists Jack Burkman and Jacob Wohl . . ." *Twitter*, 3 Oct. 2019, twitter.com/willsommer/status/1179821913385910 273?s=20.

Spender, Dale. *Mothers of the Novel*. London: Pandora, 1986.

———. *The Writing or the Sex? Or Why You Don't Have to Read Women's Writing to Know It's No Good*. New York: Pergamon Press, 1989.

Stynes, Yumi. "Solving the Mental Load—Update." *Ladies, We Need to Talk*, ABC Radio Podcasts, 11 Aug. 2020, www.abc.net.au/radio/programs/ladies-we -need-to-talk/solving-the-mental-load-update/12325472.

Teng, Emma Jinhua. "Eurasian Hybridity in Chinese Utopian Visions: From 'One World' to 'A Society Based on Beauty' and Beyond." *Positions: East Asia Cultures Critique*, vol. 14, no. 1, 2006, pp. 131–63.

Teo, Hsu-Ming. *Desert Passions: Orientalism and Romance Novels*. U of Texas P, 2012.

Teo, Stephen. *Traditions in World Cinema: Chinese Martial Arts Cinema: The Wuxia Tradition*. Edinburgh UP, 2009.

Thomas, Sherry. "Guest Author Day: Learning English the Passionate Way by Sherry Thomas." *The Good, The Bad and The Unread: Reading, Ranting and Reviewing by Readers*, 24 Mar. 2008. http://goodbadandunread.com /2008/03/24/guest-author-day-learning-english-the-passionate-way -by-sherry-thomas/.

———. *The Hidden Blade*. Self-published, 2014.

———. *My Beautiful Enemy*. Berkley, 2014.

Thompson, Lisa B. *Beyond the Black Lady: Sexuality and the New African American Middle Class*. U of Illinois P, 2012.

Thurston, Carol. *The Romance Revolution: Erotic Novels for Women and the Quest for a New Sexual Identity*. U of Illinois P, 1987.

Tiedje, Linda Beth, et al. "Women with Multiple Roles: Role Compatibility Perceptions, Satisfaction, and Mental Health." *Journal of Marriage and Family*, vol. 52, no. 1, Feb. 1990, pp. 63–72.

Vivanco, Laura. "Romance and Religion: Opiates of the People?" *Laura Vivanco*, 22 Oct. 2012, www.vivanco.me.uk/blog/post/romance-and-religion-opiates -people. Accessed 21 Nov. 2019.

Wai-Yee Li. "Heroic Transformations: Women and National Trauma in Early Qing Literature." *Harvard Journal of Asiatic Studies*, vol. 59, no. 2, Dec. 1999, pp. 363–443. *JSTOR*, www.jstor.org/stable/2652718.

Wallis, Cara. "Performing Gender: A Content Analysis of Gender Display in Music Videos." *Sex Roles*, vol. 64, no. 3, 2011, pp. 160–72.

Welles, Rosalind. *Entwined Destinies*. Dell, 1980.

West, Candace, and Don H. Zimmerman. "Doing Gender." *Gender & Society*, vol. 1, no. 2, June 1987, pp. 125–51. https://doi.org/10.1177/0891243287001002002.

Wheeler, Roxann. *The Complexion of Race*. U of Pennsylvania P, 2011.

Whittal, Yvonne. *House of Mirrors*. Harlequin, 1983.

Xia, Xiaohong. "The Great Diversity of Women Exemplars in China of Late Qing." *Frontiers of Literary Studies in China*, vol. 3, no. 2, 2009, pp. 218–46.

Young, Erin S. "Escaping the 'Time Bind': Negotiations of Love and Work in Jayne Ann Krentz's 'Corporate Romances.'" *Journal of American Culture*, vol. 33, no. 2, 2010, pp. 92–106. https://doi-org.rpa.laguardia.edu/10.1111/j.1542-734X.2010 .00736.x.

Zernike, Kate. "Forget Suits. Show the Tattoo. Female Candidates Are Breaking the Rules." *New York Times*, 14 July 2018, www.nytimes.com/2018/07/14/us /politics/women-candidates-midterms.html.

INDEX

Note: Page numbers in italics indicate a figure; a number followed by "n" indicates a note.

Acker, Joan, 105
Ahmed, Sara, 133, 149
alienation, 133–36, 138, 149, 150n8, 174–75
Allan, Kenneth, 60, 83n2
Andersen, Barbara L., 52–54n4
"Angel in the House" trope, 30, 148, 163
approach/avoidance behaviors: in *Love in the Valley* (Napier), 31, 34, 36–40; overview of, 29, 52–54n4; romance heroine's journey away from, 52. *See also* sexuality
Artist/Actress figure, 8–9
Attinger, Joelle, 100–101, 118n8
attraction behaviors, 29
authorship, female, 89–97. *See also* romance authors
avoidance behaviors, 43, 47–48

bao, 145–46
Barnett, Rosalind, 87, 117n1
beauty standards, 136–37, 150n8, 161–62
Biles, Simone, 16
binaries: of citizenship, 122–23, 155; faced by women, 16–17; and fragmented female self, 66–67; heroine's journey as rejection of, 13–14, 15–16; inherent in romance novels, 185; of work vs. motherhood, 87;

and wuxia genre, 144. *See also* virgin/whore binary
"Black lady" trope, 180n15
Boulton, Tiffany, 56
Bourne, Joanna, 123; *Spymaster's Lady*, 6, 7–9, 22, 123–32, 150n6
Bowling, Benjamin, 118–19n12, 119n13
Bradley, Harriet: on double bind for women in "male" workplaces, 105, 113; on female domestication of workplaces, 111; on gender and work, 97, 119n14; on inside/outside split of work, 119n22
"Broken Windows" philosophy, 118–19n12
Brown, Sandra, 104

Cady, Linell, 167
Cai, Rong, 142, 144, 145
Campbell, Joseph, 26n12
capitalism, 14, 85–86. *See also* employment; wealth
Carriger, Gail, 26n12
Chand, Dutee, 16
Chateauvert, Melinda, 122, 155
cheerleaders, 21, 75–77, 81, 82
childlikeness, 32, 39
Chinese diaspora, 143

national identity: fluidity of, 128–29; as natural vs. discursive, 123–24, 132; rhetoric of, as paradoxical, 127. *See also* alienation; citizenship

neoliberalism, 102

New York City, 98, 100–102, 118nn7–10, 118–19n12

New York Police Department (NYPD), 102–3, 118–19n12, 119n13, 119n15

Notaro, Tig, 83n4

Ocasio-Cortez, Alexandria, 17

Omar, Ilhan, 17

Osaka, Naomi, 16

Padavic, Irene, 104, 105–6, 110, 111, 117n2

Parton, Dolly, 65

Pearson, Carol: on female heroes in literature, 10, 25–26n8; on female Warrior, 55; on heroines vs. female heroes, 8–9; on hero vs. female Warrior, 26n9

Plüss, Caroline, 139–40

police work, 98–115. *See also* employment; *In Death* series (Robb)

Poovey, Mary, 30, 87

Pope, Katherine: on female heroes in literature, 10, 25–26n8; on female Warrior, 55; on heroines vs. female heroes, 8–9; on hero vs. female Warrior, 26n9

power relations, of gender display, 59

Price, Barbara Raffel, 119n15

Princess in Theory, A (Alyssa Cole): community support in, 178; emotion work and labor in, 169–71; family ties in, 172–74; female hero in, 7, 8; heroine's alienation in, 174–75; heroine's integrated selfhood in, 168, 171, 173, 177; identity struggles in, 168, 172–74; intersectionality in, 168–71; love plot in, 5, 6; overview of, 22, 167–68; racism in, 169–70, 172; sexism in, 171; sexuality in, 176–77; spatial dimension of, 168, 173–74

"problematic faves," 14, 26–27n13

Proctor, Tammy M., 127, 130, 131

Prokos, Anastasia, 104

public health and science, 170, 175–76

public/private spheres, 87–88, 105–6, 119n22

publishing companies, 3

race, 22, 179n5

racial passing, 134–36, 139, 149, 151–52n15

racism: "Black lady" trope, 180n15; and colorism, 161–62; intersectionality of, with sexism, 154; and "masking," 180n14; in *A Princess in Theory* (Alyssa Cole), 169–70, 172; self-alienation as effect of, 172; in STEM field, 169. *See also* racial passing

Radway, Janice, 11–12, 32, 181

rape, 70–72

Regis, Pamela: definition of romance, 1; *A Natural History of the Romance Novel*, 12; on ritual death, 76; on romance novel structure, 10

Reiderer, Rachel, 65

Reskin, Barbara, 105–6, 110, 111, 117n2

Richardson, Sha'Carri, 16

ritual death, 76, 79

Roach, Catherine M., 12

Robb, J. D., *In Death* series, 5, 6, 7, 14, 97–116

Rodsky, Eve, 88, 97

role enhancement, 45

role strain: as alleviated through community support, 46, 51; and employment, 86–87; overview of, 44–45

romance authors: "author function" vs. bio-author identity, 94–96; and financial independence, 116–17; as hypervisible/invisible, 93–94; media coverage of, 94–95. *See also* authorship, female

romance fiction scholarship: emergence of, 11–12; second generation of, 12

romance novels: cisgender focus of, 185; contradictions in, 14–15; critics as dismissive of, 93–94, 181; as "escapism," 181–82; evolution of, 2–4, 7–8; evolving genre of, 13; as fantasy solution for female economic precarity, 15; heroines as embodying genre's self-determination, 13, 17–18, 22–23, 43, 89; and identity,

Teng, Emma Jinhua, 152

Teo, Hsu-Ming, 12, 26n11

Teo, Stephen, 141, 142, 143, 152n20

Thomas, Sherry, 139; *The Hidden Blade* (Thomas), 7, 144, 153n25; *My Beautiful Enemy* (Thomas), 5, 6, 7–9, 22, 132–49, 150n–51n9, 151n12, 151–52n15

time usage, 114

Tlaib, Rashida, 17

To Die For (Howard): disfavored femininity as punished in, 76; doubling in, 77–82; "dumb blonde" stereotype, 78–79, 81; false binaries in, 77; female heroic action in, 7; and gender, 75–83; gender display in, 75–79, 81–82; heroine's integrated selfhood in, 81–83; love plot in, 5, 6; overview of, 21, 75–76; ritual death in, 76, 79; sexuality in, 77–78

"unicorn space," 97

Virgin figure, 8

virgin/whore binary: and Black womanhood, 179n3; consequences of, 52n2; historical overview, 30; in *Indigo* (Jenkins), 158–60; in *Love in the Valley* (Napier), 41–42; women's experience of, 28, 31

Vivanco, Laura, 181

Wallis, Cara, 59

Warren, Elizabeth, 27n14

Warrior figure, 148; and Campbell's hero, 26n9; and heroine's journey, 9–10; interior freedom of, 25–26n8; in *My Beautiful Enemy* (Thomas), 134, 137–39, 142–44;

overview of, 8, 9; in wuxia genre, 143–44, 152n20, 153n26. *See also* heroes, female

wealth: vs. blue-collar identity, in *In Death* (Robb) series, 103; and Cinderella trope, 86, 177; as freedom, in *Indigo* (Jenkins), 164, 165–66; and marriage, 14; as power, in *A Princess in Theory* (Alyssa Cole), 168; as solution to home/work binary, 86, 91. *See also* class status

West, Candace, 56, 71

Whannel, Paddy, 181–82

Wheeler, Roxann, 151–52n15

Wife figure, 25n7

women: binary choices as limiting, 16–17; and "Black lady" trope, 180n15; in Chinese Confucian patriarchy, 153n26; and community support, 45; economic precarity of, as resolved in romance, 15, 85; and gender display, 65; immigrants, 139; and internalized misogyny about sexuality, 51; and role strain, 44–45; romance genre as normalizing self-determination for, 116; romance novels as integrating multiple roles of, 10. *See also* virgin/whore binary

women athletes, 16, 65, 84n13

work. *See* employment

wuxia genre, 140–46, 148, 150n–51n9, 152n20, 153n26

Xia Xiaohong, 137

Young, Erin S., 85, 86

Zimmerman, Don H., 56, 71

JAYASHREE KAMBLÉ is Professor of English at LaGuardia Community College at the City University of New York. She is author of *Making Meaning in Popular Romance Fiction: An Epistemology* and editor (with Eric Murphy Selinger and Hsu-Ming Teo) of *The Routledge Research Companion to Popular Romance Fiction*. She currently serves as President of the International Association for the Study of Popular Romance.